Nineteenth-Century Cape Breton

Nineteenth-Century Cape Breton

A Historical Geography

STEPHEN J. HORNSBY

McGill-Queen's University Press
Montreal & Kingston • London • Buffalo

© McGill-Queen's University Press 1992
ISBN 0-7735-0889-9

Legal deposit second quarter 1992
Bibliothèque nationale du Québec

Printed in Canada on acid-free paper

Publication of this book has been made possible by
grants from the Canadian Embassy, Washington, DC,
and the Canadian-American Center, University of
Maine.

Canadian Cataloguing in Publication Data

Hornsby, Stephen J. (Stephen John), 1956-
    Nineteenth-century Cape Breton
    Includes bibliographical references and index.
    ISBN 0-7735-0889-9
    1. Cape Breton Island (N.S.) – History – 19th cen-
tury. 2. Cape Breton Island (N.S.) – Economic conditions – 19th century. 3. Scotland – Emigration and
immigration – Nova Scotia – Cape Breton Island.
4. Fisheries – Nova Scotia – Cape Breton Island –
History – 19th century. I. Title.
    FC2343.4.H67 1992   971.6'9'09034   C91-090620-3
    F1039.C2H67 1992

This book was typeset by Typo Litho composition inc.
in 10/12 Baskerville.

For my parents and Kathleen

Contents

Figures ix

Tables xiii

Preface xv

Introduction xix

1 Cape Breton Island at the Beginning of the Nineteenth Century 3

2 The Scottish Background of Immigrants to Cape Breton 30

3 Agricultural Settlement in the Early Nineteenth Century 48

4 The Staple Industries in the Early Nineteenth Century 85

5 The Potato Famine, 1845–1849 111

6 Agricultural Settlement in the Late Nineteenth Century 121

7 The Staple Industries in the Late Nineteenth Century 152

8 The Exodus 186

9 Cape Breton Island at the End of the Nineteenth Century 201

Notes   211

Bibliography   251

Index   269

Figures

1.1 Location of Cape Breton Island xxv

1.1 Settlement on Cape Breton Island in 1800 4

1.2 Trade connections of P. Robin & Co. (top) and
L. Kavanagh (bottom) in 1796 6

1.3 Fishermen hand-lining for cod from a whaleboat 8

1.4 Crew fishing from rail of a cod schooner 9

1.5 A late nineteenth-century view of a stage head 10

1.6 Main heights of land and rivers on Cape Breton
Island 20

1.7 Distribution of agricultural land on Cape Breton
Island 21

1.8 Forest zones on Cape Breton Island 22

1.9 Sydney, 1799 26

1.10 Plan of Sydney, 1795 27

2.1 Origin of Scottish emigrants to Cape Breton 32

2.2 Crofting township at Uig Bay, Skye, late nineteenth
century 34

2.3 Crofting township at Harrapool, Skye 35

2.4   Crofters planting potatoes in Skye, late nineteenth century   37

2.5   Kelp burning, Orkney, late nineteenth century   38

2.6   Immigration of Scottish passengers to Nova Scotia and Cape Breton Island, 1815–50   43

3.1   Crown land grants on Cape Breton Island, 1786–1820   49

3.2   Crown land grants on Cape Breton Island, 1786–1850   50

3.3   Number and acreage of Crown land grants on Cape Breton Island, 1828–50   53

3.4   Hypothetical pattern of frontland settlement on Cape Breton Island in the early nineteenth century   57

3.5   Census subdistricts on Cape Breton Island, 1851   64

3.6   Improved land on Cape Breton Island, 1851   65

3.7   Distribution of livestock on Cape Breton Island, 1851   66

3.8   Distribution of butter production on Cape Breton Island, 1851   68

3.9   Settlement along the Southwest Margaree River, Inverness County, showing the location of grants, 1831–36, and the name and place of origin of the settlers   77

4.1   Distribution of fishermen on Cape Breton Island, 1851   87

4.2   Distribution of dried- and pickled-fish production in Cape Breton, 1851   91

4.3   Production and export of coal from Cape Breton, 1827–57   97

4.4   Coal production at the principal mines on Cape Breton Island, 1827–57   98

4.5   Distribution of coal mines on Cape Breton Island and their maximum output, 1827–57   99

4.6   The GMA's village and pits at Sydney Mines, Cape Breton County, 1877   104

4.7   GMA housing, Sydney Mines   105

6.1   Origin of population of Cape Breton, 1870–71   122

6.2   Crown land grants on Cape Breton Island,
      1786–1880   124

6.3   Number and acreage of Crown land grants on
      Cape Breton Island, 1850–90   127

6.4   Hypothetical pattern of frontland and backland
      settlement on Cape Breton Island in the late
      nineteenth century   129

6.5   Census subdistricts on Cape Breton Island, 1891   132

6.6   Improved land on Cape Breton Island, 1891   133

6.7   Distribution of livestock on Cape Breton Island,
      1891   135

6.8   Distribution of butter production on Cape Breton
      Island, 1891   136

6.9   Frontland settlement, Christmas Island, Bras d'Or
      Lake, late nineteenth century   137

6.10 Backland farm, Tarbert, Cape Breton Highlands,
      c. 1890   140

6.11 Religious denominations of the Cape Breton
      population, 1870–71   145

6.12 The economic hinterland of Malcolm MacDougall,
      merchant at Christmas Island, Cape Breton County,
      1880   150

6.13 West Bay, Inverness County, 1883–87   151

7.1   Distribution of fishermen on Cape Breton Island,
      1891   153

7.2   Fish production in Cape Breton, showing three-year
      moving averages for dried and pickled fish   155

7.3   Distribution of dried- and pickled-fish production in
      Cape Breton, 1891   156

7.4   Inshore fishing craft at Chéticamp, c. 1915   158

7.5   Lobster production in Cape Breton, 1872–91   161

7.6   Fishing settlement, Arichat, Richmond County, 1883–
      87   164

7.7   Fishing settlement, Petit-de-Grat, Richmond County   165

7.8   Fishing settlements, Neil's Harbour and New Haven, Victoria County, 1883–87   166

7.9   Fishing settlement, Neil's Harbour, Victoria County   167

7.10   Distribution and output of the principal coal mines on Cape Breton Island, 1865–1866   170

7.11   Production and export of coal from Cape Breton, 1858–91   171

7.12   Distribution and output of the principal coal mines on Cape Breton Island, 1890   173

7.13   Mining scenes, Caledonia Mines, Cape Breton County, late nineteenth century   174

7.14   Colliery railways in eastern Cape Breton County   175

7.15   Men and boys employed at the coal mines in Cape Breton County, 1866–91   177

7.16   The Blockhouse and Gowrie mining villages at Cow Bay, Cape Breton County, 1877   179

7.17   Union membership among Cape Breton miners, August 1881–December 1884   182

7.18   Shipbuilding on Cape Breton Island, 1854–91   184

8.1   Distribution of male emigrants (top) and female emigrants (bottom) from Cape Breton by place or state/province of death, 1880–93   192

9.1   Distribution of population on Cape Breton Island, 1891   202

Tables

1.1 Occupations and ethnic background of heads of households on Île Madame and neighbouring fishing settlements, 1811   14

1.2 Workforce employed at Sydney Mines, 1803   17

3.1 Exports of agricultural produce outside Nova Scotia, 1843 and 1853   60

3.2 Exports of agricultural produce to St John's, Newfoundland, 1828–39   61

3.3 Exports of cattle, sheep, and butter outside Nova Scotia, 1842–48   62

3.4 Manufacturing establishments in Cape Breton, 1851   80

4.1 Occupational structure of the Cape Breton workforce, 1851   86

4.2 Boats and vessels in the Cape Breton fishery, 1851   90

4.3 Workforce employed at Sydney Mines and Bridgeport, September 1838   101

4.4 Monthly employment of colliers and labourers at Sydney Mines, Queen Pit, 1839 and 1857   103

6.1 Principal occupations of the Cape Breton workforce, 1881   123

6.2 Principal agricultural exports outside Nova Scotia, 1864–65   130

6.3 Distribution of farms by size, improved acreage, and livestock holdings, 1870–71   134

6.4 Principal manufacturing establishments in Cape Breton, 1871 and 1891   147

6.5 Capitalization and type of merchants in Cape Breton, 1870   148

7.1 Boats and vessels in Cape Breton, 1891   157

8.1 Total net migration from Cape Breton, 1871–91   188

8.2 Percentage change of population, 1851–91   189

8.3 Distribution of Nova Scotians in Canada, 1881–91   191

8.4 Distribution of Nova Scotians in selected states and territories of the United States, 1870–80   194

Preface

There is growing interest among geographers today in regional geography. This interest focuses less on the revival of the old descriptive regional geography than on using the regional concept to understand the impact of general processes on particular places. Through the regional approach, it is possible to identify broad spatial patterns of settlement, economy, and society and to delimit their interrelations. This allows a clearer picture of regional settlement and development to emerge than in a systematic or sectoral approach.

Although much regional geography concentrates on the contemporary world, *Nineteenth-Century Cape Breton* is a work of regional historical geography. It focuses on the relatively small, peripheral island of Cape Breton, part of present-day Nova Scotia, and examines its changing human geography over a hundred-year period. It sets out the basic patterns of economy, settlement, and society on the Island during the nineteenth century and considers the processes that shaped them. In particular, it looks at the impact of Scottish immigration on the Island's settlement and agricultural development, and at the role of mercantile and industrial capital in developing Cape Breton's two great staple industries (the cod fishery and coal industry). The social and economic patterns associated with each of these economies are presented, and the interrelations among the three economies are examined. The study argues that the patterns of settlement, economy, and society established on the Island during the nineteenth century were remarkably similar to patterns created elsewhere in Canada. In fact, Cape Breton can stand as a somewhat stark model of much of the settlement and economic development that occurred in nineteenth-century Canada.

The Introduction outlines the larger context for this study. It examines the importance of staple trades and agricultural settlement for early New World development and for the nineteenth-century Cape Breton experience. As in other historical geographies, the methodology employed in the substantive chapters combines cross-sectional accounts of the patterns of settlement and economy at specific times with vertical themes that discuss the processes of change. The study begins with an assessment of Cape Breton in 1800. Chapter 1 summarizes the little development that had occurred on the Island since the British take-over in 1758 and sets the scene for the massive Scottish immigrations that began in 1802. Chapter 2 considers the changing circumstances in the western Highlands and islands of Scotland during the early nineteenth century that propelled so many Scots to Cape Breton and other parts of British North America. The social and economic background of the immigrants is discussed to allow comparison with subsequent developments in Cape Breton, and the nature of the migration is outlined because of its relevance to the process of settlement on the Island. The spread of Scottish settlement and the growth of agriculture are the subjects of chapter 3. Chapter 4 deals with the Island's two staple industries – cod fishing and coal mining – and charts their evolution during the early nineteenth century. Acting as a hinge between the chapters that deal with Cape Breton in the early and late nineteenth century, chapter 5 focuses on the potato famine that occurred on the Island between 1845 and 1849. This is a convenient centre point for the study. The famine put an end to significant Scottish immigration and precipitated a massive emigration from the Island that was to run into the twentieth century. The potato famine in Cape Breton, like that in Ireland and western Scotland, was an event of singular importance.

The continued growth of population, the spread of settlement, and the increasing difficulties of farming on the Island in the late nineteenth century are examined in chapter 6. Chapter 7 considers later developments in the cod fishery and the expansion of the mining industry after 1858. Chapters 5, 6, and 7 outline the causes of the emigration from Cape Breton in the late nineteenth century, which is then dealt with in chapter 8. Chapters 6, 7, and 8 all deal with Cape Breton up to 1891, a logical point to end the study. In the early 1890s, a branch of the Intercolonial Railway was built across the Island, linking the industrial towns of eastern Cape Breton with the mainland and providing an improved market connection for farmers. More importantly, the take-over of most of the coal mines by the Dominion Coal Company in 1893 and the building of a steelworks ushered in an expansion of the coal industry so massive that the migration of Cape Bretoners was to some extent reoriented away from New England towards the mining towns of eastern Cape Breton. In many ways, the historical geography of nineteenth-century Cape Breton ends in the early 1890s and that of the twentieth century begins. A cross-section of the Island in 1891 is presented in chapter 9, a summary of the tremendous changes that had taken place over one hundred years. The chapter also draws the various themes of the study together, discusses their interrelations, and suggests some possible connections between Cape Breton, the Maritimes, and other parts of Canada in the nineteenth century.

This study has been ten years in the making, and during that time I have benefited enormously from the help and wisdom of many people. My interest in the historical geography of North America was first whetted by Peter Goheen at Queen's University, where I was on a year's exchange from the University of St Andrews in Scotland. It seems most appropriate that this book is being published under his editorship at McGill-Queen's University Press. My interest in the historical geography of North America was sustained at St Andrews by Graeme Whittington and Bruce Proudfoot, who encouraged me to do graduate work in Canada. Although warned by Cole Harris that British Columbia "really is still the North American frontier," I count it my good fortune to have done my graduate work under his guidance at the University of British Columbia. While *Nineteenth-Century Cape Breton* owes much to his ideas on the expansion of Europe overseas, his dedication to the unravelling of the fascinating human geography of Canada has been far more influential. I owe him a great debt of thanks. This study has also benefited from the enthusiasm and interest of Graeme Wynn, who has generously made many helpful comments on the text. I would also like to thank Elizabeth Mancke, who, through many spirited discussions, has helped sharpen my understanding of nineteenth-century Nova Scotia.

Research on Cape Breton would have been difficult to accomplish without the generous help of the Canadian Commonwealth Scholarship Committee. They provided support for four years in the doctoral program at the University of British Columbia and made available funds for essential travel to the archives in Ottawa, Halifax, and Sydney. Further support for research, travel, and a publication subvention was most generously provided by Canada Research

Awards from the Canadian Embassy, Washington, DC, and the Canadian-American Center, University of Maine.

Research for this study took me from Ottawa to Edinburgh via Halifax, Sydney, and Boston, and I would like to thank the staffs of the following institutions for their assistance: the National Archives of Canada, the National Library of Canada, and the Department of Labour Library in Ottawa; the Public Archives of Nova Scotia in Halifax; the Beaton Institute in Sydney; the Baker Library, Harvard University, in Cambridge; and the Scottish Record Office and National Library of Scotland in Edinburgh. Permission to quote from the R.G. Dun Collection has been given by the Baker Library, Harvard University.

Parts of this book have appeared in slightly different form in the *Annals of the Association of American Geographers*; in D. Day, editor, *Geographical Perspectives on the Maritime Provinces*; and in K. Donovan, editor, *The Island: New Perspectives on Cape Breton History, 1713–1990*. I would like to thank the editors of these publications for permission to publish copyright material.

I am also grateful for the research assistance of Victoria Hornsby and for the cartographic help of Ray Harris of the University of Edinburgh, who speedily transformed my rough drafts into clear maps. My final words of thanks are reserved for my wife, Kathleen, who has helped in numerous ways to expedite this study and has borne my interest in Cape Breton with great patience and good humour.

Introduction

The expansion of European capital and labour into North America during the colonial period created two broad patterns of regional development. The first pattern revolved around the exploitation of raw materials or staples and encompassed much of eastern Canada and the southern colonies; the second pattern focused on agricultural settlement and included the middle and New England colonies, as well as parts of eastern Canada. Together, these two patterns created a matrix in which much of the life and work of colonial North America was worked out, a matrix which also encompassed many of the developments in nineteenth-century Cape Breton.[1]

Staple trades were the earliest and longest-lived European economic activity in the New World. The discovery of a succession of raw materials – fish, fur-bearing animals, timber, minerals – and the possibility of growing plantation crops in the southern colonies, coupled with increasing international demand for these resources, led to the investment of European mercantile capital in New World staple production. Strategies of resource exploitation varied from one staple to another, but all involved the attempt to achieve economies of scale and a uniform, quality product through large-scale production. In a still pre-industrial age, labour was a vital part of the productive process and was supplied mostly by immigrant workers. At first, this labour force was transient and male,[2] but over time, wives and families reached the New World and the European populations associated with staple trades became more settled and demographically balanced. As labour was a large part of the cost of

production, capital attempted to reduce its price by importing indentured workers, by manipulating long-credit or truck payments,
and, in the southern colonies, by using African slaves. Long-distance
transportation tied staples to overseas markets, creating complex
trade networks across the North Atlantic. As demand for staple
products increased, so staple economies expanded; as demand slackened, so economies contracted. Cycles of boom and bust were common.[3] In the "timber colony" of New Brunswick, for example, the
early nineteenth-century staple economy has been described as "a
gigantic bandalore, ineluctably tied by the lines of transatlantic commerce to the rise and fall of the market for its staple product."[4]

Depending on the nature of the resource, staple economies
spawned multipliers or linkages that produced economic development in the New World.[5] Staples that were processed before
shipment generated processing industries (forward linkages).
Transportation of staples from place of production to place of shipment and from there to overseas markets required roads, wharves,
ports, wagons, and ships (backward linkages). Staple workforces consumed goods (final demand linkages) that were either imported from
Europe (a simple exchange of raw materials for manufactured
goods) or manufactured in the New World. Through taxation, staples also produced government revenue.

Although each staple trade created its own particular workplaces
– outports, fur posts, logging camps, plantations – all were highly
specialized single-industry settlements. They provided rudimentary
accommodation for management and workers, some limited processing facilities, warehouses or an area set aside for storing the
staple, and a shipping wharf. As the population became more balanced, families either rented company housing or acquired some
land and provided their own accommodation. A few service buildings, such as a church, were eventually added. Yet these larger, more
diverse settlements were still dominated by the nucleus of company
buildings, the economic heart of a staple trade settlement. Moreover,
their fortunes waxed and waned with those of the staple trades.
When market demand shifted or staple resources were exhausted,
staple settlements collapsed.[6]

Society within these settlements was stratified according to occupational ranking. At the top of the hierarchy were merchants and
planters, in the middle were skilled workers, and at the bottom were
unskilled workers and slaves. Where staple settlements were
bounded by forest, ocean, and native peoples, workforces had no
alternative employment or social groups to cushion the frequently
brutal relations between capital and labour.

In areas where staples could not be extracted, land held little attraction for European capital. Once any native population had been removed, either by disease, warfare, or land alienation, land was available relatively cheaply to immigrant European labour. The application of limited capital and massive amounts of family labour eventually yielded a farm, the basic productive unit of the rural economy. Such farms produced foodstuffs for the family and small surpluses for sale in local markets. Compared to a staple trade, the farm operation was relatively detached from the market and unspecialized. Given the availability of land, there was little need for the intensive cultivation practices and common fields of European agriculture; New World farming tended to be much more extensive and individualistic. Farms were dispersed across the landscape rather than concentrated in nucleated villages, while services were sited at accessible, central locations.[7]

So long as the market for agricultural produce was weak and population densities were low, there was considerable opportunity for settlers with limited capital to acquire land. A relatively undifferentiated rural society of family farmers appeared. To be sure, farmers on fertile land and close to markets had more commercial farms, but these were rarely equivalent to the plantations of the southern colonies or the great estates of the Old World. The availability of land and relative weakness of the rural economy had pared away the upper stratas of European society and discouraged the formation of a New World landed aristocracy. A significant degree of social and economic levelling had taken place.[8] The growth of the agricultural economy depended as much on the internal dynamic of increasing population as on the external dynamic of rising market demand. As the population grew, some farms were subdivided to accommodate the excess population, the number of landless increased, land values rose, and social and economic differentiation became marked. Yet the proximity of unsettled land frequently allowed the expansion of the agricultural frontier, relieving pressure in older settled areas. A generational cycle of immigration, population growth, and migration to new unsettled lands became part of the pattern of agricultural settlement.[9]

There was considerable variation in the regional distribution of these two patterns. In some areas, the economy was based on staple production for foreign markets; in others, it was based on the family farm and local market. Among the Thirteen Colonies, Virginia and Maryland specialized in the tobacco staple, while the Carolinas and Georgia developed staple economies based on rice and indigo. A highly stratified society consisting of a planter aristocracy, yeoman farmers, and black slaves developed. Farther north, the middle and New England colonies were more suited to family farming, although there was a good deal of regional variation. While the rich farmland of southeastern Pennsylvania was claimed to be the "best poor man's country in the world,"[10] the rocky uplands of northern New England offered only a meagre agricultural opportunity to European settlers. Within these areas, there were also considerable differences. In colonial Massachusetts, for example, the semi-subsistent family farms in Dedham contrasted markedly with the fur-trading "company town" of Springfield, which was controlled by the Pynchon family.[11] In neighbouring Connecticut, the prosperous intervale (valley bottom) farms of the Lower Connecticut River Valley, noted for their grain production, were very different from the stony hill farms of Litchfield, Windham, and Fairfield counties, where livestock raising dominated.[12] Yet whatever the regional differences in the rural economy, it was clear that agricultural land lay at the heart of early American development.

The agricultural opportunity available to European settlers in the middle and northern colonies gave powerful force to the agrarian ideal in America. Frenchman Hector St John de Crèvecour, perhaps the best known of many late eighteenth-century observers of the American scene, was quick to grasp the opportunity that these colonies offered land-starved Europeans and the social contrasts with the Old World: "The rich and the poor are not so far removed from each other as they are in Europe," he wrote. "We are a people of cultivators ... each person works for himself ... A pleasing uniformity of decent competence appears throughout our habitations ... We have no princes, for whom we toil, starve, and bleed: we are the most perfect society existing in the world." At about the same time that de Crèvecour was writing, Thomas Jefferson saw the political implications of this new rural society. "The small land holders," he declared, "are the most precious part of the state."[13] The independent yeoman farmer living on his own land was to be the backbone of the new American republic, the guarantor of American democracy. With Jefferson's purchase of Louisiana, this democratic future was secure. Vast new spaces were available for the expansion of the American agricultural empire. As settlers spilled over the Appalachians to occupy the rich agricultural lands of the Ohio Country and Mississippi Basin – "the Garden of the World" – agrarianism and individual success became central tenets of the American national myth. When the westward push eventually ran out of space in the foothills of the Rockies in the late nineteenth century, historian Frederick Jackson Turner could look back over nearly three hundred years of agrarian expansion and persuasively argue that the essence of America had lain in its agricultural frontier.

Farther north, in the territory that would eventually become Canada, the pattern of staples and agriculture continued, but the balance between the two was much different from that in the Thirteen Colonies. Exploitation of the northern staples of codfish and furs, rather than agriculture, dominated the early Canadian economy.[14] Along the barren Atlantic coasts and deep in the northern interior, European merchant capital was invested in the cod fishery and fur trade. Single-industry work camps were established in the wilderness, specialized labour was recruited, European work practices and technology were introduced, and long lines of transportation to outside markets and supplies were put in place. Where staple settlements were populated from specific areas of Europe and Old World cultural traits did not interfere with New World production, cultural replication occurred. Staple settlements were enclaves of specialized work and culture, tied by long-distance trade to the outside world. In the lee of the staple trades, a few pockets of land were available for agricultural settlement. Until the opening of the Canadian West for settlement at the end of the nineteenth century, these pockets consisted of the southern peninsula of Ontario, the Lower St Lawrence Valley, the Bay of Fundy marshlands, Prince Edward Island, and the larger river valleys of the Maritimes. Compared to the extensive farmland in the Thirteen Colonies, these pockets were a meagre endowment. They were close to the climatic limit for wheat cultivation and unsuitable for the plantation crops of the American South. Unattractive to large capital investment, they drew only a few settlers from Europe. Weakly stratified rural societies dependent upon the family farm and local markets emerged. Low immigration and plentiful land ensured that during the seventeenth and eighteenth centuries space was available for the expanding population. Where settlers were drawn from the same ethnic group, distinct regional cultures developed. A patchwork pattern of peoples – "garrison societies" Northrop Frye has called them – was created.[15]

This basic composition of staple trades and agriculture continued to shape the development of Canada during the nineteenth century. The old commercial staples of fish and fur were supplemented by new industrial economies that were based on primary resources (timber, minerals) and also produced for export. Although some of these new staples were more dependent upon North American rather than European sources of capital, labour, and technology, the basic characteristics of the earlier pattern survived. The new staples relied heavily upon external investment; they supplied distant, often fluctuating, markets; and they created compact, single-industry settlements dominated by their particular work routines. Mass immigration from Britain in the early nineteenth century led to the settlement of further patches of agricultural land. Initially, at least, these pockets offered settlers considerable agricultural opportunity. Where settlers came from the same area of the British Isles, culturally homogeneous rural societies were created. Yet by mid-century, these pockets were filled and the agricultural opportunity for new settlers was severely constrained. Rural society was increasingly marked by stratification and emigration. Some people left for the expanding agricultural frontier of the United States; others pursued an agricultural vision on the granite edge of the Canadian Shield or the northern front of the Appalachian Highlands, frequently combining subsistence farming with part-time employment in the nearest staple industry. Where local work was unavailable, people sooner or later moved into the industrializing towns and cities of Canada and the northern United States. The expansion of the Canadian agricultural empire ran into the rock of the shield and the textile towns of New England.[16]

Among the areas of Canada encompassed by these two patterns was Cape Breton Island, located at the mouth of the Gulf of St Lawrence (Figure I.1). At the beginning of the nineteenth century, Cape Breton had been part of a staple-producing world for 300 years. Cabot's discovery of the cod-rich waters of the northwest Atlantic in the late fifteenth century led to the incorporation of the inshore fishing grounds of Cape Breton, along with those of Labrador, Newfoundland, and Nova Scotia, into a massive, European-based fishery.[17] In the sixteenth and seventeenth centuries, the Island was a subordinate part of a much larger French cod fishery that stretched from the western shore of Newfoundland's Avalon Peninsula, around the Gulf of St Lawrence, and along the Atlantic shore of Nova Scotia (Figure I.1). French and Basque merchants financed a seasonal or migratory fishery to Cape Breton, sending supply vessels and fishing crews across the Atlantic each spring. Along bleak New World coasts, temporary shore stations were constructed, bases for the summer cod fishery. After a season's fishing, the fishermen loaded their dried and salted cod onto vessels and returned to Europe. In the early eighteenth century, the French, displaced from their fishing bases in Newfoundland by the English, supplemented the migratory fishery to Cape Breton with a permanent fishing station at Louisbourg (Figure I.1), an ice-free harbour on Cape Breton's southern shore. The port soon became a major centre for the cod fishery, an important naval base, and an entrepôt

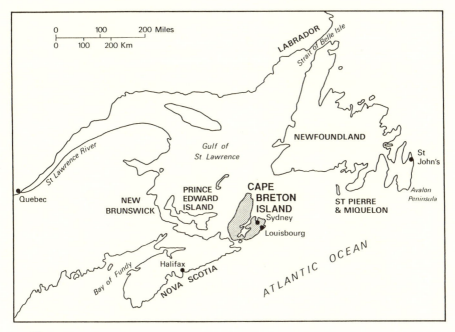

Figure 1.1
Location of Cape Breton Island

of French trade in the North Atlantic.[18] Among the most important commercial centres along the eastern seaboard and an outer bastion of New France, Louisbourg was defended by the largest, most sophisticated fortifications in North America. Yet the Seven Years' War (1756–63) between Britain and France led to the destruction of Louisbourg, the capture of Quebec, and the end of the French regime in North America. The victorious British took over Cape Breton, deported most of its French inhabitants, and quickly set about restoring the Island's cod fishery. Although numerous small Nova Scotian merchants became involved in the fishery, a handful of merchants based on the English Channel Islands soon controlled much of the industry. They established large fishing stations on the Island, imported supplies and seasonal labour from the Channel Islands, outfitted Acadian, Irish, and Scottish settlers for the fishery, and exported dried fish to overseas markets. By the early nineteenth century, a series of staple enclaves, each heavily dependent upon external capital and markets but marked by considerable individual cultural distinctiveness, had been created around the coast of Cape Breton.

Soon after the fishery was re-established, the second pattern began to be put in place on the Island. Successive restructurings of the agricultural economy of the western Highlands and islands of Scotland in the late eighteenth and early nineteenth centuries led to the displacement of thousands of people, many of whom emigrated to British North America. The Scottish settlers who arrived in Cape Breton found only a meagre agricultural base. Constrained by rocky uplands and a short growing season, early settlers occupied the few patches of good land on the Island. After a lifetime's hard work, a few achieved a modest independence on the land. Later arrivals, however, were forced onto the uplands of Cape Breton, where they struggled to make a living. Mixed livelihoods were cobbled together from farming, fishing, and mining. An independence on the land depended upon part-time, wage labour elsewhere. A vibrant Gaelic culture, under siege in Scotland, was also transplanted to Cape Breton, the basis of a distinctive regional culture. Yet once the available agricultural land had been settled, people drifted away in search of work. By the late nineteenth century, Cape Bretoners were leaving the Island, most destined for the towns and cities of New England. Cultural replication would be difficult, if not impossible, in the cultural melting pot of the United States.

At about the same time that Cape Breton was providing a meagre agricultural niche for thousands of Scottish emigrants escaping the changes engendered by British industrialization, the Island began to be incorporated into the new industrial world. Just as Cape Breton's rich cod fisheries had attracted British mercantile capital, so the Island's coalfield, among the largest in North America, drew British industrial investment. Over the course of the century, British and American mining companies sank numerous mines, imported management and labour, employed the latest mining technology, laid out company villages, and created a full-time mining workforce. As in the fishery, the investment of external capital in the Island's natural resources had produced a staple economy, settlements, and workforce heavily dependent upon the outside world.

The intersection of these two patterns on Cape Breton Island in the nineteenth century gave rise to a distinctive regional geography. While the details and circumstances of this geography were unique to the Island, elements of the Cape Breton experience were found in other parts of Maritime Canada. Viewed more generally, the historical geography of this small, peripheral island offers a simple, somewhat stark encapsulation of some of the salient developments in settled Canada during the nineteenth century.

Nineteenth-Century Cape Breton

1 Cape Breton Island at the Beginning of the Nineteenth Century

At the beginning of the nineteenth century, Cape Breton Island was a thinly settled, extensively forested, and relatively undeveloped colony of Great Britain (Figure 1.1). Barely 2,500 people lived on the Island. Most of them dwelt in a few settlements scattered around the coast: some 800 in Sydney and along the shores of Sydney Harbour; almost 200 in Main-à-Dieu, Louisbourg, and Gabarus; and about 1,500 split between Arichat and the northwest coast.[1] About half the population were French-speaking Acadians concentrated in Île Madame and Chéticamp; most of the rest were Loyalists settled in Sydney and Baddeck River. The remainder were Southern Irish and New Englanders settled along the southeast shore, Gaelic-speaking Scots dispersed along the west coast, and Micmac Indians in the interior woods.

The economy of Cape Breton, like that of much of Atlantic Canada, was dominated by the cod fishery.[2] It supported about two-thirds of the population, attracted British mercantile capital and skilled labour, and tied the colony into the North Atlantic commercial world. Coal mining, the Island's other staple industry, employed few people, rarely made money, and fed into a more local, regional economy. Together, these staples generated some shipping and ship-building. Farming, employing most of the remaining population, was largely subsistent; only a few sales were made to the fishery and regional markets. Superimposed upon this economic structure was the colonial regime at Sydney, the Cape Breton capital, which supported barely 200 people and scarcely extended beyond the town.

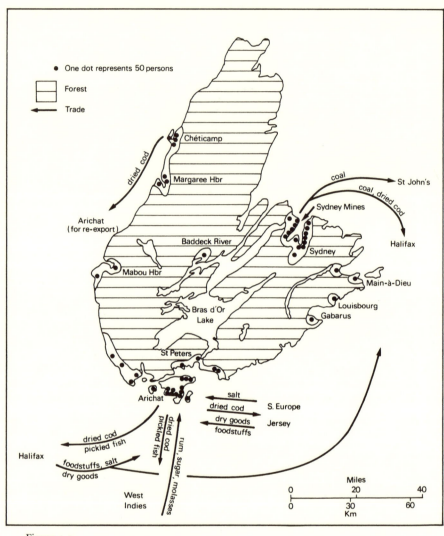

Figure 1.1
Settlement on Cape Breton Island in 1800
Source: Return of population enclosed in General Despard to Lord Hobart, 24 December
1801, CO/CB/A/22, National Archives of Canada.

THE COD FISHERY

After the French withdrawal from Cape Breton in 1758, British and
colonial merchants moved in to rebuild the cod fishery.[3] In 1765,
merchants from the English Channel Islands opened a fishing station

at Arichat on Île Madame and, a few years later, another at Chéticamp on the northwest coast. In the early 1760s, a Newfoundland
merchant established a station at Louisbourg, and several New England traders also operated along the south shore. At the same time,
some of the Acadian fishermen who had been deported from Cape
Breton after the capture of Louisbourg returned to settle at Île
Madame and Chéticamp. In addition, a few Irish migrants from the
Newfoundland fishery settled at Louisbourg, and English fishermen,
a mixture of New Englanders and disbanded soldiers, settled at
Main-à-Dieu, Louisbourg, and Gabarus.

At the beginning of the nineteenth century, the cod fishery was
concentrated at Arichat and a few outports around the coast (Figure 1.1). With some 350 inhabitants, Arichat was by far the biggest
place in Cape Breton. It served as the main fishing port on Île
Madame, as one of the colony's two customs ports, and as the Island's
principal centre for the distribution of imported supplies to the
outports and for the collection and export of dried fish; in 1796, 81
percent of Cape Breton's dried-fish exports passed through the
port.[4] Elsewhere on Île Madame, there were fishing settlements at
Petit-de-Grat and D'Escousse, each with about 150 inhabitants. On
the opposite Cape Breton shore, River Bourgeois and St Peters
shared some 100 people, and nearby L'Ardoise had another 100.
Farther east, Gabarus, Louisbourg, and Main-à-Dieu each had about
50 inhabitants. The only other sizeable place associated with the
fishery was Chéticamp with some 200 people.[5]

The cod fishery was dominated by three Channel Island merchants: Janvrin & Co., Remon & Co., and Philip Robin & Co.[6] Although based in Jersey, they had extensive interests in North Atlantic
trade and the New World cod fishery.[7] Janvrin owned fishing stations at Île Madame, the Magdalen Islands, and Gaspé; Remon had
stations in eastern Cape Breton and at Chaleur Bay; Philip Robin
had stations at Arichat and Chéticamp and was connected to Charles
Robin & Co., the most important fish merchant in Gaspé.[8] The
merchants manned these stations with company agents and seasonal
labour, imported supplies to outfit local fishermen, sent vessels
along the coast to collect fish, and exported cod. In 1796, the three
merchants shipped 13,059 quintals (1 qtl = 112 lbs = 51 kgs) of
cod from Cape Breton, 63 percent of the colony's total dried-fish
exports.[9]

Cod exports allowed the Channel Island merchants to participate
in an extensive triangular trade around the North Atlantic
(Figure 1.2). Prime-quality dried cod was shipped to southern Europe, where wines, nuts, and olive oil were purchased for the British

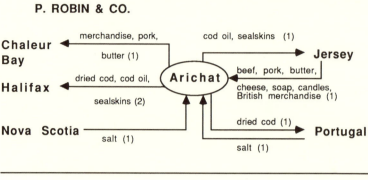

P. ROBIN & CO.

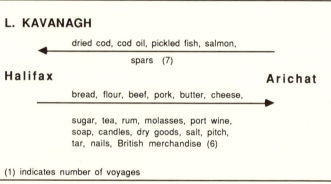

L. KAVANAGH

(1) indicates number of voyages

Figure 1.2
Trade connections of P. Robin & Co. (top) and L. Kavanagh (bottom) in 1796
Source: Shipping Returns for Arichat, 1796, co 221/34, National Archives of Canada.

market, and salt for the Cape Breton fishery. Inferior dried cod was exported to the Caribbean, where rum, sugar, and molasses were bought, either for consumption in Cape Breton or to sell in Europe. The goods sold in Britain provided cash to buy manufactured goods and foodstuffs, which were exported, via Jersey, to Cape Breton. Such trade was tightly controlled; on every leg, cargoes were transported in company vessels, and at some ports, business transactions were carried out by company agents. Yet such long-distance trade was vulnerable: shipwreck and war took their toll, competition from rival producers was a constant threat, and the rise and fall of the market was beyond the merchants' control.

The rest of the Cape Breton fishery was organized by a few local merchants and numerous planters. In 1796, there were only three Cape Breton merchants of any importance: Lawrence Kavanagh at St Peters and the partnership of Tremain & Stout at Sydney.[10] They were general, all-purpose merchants with fishing as one interest among others. They imported supplies, outfitted fishermen, sold seed and provisions to farmers, and exported fish and country produce. Tremain & Stout, "the principle and indeed the only respectable merchants in Sydney," also ran the local coal mine and exported coal to Halifax.[11] In 1796, Kavanagh and Tremain & Stout handled 3,661 quintals of cod, 18 percent of the Island's total dried-fish exports. The planters owned a fishing station and a fishing boat or small schooner and hired men as crew. They drew supplies from Cape Breton, Channel Island, or Halifax merchants and sold fish in return.[12] In 1796, 25 planters exported 3,952 quintals of cod, with individual cargoes ranging from 20 to 570 quintals.

Cape Breton merchants and planters had insufficient capital to trade directly with overseas markets; instead, they dealt with middlemen in Halifax. Compared to the intricate, international dealings of the Channel Island merchants, this was a simple trade: dried cod and cod oil were shipped along the coast to Halifax merchant-wholesalers for re-export; salt, supplies, foodstuffs, and British merchandise were shipped back to Cape Breton (Figure 1.2). In 1796, the Cape Breton merchants and planters exported 7,293 quintals, 96 percent of their cod exports, to Halifax. The port dominated more than a third of the Island's cod trade.

The Cape Breton cod fishery was almost entirely an inshore fishery. During late spring, cod spawn on the offshore banks and then move inshore to feed on herring, mackerel, and capelin.[13] Although the exact time varies from place to place, cod usually arrive around the coasts of Cape Breton in early May and stay until mid-December, when they return to the banks. They appear to be most plentiful in inshore waters during June, July, and August. Although cod were intercepted on the banks by Nova Scotian fishermen (the bank or offshore fishery), the fish had to be heavily salted to preserve them during the weeks at sea, which produced a poor-quality cure. But cod caught inshore could be landed the same day and processed quickly, producing a high-quality cure. Cape Breton, like parts of Newfoundland and Gaspé, was ideally situated for the inshore fishery.

By the turn of the nineteenth century, the techniques and technology of the inshore cod fishery were well developed. The principal fishing crafts were the shallop or whaleboat, which had been used for fishing in New World waters since the sixteenth century, and the schooner. The shallop was an undecked or partially decked rowing boat with one or two masts that could be set up as necessary (Figure 1.3).[14] It was usually clinker-built, 15–30 feet long, and ta-

Figure 1.3
Fishermen hand-lining for cod from a whaleboat
Source: G.B. Goode, *The Fisheries and Fishing Industries of the United States*, section 3 (Washington, DC: US Government Printing Office, 1887).

pered from the middle to each end. The boat was rigged with two spritsails or gaff-sails, but could be fitted with a schooner rig for deep-sea voyages. Two or three men crewed the boat, sufficient to handle it in the roughest of weather. The schooner was a versatile vessel used for trading and fishing (Figure 1.4). It was 30–60 feet long, between 20 and 120 tons (although schooners in Cape Breton were usually 35–45 tons), and crewed by two or three men for trading voyages and four to six men for cod fishing.[15]

Fishing was done with hook and line.[16] Each fisherman was equipped with four lines for shallow water (less than ten fathoms) and two for deeper water. Each line had a lead sinker, weighing from two to three pounds according to the depth of water and strength of current, and a double hook baited with fresh herring, mackerel, capelin, squid, or cod offal. If cod were biting, as many as three or four quintals could be taken by each fishermen in a day. Shallop fishermen were usually out on the grounds from dawn until late afternoon, although a freshening wind or a lack of bait could

Figure 1.4
Crew fishing from rail of a cod schooner
Source: G.B. Goode, *The Fisheries and Fishing Industries of the United States*, section 3
(Washington, DC: US Government Printing Office, 1887.

shorten the day's fishing. Schooner fishermen could be out longer, in which case the fish had to be salted on board.

The catch was landed on the beach or at the stage head of a fishing station. If the fish were being delivered to a merchant, the catch was weighed and the fisherman's tally recorded in the merchant's day-book. The cod were then "dressed" before they became warm and spoiled, a process that took place either on a table set up on the beach or on the stage head (Figure 1.5). The fish were sliced open from the throat to the navel, the entrails removed and thrown away, the liver detached and saved in a barrel, and the head cut off. Their bodies were then opened up from the neck to the tail and the back-bone removed. After that, the fish were ready for curing, a long, complex task upon which their price depended. The fish were spread in a pile, flesh side up, and covered with a layer of salt. After five or six days drying, they were placed in a trough, where they were washed to remove all the salt, and then stacked to dry further. A day or two later, providing the weather was fine, the fish were laid out, again flesh side up, on flakes (raised timber platforms) for the

Figure 1.5
A late nineteenth-century view of a stage head. Apart from the old dory being used for washing cod, scenes similar to this would have occurred at the Channel Island fishing stations in Cape Breton in the early nineteenth century.
Source: G.B. Goode, *The Fisheries and Fishing Industries of the United States*, section 3 (Washington, DC: US Government Printing Office, 1887).

third drying process. After the first day, the fish were turned over, skin side up, to protect them from the night's dew. Thereafter, they were laid out, flesh side up, each morning and collected up and made into piles of 20 to 30 in the evening. After two or three days drying, the fish were placed in large piles, each containing about 125 quintals, and covered with birch-bark or canvas weighted down with stones. This process aimed to squeeze out the last remaining moisture and lasted several weeks. Once completely dry, the fish were housed in a dry fish store. On a fine day, just before shipping, the fish were taken outside and spread on the ground for a "last sunning" or "parting sun" to extract any dampness that might have been absorbed in the fish store. The fish were then packed in tubs ready for export. Such "kench curing," as it was called, produced prime, merchantable dried fish, suitable for the best markets.

Obviously the weather was critical to the success of the cure. Warm air rather than sunshine was most needed; a west wind bringing warm, dry air off the continent was the best drying weather. Easterly or southeasterly winds off the Atlantic tended to bring cloud, rain, or, in the words of a Robin agent, "our usually constant friend the fog."[17] If fish were still lying flesh side up when it began raining, the flesh quickly deteriorated. Cut branches (dinnage) were always at hand to cover the fish at the first sign of rain. Protected by the Cape Breton Highlands from the Atlantic fogs, the fishing stations along the gulf shore of Cape Breton, particularly Chéticamp, were the best placed for making dried fish.

Apart from the cod fishery, Channel Island and Cape Breton merchants were involved in several subsidiary fisheries.[18] The most important were the herring and mackerel fisheries, which provided fresh bait for the cod fishery and pickled fish for export. In 1796, Janvrin exported 660 barrels of pickled fish to Barbados, while resident merchants and planters shipped 582 barrels to Halifax, 277 to other parts of Nova Scotia, and 100 to New Brunswick. Like cod, herring and mackerel were caught in inshore waters; particularly good runs were intercepted along the west coast and the Strait of Canso in late summer when the fish migrated from their feeding grounds in the Gulf of St Lawrence to deep water in the Atlantic. The fish were caught in gill-nets set overnight, landed the next day, gutted, and pickled in barrels. The merchants also dealt in the salmon fishery; in 1796, Janvrin shipped 102 barrels of pickled salmon to Portugal and 35 to Ireland, while resident merchants and planters sent 598 to Halifax. The salmon fishery was prosecuted around the Island's coasts, particularly at river mouths where the fish were caught as they migrated upstream; the Margaree River was the most important salmon fishery in Cape Breton. The fish were caught in nets and then split and pickled in barrels. A few planters, mainly those at Margaree Harbour and Chéticamp, were also involved in the hazardous seal fishery. Sealing usually took place along the west coast of Newfoundland and around the Magdalen Islands in March, when harp seal pups were still on the ice. In 1796, three puncheons and 340 sealskins were exported to Halifax, and 525 skins to Jersey.

Fishing, like other pre-industrial occupations, was labour intensive. Men were needed for fishing, processing the catch, curing the cod, making barrels, building shallops and trading vessels, and maintaining fishing premises. At the turn of the nineteenth century, there were two sources of labour: migrant workers from Europe and resident fishermen in Cape Breton. Migrant workers had been crossing the Atlantic from Europe to the New World cod fisheries since the early sixteenth century, but their numbers were declining as the resident European population increased during the late eighteenth century.[19] Even so, Channel Island companies in Cape Breton and the Gulf of St Lawrence and some English companies in Newfoundland and Labrador continued to import men for the fishery. In the mid-1790s, a Cape Breton official reckoned there to be "above 100 Jersey men attending the curing of fish who spend but six months in the year in the Island."[20] Most of these men were recruited from small farms in the Channel Islands; the cash wages paid by the companies provided a much-needed supplementary income.[21] The men left in spring and returned in late fall, a seasonal transhumance across the Atlantic that fitted neatly into the agricultural calendar. Crops were planted before they left; potato raising, ploughing, and sowing were done after they returned.

Most of the labour, however, was drawn from the resident population. In 1800, the majority of fishermen were Acadians living at Arichat and Chéticamp; the rest were Irish and New Englanders at Main-à-Dieu, Louisbourg, and Gabarus. Some of these men were planters and relatively independent; they owned their own boat and gear and exchanged their catch for provisions. Others lacked the means to fish and had to serve as crewmen on shallops and schooners belonging to the planters and merchants. They were credited with their catch or shares of a catch and paid in provisions.

Considerable differences existed between the Channel Island and resident workforces. Channel Islanders worked in fish-processing factories, in which there was a highly specialized division of labour.[22] Some men were assigned to fishing and employed as shallop masters, fishermen, or stowers; others were engaged on shore, either as cut-throats, headers, splitters, and salters in the fish-processing sheds or as labourers at the fish-drying flakes. There were also numerous support staff – clerks, bookkeepers, storekeepers, carpenters, black-smiths, shipwrights, and cooks – who maintained and facilitated the daily running of the station. All these employees were supervised by company overseers: a beach master kept an eye on the critically important curing process, while a company agent, in frequent contact by letter with headquarters in Jersey, was responsible for the fishing station.

Although the stratified and occupationally specialized nature of these workforces was similar to that of the factory workforces in industrializing Britain, the routine of work was essentially pre-industrial.[23] Fishing and processing crews could work only when cod and fresh bait were available and the weather was fair; at other times, they were employed in maintenance work, shipbuilding, or labouring on the station's farm. Moreover, when fish were drying, the threat of rain would bring every man on the station out to the flakes to turn and cover the fish. The dictates of weather, fish, and curing set very different rhythms from those of a mechanized factory.

Resident fishermen were less specialized and even more flexible in their work than the Channel Islanders. Because the unit of production was small, usually consisting only of a planter and his crew or family members, individuals had to do a variety of tasks that would have been the sole responsibility of one or two men in the much larger fishing stations. Men fished, processed the catch if necessary, built shallops, and maintained smallholdings. Sons helped fathers fish; wives and daughters spread fish and tended crops and livestock. Moreover, resident fishermen enjoyed a greater degree of independence in the workplace than the Channel Islanders. Although planters must have kept a close eye on their fishing crews, merchants had little direct control over the fishermen they outfitted beyond the ability to threaten and exact financial penalties if a boat and gear were lost or damaged. Fishermen who owned their own boat could work as they pleased. For those Cape Breton fishermen, fishing was a way of life rather than a contractual employment.[24]

The principal fishing settlements on the Island were dominated by large fish-processing factories. At Arichat and Chéticamp, Channel Island merchants owned extensive properties covering several hundred acres,[25] sufficient land for a farm, woodlots, and numerous company buildings.[26] A typical Channel Island fishing station consisted of a long deep-water stage for unloading fishing boats and supply vessels; covered sheds for splitting and salting the catch; drying flakes, often covering several acres of beach; net-drying racks; dry fish and salt stores; rigging and sail lofts; a forge and cooperage; separate cookhouses for the migrant and resident employees; an agent's or merchant's house; a retail outlet for supplying fishermen; and a shipyard consisting of launchways, a covered sawpit, and timber sheds. Such premises were among the largest of any industry in Atlantic Canada. The planters' fishing rooms were much smaller, comprising a stage, shed for processing the fish, flakes, and another shed for storage. The remaining buildings in the outports were the homes of resident fishermen, usually little more than log cabins, roofed with bark or turf. Many fishermen also had gardens, small plots of land for growing hay, pasturing a cow, and cultivating potatoes and other vegetables.[27]

The population of the outports depended almost completely upon the fishery. In the southwest corner of the Island, the centre of the fishery, most heads of households in 1811 were employed in either the fishery or the coasting trade (Table 1.1). There were very few jobs in manufacturing or services, and virtually all of them were concentrated in Arichat. Within these outports, society was stratified

Table 1.1
Occupations and ethnic background of heads of
households on Île Madame and neighbouring
fishing settlements, 1811

Occupation	Acadian	Others
Fisherman	79	2
Mariner	139	8
Yeoman	30	10
Blacksmith	1	1
Shoemaker		1
Tailor		2
Priest	1	
Trader		2
Merchant		3
Innkeeper	2	
Customs officer		1
Civil officer		1
Doctor		1

Source: Nominal census of Arichat, Little Arichat, Upper Ari-
chat, Barrachois, Petit-de-Grat, D'Escousse, Grand Digue, River
Bourgeois, St Peters, and L'Ardoise, 1811, RG 1/333/84–98,
Public Archives of Nova Scotia.

according to occupational ranking. At the top of the social and economic hierarchy were the merchants, the facilitators of trade and
the greatest investors in the fishery. They imported supplies and
advanced them to planters and fishermen in return for fish; a system
similar to the putting-out method of production in the English cloth
industry. Planters, standing midway between merchants and fishermen, were dependent upon merchants for supplies and a market
connection, but ownership of boats and a fishing room gave them
power over their fishing crews. Fishermen had little or no capital
and were dependent upon merchants and planters.

These three groups were bound together by lines of credit and
debt. In good seasons, when codfish were in demand and prices were
high, fishermen could get a good return on their catch; in bad,
fishermen could not repay their advances and fell into debt. Further
debts quickly accumulated. More supplies and provisions were
needed for the winter and additional fishing gear for the following
summer. Once in debt, fishermen lost all power and were easily
exploited. As one Arichat priest observed, "Most of the people are
deep in the books of the merchants, who treat them with horrible

tyranny."[28] Planters, too, were frequently indebted to the merchants; with limited capital, they were easily squeezed out of business. Merchants were indebted to their suppliers, but at least the Channel Island companies were usually large enough to ride out a bad year and pay off their losses.

Outport society was also marked by sharp ethnic differences. Most of the merchants in Cape Breton were British and Protestant (the Channel Island merchants were originally French Huguenots). The majority of the fishermen, including the planters, were either Acadian or Irish and Roman Catholic (Table 1.1). Each group inhabited different social worlds: merchants knew each other and dealt with officials in the colonial capitals of Sydney and Halifax; fishermen lived in communities of friends and family. Among the Acadian population of Arichat, 12.5 percent of families had the most common surname and 56.25 percent had one of the seven most common names in 1811. Bloodlines were so intertwined among the Acadian population that as early as 1790 Catholic missionaries were requesting special dispensations to allow kin to marry.[29] Such tightly knit communities provided moral and familial support to individual fishermen, a cushion that helped blunt some of the power of mercantile capital in the Cape Breton outports.

THE COAL INDUSTRY

The French had mined coal on the north side of Sydney Harbour in the early eighteenth century, and after the Loyalist plantation at Sydney in 1785, the mine was reopened to supply the naval yards at Halifax and St John's (Figure 1.1).[30] As the coal deposits were claimed by the Crown, the colonial government at first ran the mine, but in 1788 it began leasing it to local entrepreneurs. Rent from the mine, consisting of royalties on coal sales, provided the government with its main source of revenue. Yet although Tremain & Stout, the tenants between 1791 and 1799, raised the annual output from a little over 2,000 tons to almost 9,000 tons, the mine was not profitable and, at the end of their lease, the government had to take over the operation.[31]

The major problems in the industry were the high costs of production and transportation and small markets. Wage costs, comprising four-fifths of the total expense, were considered "extravagant," and the lack of return freights raised the price of shipping.[32] The mines were distant from major markets, relying instead on minor local demand (Halifax consumed about three-quarters of output and St John's much of the rest), which one informed observer thought had "attained its medium."[33] Even in these markets, the high price of Cape Breton coal made it barely competitive against British coal shipped to North America as ballast.

With a trifling and scarcely profitable coal trade, the extensive bituminous coal deposits that outcrop along the Island's east coast lay largely undeveloped. The colliery at Sydney Mines was small, primitive, and pre-industrial. Adits driven from the foreshore gave access to the coal seams and drained off excess water, while shallow shafts sunk from the surface shortened underground haulage and provided ventilation. Rooms or "bords" were cut into the coal, and "pillars" were left to support the roof. Coal was cut with picks and shovels and dragged in tubs to the shaft bottom. There, it was raised to the surface by a double-horse gin, tipped into horse-drawn carts, and transported to the shipping wharf. Such mining was simple and rudimentary, dependent upon the muscle of men and animals and on an easily accessible technology.[34]

Some 50–100 men worked at the colliery.[35] Mostly Irishmen from the Newfoundland fishery or recently arrived Loyalists, they had cabins or farms nearby. They worked at the mines during the summer shipping season and were occupied on their farms in spring and fall.[36] Even during the summer, mining was intermittent, dependent upon the arrival of vessels and orders for coal. Some men worked 30 days per month, others less than a week, and a few only part-days.[37] The workforce was divided into underground workers, surface workers, and wharf men, and within each group there were specific jobs (Table 1.2). Even so, the division of labour was not rigorously kept to. Some men turned their hands to a variety of tasks. Coal-cutters, for example, mined coal, hauled tubs, and timbered levels; between 25 September and 24 October 1807, one James Cann earned 4s. 4½d. for cutting 2.5 chaldrons of coal, 2s. 6d. for hauling, and £2 11s. 6d. for 25.75 days' work.* In the same period,

---

* Three currencies were used in nineteenth-century Cape Breton: British sterling and Halifax currency were used concurrently to 1860, and the decimal system thereafter. British sterling and Halifax currency were slightly different in value (£1 sterling = £1 5s. Halifax currency) but the records used in this study do not always identify which currency prices were in. It can be fairly assumed that local prices were in Halifax currency. Where the prices are known to have been in sterling, they are identified as such. Between 1860 and 1871, £1 sterling was equal to $5.00 in Nova Scotia. After 1871, it was worth $4.86. For more information on currency conversion, see A.B. McCullogh "Currency Conversion in British North America."

Table 1.2
Workforce employed at Sydney Mines, 1803

Description	Sydney Mines
Coal-cutters	18
Haulers	9
Puncheon setter	1
Lamp lighter	1
Pit-bottom man	1
Pit-board makers	2
Pit-top man	1
Gin driver	1
Hopper man	1
Heap man	1
Cart men	9
Blacksmiths	2
Carpenters	2
Sawyers	2
Woodsmen	2
Ostler	1
Cook	1
Labourer	1
Overseers	3
	Sydney Mines wharf
Boat men	7
Heap men	5
Wharf men	2
Cart men	8
Ostler	1
Blacksmith	1
Carpenters	2
Cook	1
Labourer	1
Overseers	3

Source: Memorial from William Campbell, leasee of coal mines, to General Despard, 17 January 1803, CO/CB/A/24, pt. 2, 277–87, National Archives of Canada.

another cutter, George Long, earned £1 4s. 6d. for cutting 14 chaldrons, 13s. 6d. for hauling 13.5 chaldrons, £1 16s. for "water work," and 2s. for two days' work.[38] Moreover, with no previous experience of mining, the men were not particularly skilled; the overseer of the mines in 1795 was said to have been "bred a blacksmith near a coalery in England."[39]

During the summer, men were accommodated in a ramshackle mining camp consisting of two log cookhouses, half a dozen log and sod huts, a framed house, a couple of sheds and stables, and a hay "barrack." The men boarded in the cookhouses: bunk-beds lined the walls and a fire occupied a central hearth. Washing facilities were non-existent, and in the summer many men preferred to sleep outside. The colliery agent lived in the framed house, a dwelling considerably damaged by underground subsidence.[40] By 1808, all of these buildings were "in a decayed and ruinous state ... entirely unfit for their respective purposes, not affording common shelter from wind rain or snow."[41]

Largely because of the shortage of labour and the high cost of living, the workforce was comparatively well paid.[42] In 1794, the wages of a common labourer were $8 per month or about £1 12s. sterling; those of a coal-cutter between $8 and $10, sometimes $12 or about £2 sterling.[43] In 1807, the monthly wage was about £2 8s. sterling.[44] Despite these wages, the truck system operated by the colliery tenants left few miners with much money. Wages were paid irregularly and usually credited at the company store, where the miners were allowed "to have a running account ... until the time of settlement; when, notwithstanding their high wages ... little remains due to them."[45] The large premium Tremain & Stout charged on imported goods recouped much of the money paid out in wages. James Miller, an English mining engineer sent out to assess the mines, was assured by "several of the colliers ... [that] they would be contented with one fourth less allowance, were they to be paid regularly in cash, to buy their necessaries where they pleased, & be permitted to maintain themselves."[46] Yet given the merchant-employer monopoly, such independence was unobtainable and no doubt many men were tied by debt to the mine summer after summer.

SHIPPING AND SHIPBUILDING

While the cod fishery and coal industry had substantial impact on the growth of the Cape Breton economy, they also produced economic spin-offs or multipliers that allowed some economic development around the export base.[47] Although forward linkages were minimal because the staples required little or no processing, important backward linkages did develop. The fishery generated considerable demand for containers (tubs and barrels) for packing dried cod and pickled fish and for importing dried and liquid goods. Several thousand barrels and tubs were produced each year on the

Island, giving part-time employment to farmers and fishermen and, possibly, full-time work to coopers. A more important linkage, though, was transportation. Both staple trades were completely dependent upon water transportation to ship their products to market: shallops and schooners took fish and coal along the coast to local buyers, ocean-going vessels carried fish across the Atlantic to foreign consumers. Goods and foodstuffs also had to be imported into Cape Breton. Although some of the shipping was registered in Halifax, St John's, and Jersey, numerous vessels were registered in Sydney and based in either Sydney or Arichat. In 1796, for example, 69 Sydney-registered vessels cleared outwards from the two ports;[48] other vessels, not recorded in the shipping returns, also worked around the Island. Such coasting trade earned profits for Cape Breton shipowners and provided considerable local employment; 152 men were on the Cape Breton vessels cleared out of Sydney and Arichat in 1796, a workforce larger than that at Sydney Mines.[49] Many of these men were from fishing villages in the Îsle Madame area. A census of Arichat, River Bourgeois, St Peters, and L'Ardoise taken in 1811 reveals that 147 heads of families, 52 percent of the total, were mariners (Table 1.1).[50] No doubt many male family members were also in the same occupation. These men were the masters and crew of Arichat-based vessels engaged in local coasting and the cod fishery.

Coasting and oceanic trades, as well as the British export market for vessels, generated a small shipbuilding industry in Cape Breton.[51] Although data are sketchy, it seems clear that many of the vessels registered in Sydney were built on the Island, most of them at Arichat.[52] In 1804, it was reported that 8–12 schooners of 40–80 tons were built at the port each year, usually during the slack winter months. As timber was in short supply on Isle Madame, black birch, yellow birch, maple, and black spruce – the main timber used in shipbuilding – were ferried across from the Cape Breton shore. Rigging and other ship's gear were imported from Halifax or Britain. The cost of construction was estimated to be not less than £4 per ton.[53] The industry made profits for local shipbuilders and gave employment to lumberers, shipwrights, blacksmiths, riggers, and sailmakers. Overall, the carrying trades and shipbuilding industry were at least as valuable as coal mining to the Cape Breton economy.

AGRICULTURAL SETTLEMENT

The agricultural settlement of Cape Breton Island began in the mid-1780s when several thousand Loyalist refugees from the United

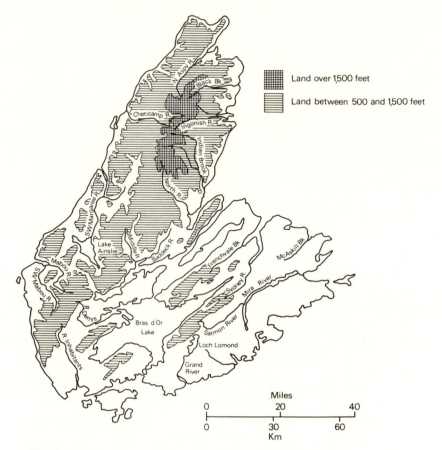

Figure 1.6
Main heights of land and rivers on Cape Breton Island
Source: After map in D.B. Cann, J.I. MacDougall, and J.D. Hilchey, *Soil Survey of Cape Breton Island Nova Scotia* (Truro, NS: Nova Scotia Soil Survey, 1963), 18.

States spilled into British North America. Although most went to Quebec, Nova Scotia, and the newly created colony of New Brunswick, some 300–400 arrived in Cape Breton.[54] The majority settled in Sydney, the rest took up agricultural land around Sydney Harbour and at Baddeck River (Figure 1.1). A decade later, a trickle of Highland Scots arrived on the Island, land-seekers from the Scottish settlements in eastern Nova Scotia and Prince Edward Island, and settled along the Strait of Canso shore and around Mabou Harbour.[55] A few Acadians at Margaree Harbour and along the Chéticamp coast also farmed. In 1800, some 750 people, a third of the Island's population, depended on farming.[56]

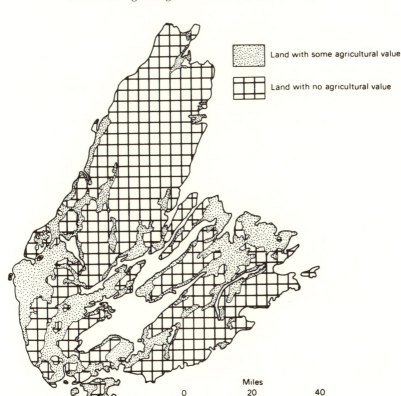

Land with some agricultural value

Land with no agricultural value

Miles
0   20   40
0   30   60
Km

Figure 1.7
Distribution of agricultural land on Cape Breton Island
Source: After map in D.B. Cann, J.I. MacDougall, and J.D. Hilchey, *Soil Survey of Cape Breton Island Nova Scotia* (Truro, NS: Nova Scotia Soil Survey, 1963), 57.

Many of these settlers must have found Cape Breton discouragingly bleak.[57] More than half of the Island is composed of rough, glaciated upland, part of the old, worn-down Appalachian mountain range (Figure 1.6); the rest comprises gently rolling lowlands that are covered with thick layers of boulder clay and outwash deposits and pockmarked by glaciated lakes and rock outcrops. Water-logged gley soils and well-drained, nutrient-leached podzols are widespread. Liming is needed to counteract the natural acidity of the soil. The best farmland is confined to parts of the coast and the few river valleys (intervales) where the flood plains provide rich alluvial sediments (Figure 1.7).

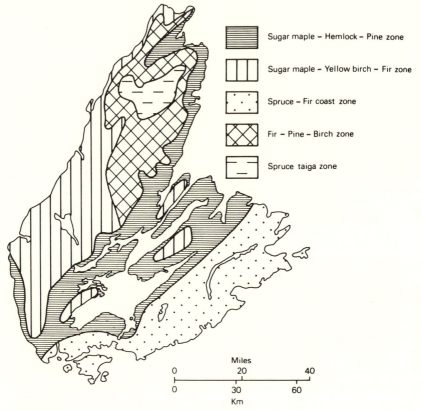

Sugar maple – Hemlock – Pine zone

Sugar maple – Yellow birch – Fir zone

Spruce – Fir coast zone

Fir – Pine – Birch zone

Spruce taiga zone

Miles
0   20   40
0   30   60
Km

Figure 1.8
Forest zones on Cape Breton Island
Source: O.L. Loucks, "A Forest Classification for the Maritime Provinces."

At the turn of the nineteenth century, virtually all this land was covered with a mixed coniferous-deciduous forest (Figure 1.8).[58] Along the Atlantic coast, coniferous species, mainly spruce and balsam with some patches of larch, predominated. Around Bras d'Or Lake and along the east and west coasts, the forest was more mixed, comprising sugar maple, hemlock, spruce, and pine, with elm, "very fine and in great quantities," on the intervales.[59] On higher, cooler slopes were found sugar maple, yellow birch, balsam fir, and white spruce. In the Cape Breton Highlands, balsam fir, white birch, and spruce were most common, while on the plateau summit grew dwarf conifers, some white spruce, and mountain ash.

Although clearing the forest was an exhausting task, a more important handicap to agricultural development was the Island's severe continental climate.[60] Then, as now, the winters were frequently bitterly cold (January temperatures average − 5.5° C at Sydney), the snowfall heavy (five feet per annum), and the spring late. Snow was common in May and ice lingered along the coast, depressing land temperatures, until early June. Moreover, the freezing Labrador current that sweeps the Atlantic coast kept the Island cool during the summer (July temperatures average 17.6° C at Sydney) and shortened the growing season (156 days at Chéticamp, 62 days at Margaree ten miles inland, and even less at high elevations). Such conditions limited the range of crops to hardy varieties from northern Europe: hay, coarse grains, potatoes, turnips, and some vegetables. Wheat was a marginal crop.

Markets, too, were limited. Cape Breton was distant from export markets and local ones were small. In 1796, only 100 bushels of potatoes, 4 oxen, and 80 sheep were shipped to Halifax, and 64 bushels of potatoes to St John's.[61] There were no other agricultural exports. Within Cape Breton, the principal markets were the fishing stations, outports, and Sydney, but many fishermen and townspeople in these small settlements grew their own root crops and vegetables, kept dairy cows, and purchased imported flour.

Crown land regulations further discouraged settlement. Grants in fee simple (freehold ownership) were available only to fish merchants, bona fide Loyalists, and soldiers demobilized after the American War of Independence. Loyalists and soldiers were entitled to 100 acres for each family head and a further 50 acres for each member of the household. Additional land was also available to commissioned and non-commissioned officers according to rank.[62] Other settlers, however, could only lease land from the Crown and were subject to eviction "at will."[63] A government report noted in 1814 that tenants "finding they can neither dispose of, or bequeath [land], with their families, have become careless in their cultivation, and are not inclined to labor, but for a mere subsistence."[64] Few wanted to improve land that did not belong to them.

In these circumstances, most farms in Cape Breton were subsistence operations. A few Loyalists close to Sydney and some Acadians at Chéticamp, known for their "raising of cattle" and growing of grain, had farms that produced regular, commercial surpluses, but most farms had only occasional spare produce.[65] Essentially, their farms produced food for a family. Clearances on these farms were small – an average of 9–13 acres according to an estimate made in 1813 – and combined arable and pasture land.[66] An acre or two would have been sown in potatoes and vegetables, several acres in oats and barley, and on fertile, new burnt land, wheat. An area roughly equivalent to the arable was sown in grass. Hay was a vital crop, needed to support the livestock through the Island's six-month winter. The farms would have been stocked with about 6–12 cattle, a similar number of sheep, a pig, and a horse.[67] Nearby forests and streams provided game, fish, berries, and maple sugar.

Economic differentiation was not marked in these agricultural communities. To be sure, pioneer squatters had not achieved as much as more established settlers, but among the relatively long-settled Loyalists and Acadians a rough parity prevailed. Semi-subsistence farming hardly attracted wealth or supported it. There were no large estates or great plantations on the Island. The few small farms provided a minimal livelihood for settlers and their families but little more.

Given the availability of land in the colony, there was no need for nucleated villages. Instead, settlements consisted of straggling lines of dispersed farms. Where land had been granted and surveyed, as around Sydney Harbour, farms consisted of parallel rectangular lots of 100–200 acres running back from the shore or riverbank.[68] On most lots stood a farmhouse, several hundred yards from its nearest neighbour and within a stone's throw of uncleared forest. Along the Strait of Canso, where some of the Scottish settlers were squatting illegally on Crown land, settlement was less orderly, just a patchwork of ragged clearings in the bush.

Farmhouses varied in construction, style, and comfort. Pioneer shanties, common among the Highland Scots, were usually con-structed from round logs cross-notched at the corners, their single-slope roofs from battens covered with turf or bark. The one-room interior would have had a dirt floor and minimal furnishings. In the Loyalist settlements, more substantial, second-generation houses would have been numerous. Such houses were constructed from squared logs, dovetailed at the corners, and had gable roofs covered with shingles. Inside, there were usually two or three rooms on the first floor, further accommodation in the attic space, and a root cellar. A few farmhouses might even have been of framed construction with shingle or clapboard siding; certainly, several such houses had been built in Sydney by the 1790s.[69]

In general, the farm communities were isolated from each other. Distance, forest, rough terrain, and a lack of roads hindered com-munication and prevented the intermingling of settlers that was common on many frontiers. There was little pressure on the French-speaking Acadians and the Gaelic-speaking Scots to conform to the Standard English of the Loyalists. A good deal of orally transmitted folk culture was maintained. Within these communities, social institutions were few. Churches had not been built and missionaries were infrequent visitors to the Island. The only resident clergyman, an Anglican, served the Loyalist congregation in Sydney.[70] Local government was significant by its absence: no taxes appear to have been raised, and with no House of Assembly in the colony, there was no political representation. The settlers' world revolved around family and close neighbours. By 1800, close ties existed among the Acadians and were also beginning to form among Loyalist families.[71] No doubt the same was true of the Highland Scots. Although most farmers lived closely bounded lives, the constraints had more to do with the demands of everyday subsistence in forest-bound, isolated environments than with pressures from government or merchants.

THE TOWN OF SYDNEY

Sydney was founded in 1785 as the capital of the new Loyalist-dominated colony of Cape Breton.[72] Distant from the main fishing grounds and ten miles from Sydney Mines, the town had no export staple to support it and in 1800 remained completely dependent upon its role as the colonial capital (Figure 1.9). In 1795, Sydney had about 120 inhabitants, of whom 50 had "only salaries to depend upon for subsistence."[73] Among these officials were the governor, chief justice, auditor, clerk of crown, and clerk of council. With little commercial trade, few people were employed in processing and service occupations; a census in 1795 listed a carpenter, two shoemakers, a butcher, two merchants, two publicans, and a brothel owner. Business was so bad, however, that several were threatening to emigrate to the United States. [74]

Situated on a defensible neck of land jutting into Sydney Harbour, the town was laid out in 1785 according to an ambitious formal plan drawn up by the first governor (Figure 1.10). Perhaps influenced by the classical revival New Town of Edinburgh, Sydney was to have a series of wide avenues that intersected cross-streets bearing such grandiloquent names as Great George Street and Prince William Henry Street. Ten years after the plan was drawn up, only two streets kept to the original layout. Elsewhere, birch trees covered proposed city blocks and a cattle track distorted what were to have been straight-lined avenues.

According to one visitor, most of the houses in Sydney were ruined and deserted.[75] Public buildings, paid for by British money, built by the army, and reflecting European architectural styles, were the most impressive buildings in the town. The governor's residence appears to have been a large classical building.[76] The garrison church, also

Figure 1.9
Sydney, 1799
Source: John Hames, "View of Sydney in the Island of Cape Breton," c-24939. National Archives of Canada.

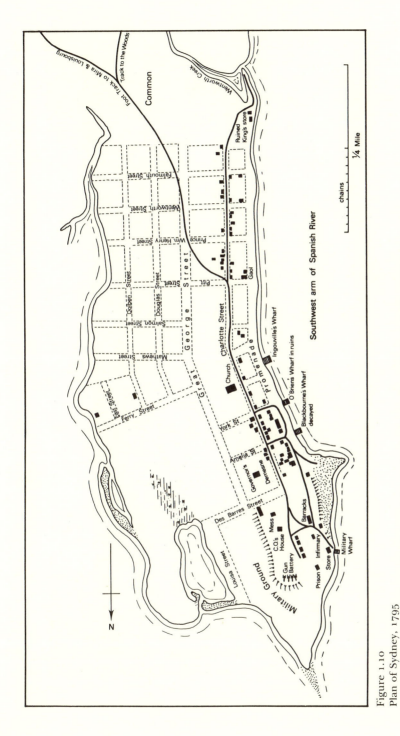

Figure 1.10
Plan of Sydney, 1795
Source: After "Map of the Town of Sydney, 10 July 1795," H3/240/Sydney/1795, National Archives of Canada.

in the prevailing classical style, consisted of a nave about 60 feet long, lit by six round-headed side- windows and a venetian window at the east end. The building was constructed from ashlar salvaged from the ruined fortress at Louisbourg.[77] A few New England frame houses also lent some dignity to an otherwise foresaken town.

Army and government salaries supported social pretensions. During spring, the governor loaned his sedan to carry guests across the "great thaw of deep mud" to Government House, where balls, dances, and dinner parties were held within sight of uncleared forest.[78] Officers' wives affected metropolitan fashions with the meagre resources at hand. One lady noted in her diary: "Charlotte call'd & brought home my lace cap after altering it ... it was old point once my poor mother's that had long lain useless in my drawers but now by the variation of fashion is metamorphosed into a handsome head dress."[79] Such self-sufficiency reflected the isolation of the town. 2,500 miles from Britain, several days' sailing from Halifax, hemmed in by forest and winter ice, Sydney was isolated and insular. Self-important officials bickered and army officers grew morose.[80] One soldier, recently arrived in 1789, reflected that having "passed a great part of my life in America and been in many unpleasant and disagreeable situations ... I so declare without exaggeration that I think Sydney by far the worst."[81] Strategically unimportant and peripheral to the fishing economy of the Island, Sydney was an enclave of government amid the bush.

Many of the elements of the nineteenth-century pattern of development on Cape Breton Island were in place by 1800. British mercantile capital had created a few highly specialized settlements around the coast that were overwhelmingly dependent upon the cod fishery and the ebb and flow of international trade. To all intents and purposes, they were export enclaves. Hampered by small markets and British competition, local capital had done little in developing the Island's coalfield. Nevertheless, an export-oriented coal trade had been established. Away from the staples, a handful of settlers were struggling to create a viable farming economy. Although occasional sales of agricultural produce were made to local markets, the farm economy was mainly subsistent. To make a living, some farmers had to combine farming with seasonal work in the coal mines – a pattern of mixed employment that was to persist throughout the century. With the major profits from the fishery drained away to the Channel Islands, few profits from the coal mines, and a largely subsistence agricultural sector, there was little surplus capital to reinvest in the Island. Moreover, the small population and poverty of the workforces hardly encouraged the development of manufacturing or service industries in the colony. There was little immediate prospect of a larger, more mature economy developing. Within the Island's scattered settlements, society varied considerably. The stratified world of the outports was far removed from the essentially egalitarian communities of the farm settlements. Differences in language, religious affiliation, and cultural background further complicated the social mix. Although geographically and politically distinct, the colony of Cape Breton in 1800 was socially and economically fragmented.

2 The Scottish Background of Immigrants to Cape Breton

In the first half of the nineteenth century, almost a million people emigrated from the British Isles to British North America. Many of these emigrants were displaced by the social and economic changes associated with the agricultural and industrial revolutions and by the economic recession that affected Britain after the end of the Napoleonic Wars. Small tenant farmers and marginal cottars were squeezed off the land by enclosures and the general improvement of farming; hand-loom weavers were put out of business by the spread of the textile industry; and rural tradesmen suffered from the postwar depression. Although some of these emigrants were destitute, victims of famine or eviction, and had their passages across the Atlantic sponsored by government or landlords, most were in middling circumstances, able to pay their way, and had consciously decided to emigrate. Used to a rural way of life and facing impoverishment or employment in the growing industrial towns of Britain, they preferred to settle overseas, hoping to preserve a traditional, family-centred independence on the land.[1]

Among the areas of Britain where agricultural change and emigration were particularly marked were the western Highlands and islands of Scotland. Nominally a part of Britain since the Union of the Crowns in 1707, the Highlands and islands were a remote and rebellious part of the country until the crushing of the Jacobites at the Battle of Culloden in 1746. Once law and order had been established, the region was quickly integrated into the British economy.

With no need to support reserve armies of clansmen, Highland landlords put their estates to more productive use, concentrating on the production of staple exports for the growing markets of industrial Britain. The traditional rural economy was reorganized, dislocating thousands of people from their familiar surroundings.[2] Although a few moved to the industrial towns of Lowland Scotland, most emigrated overseas. In the late eighteenth and early nineteenth centuries, the principal migration streams were to British North America, one tributary going to the Canadas, another to eastern Nova Scotia, Prince Edward Island, and Cape Breton.[3] Between the arrival of the first emigrant ship in 1802 and the last trickle of immigrants in the early 1840s, some 20,000 mainly Gaelic-speaking Highland Scots settled in Cape Breton.[4] At the height of the migration, during the late 1820s and early 1830s, more Highland Scots were moving to Cape Breton than to anywhere else in North America.[5] The effect on the Island was dramatic. The population increased from fewer than 3,000 in 1801 to almost 55,000 in 1851, and the ethnic composition changed greatly. By the early 1820s, Scots made up a majority of the population; by 1871, 50,000 of the 75,000 Islanders were of Scottish origin, outnumbering by two to one the descendants of Acadian, Irish, and Loyalist families who had settled in Cape Breton before 1800.[6] In large part, Cape Breton had become a Scottish island.

THE PLACE OF ORIGIN

Throughout the period of immigration, officials in Cape Breton reported that the Scottish settlers were from the "Western Highlands of Scotland" and the "Western Islands."[7] Such observations are confirmed by gravestone inscriptions of 301 male and female settlers in Cape Breton and genealogical records of 510 male settlers in Inverness County,[8] which show that most immigrants were from northwest Argyll, western Inverness-shire, Wester Ross, and the Hebrides (Figure 2.1). More specifically, those from the mainland left the coastal parishes between Loch Linnhe in Argyll and Loch Torridon in Wester Ross (Ardamurchan, Arisaig, Moidart, Glenelg, Kintail, Loch Alsh, Loch Carron, and Applecross), while those from the islands came from some of the Inner Hebrides (Mull, Coll, Tiree, Rhum, Eigg, Muck, Canna, Skye, and Raasay) and from the entire string of the Outer Hebrides (Barra, the Uists, Benbecula, Harris, and Lewis). A few others were from adjacent areas such as Gairloch (the parish north of Applecross) and the interior Highland valleys

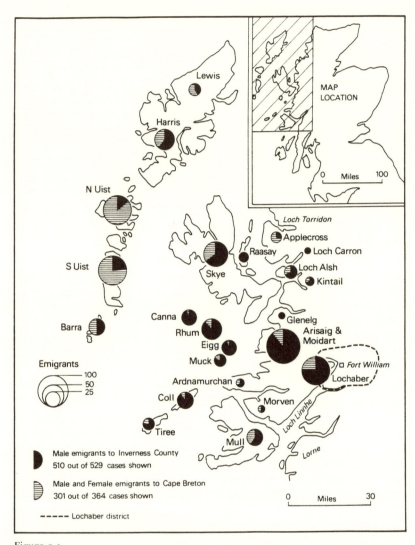

Figure 2.1
Origin of Scottish emigrants to Cape Breton
Source: J.L. MacDougall, *History of Inverness County Nova Scotia* (Truro, NS, 1922), Ferguson Mss., Beaton Institute.

of Glengarry, Strath Glass, and Glen Orchy, but virtually none came from Sutherlandshire or from southern Argyll. The distribution was remarkably confined to a triangular wedge of territory that had its eastern point at Fort William in Lochaber, its southwestern in Barra, and its northwestern in Lewis.

ECONOMIC AND SOCIAL BACKGROUND

Towards the end of the eighteenth century, most of the population of the western Highlands and islands lived on the large estates of a few clan chiefs. They depended upon farming and lived in nucleated villages or clachans dispersed around the coast and along the interior valleys. Each clachan usually consisted of an irregular cluster of stone-and-turf houses set amid a large, arable open field and surrounding common grazings, which included distant upland pastures or shielings. Among the inhabitants were a few substantial tenant farmers who rented land either from a tacksman (an old clan lieutenant) or directly from the clan chief. Few of them had written leases, and without leases they could be evicted "at will." Each tenant had shares in the open field and grazing rights on the commons, a system known as runrig. These shares and rights were protected by collective rules and practices overseen by a township council. Tenants also sublet land to cottars, the landless poor who made up much of the population of each village. Tenants drew a living from subsistence crops of oats, potatoes, and barley and from sales of black cattle to southern drovers – the market connection that paid the rent. Cottars laboured for the tenants. Such an agricultural system, unchanged for generations, was relatively self-sufficient and aimed to accommodate as many clansmen on the land as possible.[9]

In the 1790s and early 1800s, all of this was disrupted. Rising prices for wool and meat during the Napoleonic Wars (1793–1815) encouraged Highland landlords to clear many of the agricultural villages in the interior and to lease the vacated land to large, progressive sheep farmers. A French embargo on the export of Spanish barilla (alkali) to Britain also pushed up the price of domestically produced alkali, stimulating the expansion of kelping (the gathering and processing of seaweed to produce alkali) along the west coast of Scotland and in the Hebrides.[10] As kelping was labour intensive, tenants were removed to coastal districts so that they could work in the kelp industry. To accommodate this workforce, many clachans were turned into crofting townships (Figure 2.2). Following the advice of agricultural improvers, who stressed the value of individual holdings, open fields were consolidated and arable land divided into separate crofts (of about five or six acres), each of which was allocated to a tenant farmer or crofter.[11] To squeeze more tenants onto the land, new areas were also taken into cultivation. The resulting ladder-like arrangement of crofts rarely bore much relation to the terrain. At Harrapool, a crofting township laid out in Strath on the Isle of Skye for Lord MacDonald in the early 1800s, long, thin lots

Figure 2.2
Crofting township at Uig Bay, Skye, late nineteenth century. Note the unenclosed arable strips running down to the shore.
Source: George Washington Wilson Collection, Aberdeen University Library.

were superimposed upon moss (peat bog), arable, and hill pasture (Figure 2.3). Some crofts were composed almost entirely of bog, while much of the old runrig arable land was turned over to pasture. In some townships, particularly those in the Outer Hebrides, the soil was so wet that arable strips were reduced to "lazy beds", corrugated ridges built up from earth removed from drainage ditches.[12] Apart from an earth baulk between the strips, few, if any, crofts were enclosed, and for purposes such as fallow grazing still constituted an open field. A stone dyke or wall divided the township arable land from the common pastures and shielings, usually left unchanged from the old clachan.

Crofts were expected to provide a meagre agricultural subsistence. On the tiny arable strips, the crofter grew the traditional Highland crops of oats, barley, and potatoes. The relative proportions of each crop grown varied from township to township according to soil quality and terrain. More barley tended to be grown on the light sandy soils of the Outer Hebrides than on the heavy clay and peat soils of the mainland.[13] In general, however, potatoes gradually replaced grains as their nutritional value was recognized and as crofts got

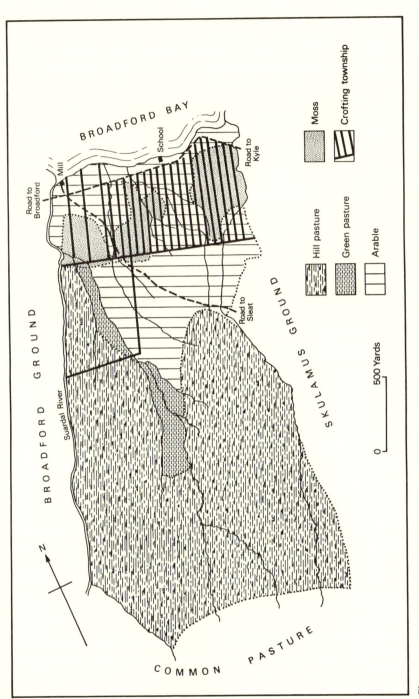

Figure 2.3
Crofting township at Harrapool, Skye
Source: After "Plan of Harraple," RHP 5998/16, Scottish Record Office.

smaller. By the 1840s, many crofts in the western Highlands and islands had at least half their ground in potatoes; the crop had become the buttress of the crofter's existence.[14]

Farming was extremely intensive. Arable strips were usually cultivated year after year with only an occasional fallow rotation. Considerable manuring was needed to maintain soil fertility; byre muck (manure), sea shells, and old thatch were all spread on the fields before planting.[15] In addition, livestock were pastured on the strips after harvesting, adding their dung to the soil. Individual crofters were responsible for their own strips and family members did much of the weeding, but tasks such as digging, ploughing, planting, and harvesting were often done in cooperation with other crofters. Given the variable weather in spring and fall, planting and reaping had to be done quickly and required many hands. As well, because few crofters owned sufficient horses to make up a plough team, they had to share their resources. In areas unsuitable for ploughing, spades were used – either the *cas dhireach* (straight spade) or the *cas chrom* (crooked spade) – and spadework, too, was often done in teams (Figure 2.4). Twelve men using *cas chroms* could till an acre in a day.[16] With such intensive cultivation, potato patches could yield eight or nine barrels for each one sown.[17] Grains received less effort and fertilizer, and yields were pitifully small, usually two or three seeds for each one sown.[18]

According to the size of his arable holding, each crofter was entitled to a share of the common pastures. In general, this allotment worked out to roughly one cow or its equivalent per arable acre, about half a dozen livestock per croft. For example, each crofter in South Uist in 1827 held on average three ponies, three cows, and two or three young cattle. Prosperous crofters, who paid £10 to £12 rent, usually had three ponies, four or five cows, and three or four young cattle. Poor tenants, who paid £4 to £5 rent, had two ponies, two cows, and a young beast or two. Some of these livestock, however, belonged to landless cottars who purchased pasturage rights from crofters.[19] Most cattle, sheep, and goats were of indeterminate breed, underfed, and scraggy. Common pasturing hardly allowed pure breeding, and a perennial shortage of winter fodder was a severe problem. Cattle housed indoors during the winter were often so weak by spring that they had to be carried out of their shelter. Of those left outside to gnaw the stubble "to the quick," one in five died in a normal winter.[20]

Huddled on tiny farms on some of the worst agricultural land in the British Isles, crofters were forced to exploit local resources to the full. Natural grasses were cut from green meadow to provide

Figure 2.4
Crofters planting potatoes in Skye, late nineteenth century
Source: George Washington Wilson Collection, Aberdeen University Library.

winter livestock fodder; reeds and heather were used for thatch; peat was cut and dried for fuel; lakes, rivers, and streams were fished for salmon and trout; beaches were scoured for shellfish; and cliff-top nests were raided for eggs and seabirds. Seaweed, a possible source of fertilizer, was reserved for the kelp industry, and stiff fines were levied on crofters who applied it to their fields – a serious constraint, especially when potatoes were being grown on the same land year after year.

The crofters' principal supplementary income came from kelping. From early May to the end of August, men, women, and children were involved in the laborious tasks of cutting and processing kelp. As growing weed was preferred to that thrown up on the beaches by Atlantic storms, kelp had to be cut at low tide from along the coast and the innumerable rocky islets offshore, a bitterly cold and sometimes dangerous job. After being cut, the kelp was spread on the beach to dry and then incinerated in low kilns (Figure 2.5).[21] The resulting ash, high in alkali content, was sold to the landlord, who, in turn, exported it to chemical, glass, and soap manufacturers in Lowland Scotland and England.[22] While kelping was going on,

Figure 2.5
Kelp burning, Orkney, late nineteenth century. Similar scenes occurred along the
west coast of Scotland and in the Hebrides earlier in the century.
Source: Edinburgh City Libraries.

farming was often neglected: fields became choked with weeds, un-
attended cattle made depredations on the crops, and tasks such as
peat cutting, haymaking, and farm maintenance had to be left until
the fall, when the weather was often poor.[23] Although landlords
had designed kelping to be an adjunct of crofting, the two activities
were barely compatible.

Together, money from kelping, cattle sales, and farm produce
yielded crofters a meagre living. Most of their income went out in
rent, although rents were usually less than £5 or £6 a year.[24] In
1827, 481 crofters in South Uist paid rents of between £4 and £13,
with an average of about £6 10s.[25] Most of the rent was paid from
kelp earnings rather than farming. As the landlord's factor (estate
manager) in South Uist explained: "If the kelp is given up small
tenants cannot continue to pay the present rents because the work
they got enabled them to pay rents for portions of ground so small
that they could pay nothing from the produce."[26] Through high
rents, landlords recouped much of what they had paid crofters for
kelp. Tenants were also charged when they ground their grain at

the estate mill. In good years, crofters made enough to get by. In bad, when the price of kelp or cattle fell, many found themselves in debt, facing the loss of their possessions and eviction from their holding. Crofters lived on the very edge of destitution.

Most of the crofters' spare income was spent on imported meal and salt, but diet was generally poor, usually some combination of milk, cheese, oatmeal, potatoes, and fish.[27] Red meat was rarely eaten, except when calves or lambs had to be killed because there was a lack of milk to rear them. Visitors to the Highlands noted that people were small and underfed.[28] Living conditions, too, were spartan. The typical crofter's house was the "blackhouse," a small, unadorned shelter about 40–50 feet long and 10–12 feet wide inside and not much more than a man's height (Figure 2.2). Its construction made the most of local resources and was minutely adjusted to the terrain. The dry-stone walls of the house were usually double-skinned (the intervening earth core providing extra insulation) and rounded at the corners to lessen wind resistance. Rafters, made from driftwood, rested on the inner wall and supported the roof members, which were covered with turf or thatch made from rushes, ferns, heather, or straw. The roof was lashed down by heather ropes fastened to stones. Inside, there was a living-room where the family ate and slept; a byre for cattle, pigs, and poultry; and at the rear, a barn for storing oats, barley, potatoes, salted food, and threshed fodder (Figure 2.2). One door gave access to these various compartments, and there were few, if any, windows. The floor usually sloped to help drain away slops and byre muck. In the middle of the living-room was a hearth for cooking; a hole in the roof allowed the smoke to escape. The few furnishings included bunk-beds, often let into the walls to save space; some hassocks stuffed with straw, or logs, salvaged from timbers of wrecked ships, for chairs; a cooking pot and plates; a spinning wheel; a wool basket; and a chest for storing foodstuffs. The crofter also had a few agricultural implements (a crooked spade, a straight spade, a scythe, a sickle, a rake, and a flail), some fishing gear (hand-lines, nets, and sheepskin buoys), and creels for carrying kelp and potatoes. Few had much more than these scanty, utilitarian possessions.[29]

Yet the crofters were relatively well off compared to the cottars, who had "no means of subsistence but what they derive from the tenants their relatives."[30] In return for a patch of soil in which to grow potatoes and for the right to pasture a cow on a grass border, cottars paid rents in the form of labour (weeding, digging, and kelping), money, or kind (a few fowls, a calf). They also derived some income from kelping, from harvesting on Lowland farms, and from begging, scavaging, and knitting sweaters for sale.[31] The diet of the cottars must have been less nutritious than that of the crofters, scarcely more than milk, potatoes, oatmeal, and shellfish. Their housing, too, was considerably less substantial. With no firm hold on land, they lived in hurriedly constructed earth-and-stone hovels, partly burrowed into the ground, with roofs made of driftwood covered with heather and turf. Cottars were hardly better off than beggars.[32]

If late nineteenth-century Tiree is any guide, the nuclear family was the most basic unit of crofting society.[33] Most households comprised parents and children; the rest consisted of extended families of parents, newly married children, and grandparents. Other relatives often lived nearby. For many crofters, their "chief earthly anxiety was to pay their rents, retain their small possessions and keep their families about them."[34] To ensure this in densely crowded townships, crofters relied on mutual aid and assistance from kin and on the rules and regulations governing the collective use of the commons. A township constable was elected to protect crofters' rights, and he rigorously checked the stocking of grazings and cutting of peat on the commons. Beyond the township, the crofter had few people to rely on. The few tacksmen who remained were poor and probably detested by their tenants. In the 1780s, if not later, some tenants, as part of their rent, spent several days each year working on the tacksman's farm, a "manerial bondage" that was greatly resented.[35] Personal bonds between clan chief and tenants, once so strong, were no longer important. Most chiefs were absentee landlords who were represented on their estates by a factor, often a Lowlander, who had no intimate personal connection with the people. Priests and ministers were the only other people of consequence in the lives of the crofters. Many Roman Catholic priests took considerable interest in their pastoral charges and, in the face of landlord hostility, encouraged their congregations to emigrate.[36] Presbyterian ministers, however, were often on the side of the laird and factor, rather than the crofter. They depended upon landlords for financial support, and some, at least in Skye in the 1820s and 1830s, acted as estate factors and ran sheep farms. According to a statement read to the General Assembly of the Church of Scotland in 1824, the clergy of the northwest Highlands were in general "inattentive to the interests of religion" and often lacked a working knowledge of Gaelic.[37] The lack of official church interest in the crofters was exploited by evangelicals who preached in the townships and distributed Gaelic Bibles. They at least offered some moral and spiritual support to a people struggling to eke out a livelihood.

THE CLEARANCES

Neither the destruction of the traditional agricultural economy nor its replacement by crofting and kelping was readily accepted by the people. On Lord MacDonald's estate in Skye, the surveyor responsible for laying out the new crofts reported in 1799 that the tenants' "adherence to inveterate opinions and old uncorrected customs operates powerfully against improvements or even alterations." Similarly, in North Uist, the tenants were "equally averse to settle in situations for villages or to take moor crofts for improvements."[38] Fearing that they would lose land, rights, and status in the transition, many tenant farmers preferred to emigrate, hoping to recreate overseas something of the life that was being destroyed in Scotland. During the peace between Britain and France in 1802–3, nearly 7,000 Highlanders left for British North America.[39] With relatively cheap passages available on timber ships returning to the Maritime provinces (a family of five could cross the Atlantic for about £15),[40] the British colonies were a less expensive destination than the United States. Astride the main shipping lanes and almost the closest North American landfall to Europe, Cape Breton was easily accessible. In August 1802, the first emigrant ship to sail directly to the Island arrived in Sydney, and that year at least 400 new settlers took up land on the Island.[41] Concerned that their estates would be depopulated and that cheap labour for the kelp industry would disappear, Highland landlords joined humanitarians in lobbying the government for an act to improve conditions on emigrant ships. Stricter regulation of the emigrant trade would, of course, raise the price of a berth and help stem the exodus.[42] Although the Passenger Vessel Act was passed in 1803, doubling the price of a transatlantic berth, the renewal of hostilities between Britain and France in the same year probably did more to curtail the outflow. The disruption of shipping, army recruiting in the Highlands, and the kelp boom reduced the emigrant flow to a trickle; between 1803 and 1812, only about 2,500 people left the Highlands for British North America.[43]

After 1815, as the British economy slid into postwar depression, cheap, foreign alkalis and the greater use of salt in chemical and soap manufacturing weakened the market for kelp. From an all-time high of £20 per ton in 1808, the price of kelp declined to about £10 for the highest grades in 1815.[44] Falling cattle prices undermined the other essential foundation of the crofting economy. In 1810, a three-year-old sold for about £6; in the 1830s, the price was £3 10s.[45] "Had the prices [of cattle] continued as high as formerly," reported one factor in 1823, "it is likely that no great sums of arrears would have been lost."[46] All the while, rents remained stable, set at their inflated wartime levels. South Uist, for example, was rented at £2,408 in 1811 and £3,000 in 1830.[47] Few landlords wished to jeopardize their standard of living by lowering rents, as Lord MacDonald made clear in 1817. "It is impossible I can forego the present rent," he declared, "without extreme inconvenience to my affairs."[48]

Faced with shrinking incomes, indebtedness, and the prospect of further agricultural reorganization, many crofters decided to emigrate while they still had the means.[49] Between 1815 and 1825, at least 9,000 Scottish passengers, virtually all of them Highlanders, arrived in Nova Scotia, more than 2,000 of them in Cape Breton (Figure 2.6). Most of these crofters must have had some capital, for despite the gradual relaxation of the Passenger Vessel Act after 1815, a passage across the Atlantic remained expensive. In 1817, the 382 passengers from Barra who arrived at Sydney on board the *Hope* and *William Tell* had paid eight guineas for each adult and six guineas for each child under the age of seven.[50] A family of five would have paid almost £40, a sum equivalent to eight years' rent. Contemporary observers in Scotland confirmed the pattern. In 1826, a factor of a West Coast estate reported that emigrants were mostly "what we call Crofters, in the islands, and some of them were farmers, some of these people had money, a good deal of money." In 1827, just before the mass emigrations began, the factor of the Seaforth estate in Lewis feared that "several of the best tenants" would emigrate unless they got "tenures of a fixed duration," and concluded that "the evil of this kind of emigration is that the best and most active tenants go and leave the poor and weak behind." Similar sentiments were expressed that same year by Clan Ranald's factor in South Uist, who thought that if emigration was sponsored by the government, the proprietors should have the right to select the emigrants, otherwise "the most wealthy and industrious of our population will emigrate, and we will be left with the dregs."[51]

Yet these early emigrations to Cape Breton were dwarfed by the massive outflow of Highlanders that took place between the mid-1820s and the early 1840s. During those years the crofting economy fell apart. In 1825, the government, bowing to pressure from chemical and soap manufacturers, removed the tax on salt. Kelp prices collapsed. Kelp that brought £9 4*s*. in 1823 fell to £6 16*s*. in 1826, £4 14*s*. in 1827, and £3 13*s*. in 1828.[52] In 1827 the price was lower than the cost of production and transport, and throughout the West Coast and Hebrides, the industry was finished. That year, Clan Ranald's factor in South Uist reported that "owing to the fall in the price

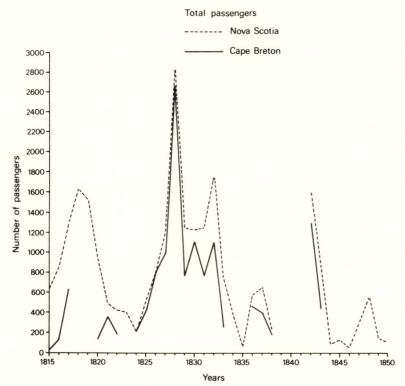

Figure 2.6
Immigration of Scottish passengers to Nova Scotia and Cape Breton Island, 1815–50. This graph does not show all Scottish emigrants to the region.
Source: J.S. Martell, "Immigration to and Emigration from Nova Scotia 1815–1838," and R.G. Flewwelling, "Immigration to and Emigration from Nova Scotia 1839–1851," Appendix 2 (Mss in Public Archives of Nova Scotia).

of kelp it would be convenient to discontinue the manufacture of that inferior kelp for a season ... inferior kelp will not be saleable at any price."[53] By 1830, production had stopped in the kelp areas along the west coast – Ardamurchan, Sunart, and Morvern – and only the highest grades were still being produced in the Hebrides.[54]

The effects of the price collapse reverberated throughout the region. As rents were paid by kelp earnings, crofters were soon in debt. Although some paid their rent by working on the estates, improving roads, bridges, and drains, such work could only go on for so long.[55] As far as the landlords were concerned, the crofters were now a "redundant population"; they had served their economic purpose. Moreover, with no income from rent rolls, the estates had to be reorganized in order "to draw a revenue from the lands altogether independent of kelp."[56] There was little alternative but to turn to sheep. Sheep farming, which had reached the borders of the western Highlands and islands in the early 1800s, swept into the region in the 1820s and 1830s.

In many crofting townships and the few remaining clachans, tenants were evicted, houses demolished, and arable land turned over to sheep pasture. In South Uist, the process began when the central and northern townships were cleared in the late 1820s and continued on the rest of the island and in Benbecula in the early 1830s.[57] Similar evictions occurred in Lewis, where about 28 settlements were removed in the 1820s and 1830s, while in Harris some 13 townships along the west coast were cleared.[58] In Skye, the Clearances, begun in the first two decades of the century, continued. Large areas of the Dunvegan estate, particularly the parts of it in the parish of Bracadale, were let to sheep farmers. In 1821, the parish's population was 2,103; a decade later, it was 1,769, a decrease, according to the parish minister, "solely to be ascribed to the system of farming which had for some time been adopted, viz. throwing a number of farms into one large tack [lease] for sheep grazing and dispossessing and setting adrift the small tenants."[59] Similar occurrences were taking place in Barra, Coll, Rhum, Eigg, and the coastal parishes of the mainland.

Some of those evicted were resettled on new crofts laid out on rocky moorland. In South Uist, for example, nine-tenths of the population were squeezed onto less than one-third of the land. Years later, one crofter complained that "the whole of the people of this country have been blocked up like sheep in a fank [sheep-pen] huddled together so that it is impossible for them to live."[60] A few crofters made their way to Britain's growing industrial cities; most took a passage overseas. Some had enough money for the transatlantic crossing, particularly after the Passenger Act was temporarily removed in 1827, but many were so in debt that their passages had to be subsidized. Eager to clear their estates, several landlords abolished rent arrears to allow tenants to raise some capital from the sale of livestock and equipment. Clan Ranald's factor in South Uist thought that most of those about to be evicted "would emigrate on their arrears being given up indeed it is believed the whole would emigrate on these conditions." On the island of Eigg, the tenants, who were "very much in arrears," presented a memorial to the trustees of Clan Ranald's estate in 1827, proposing to emigrate "on being allowed to retain the arrears due by them." But many tenants were so destitute that even when arrears had been waived, they lacked sufficient possessions to sell. On the small island of Sanday, off the coast of the island of Canna, the tenants were reported to be "even in a worse condition than those of Cliadel on Eig," and were their arrears cancelled, "they would still be unable to emigrate."[61] In such circumstances, landlord assistance was the only recourse. In 1831, one Nova Scotian newspaper reported that "a great number of those who have come out this season have been sent to our shores at the expense of the landed proprietors, as the most economical means of getting rid of a pauper population."[62] A few years earlier, in 1826, MacLean of Coll shipped about 300 people from his Rhum estate to Cape Breton, cancelling their rent arrears, paying £5 14s. for each adult passage, and providing them with "a little money in their pockets" – charity he could afford after leasing the entire island as a single sheep farm for £800 per annum, an increase of about £500.[63] Lord MacDonald also helped about 1,300 people to emigrate from his North Uist estate between 1838 and 1843.[64]

The numbers leaving were considerable. Between 1826 and 1827, about 1,300 people left Skye for British North America; the following year, over 600 left North Uist and 600–800 left Harris.[65] There were also substantial emigrations from South Uist and Barra at the same time. As Figure 2.6 shows, many of these emigrants were fetching up in Nova Scotia, particularly in Cape Breton. Between 1827 and 1832, Customs House records from Sydney document the arrival of 7,300 Scots; 2,600 disembarked in 1828 alone. Many more came ashore unrecorded, as the customs officers admitted in 1831: "Several vessels arrive annually and land their passengers on the Western shore of this Island, the Masters neglecting to make any report of the number, in consequence of an officer not being stationed at Ship Harbour [Port Hawkesbury]."[66] Moreover, many of the Scottish passengers who landed in Halifax and Pictou, as well as in Charlottetown, Prince Edward Island, later moved to Cape Breton. Although the number of immigrants declined after 1832, there were further large influxes in the late 1830s and early 1840s. In the 20 years before 1845, when the potato blight and famine brought a virtual end to immigration to Cape Breton, some 17,500 Scots migrated to the Island.

THE CONDITION OF MIGRATION

The Scottish emigration to Cape Breton appears to have largely been composed of families. When a landlord cleared the population from a township and paid for their passage overseas, families and extended kin groups usually embarked together. For example, in the summer of 1828, the Leith-registered *St Lawrence* carried 208 passengers from Rhum – the last inhabitants to be removed from that island – to Port Hawkesbury. Of 13 surnames listed on the passenger list, 4 (McKinnon, McLean, McKay, and McMillan) accounted for 170 people, 81 percent of the total. Sixty-five of the passengers were 15 years of age or under, and 20 were 60 or over.[67] Even when wholesale removal did not take place, family migration was common. As one close observer of British emigration to North America noted in 1829, "The following very prudent plan has long prevailed in Scotland ... When a family, or a few families, determine on emigrating, some of the sons or relations that are grown up, are sent forward to prepare for the reception of the families, who are to follow afterwards. It often occurs that the young men thus sent to America have, for two or three years, to earn the money, which they remit to pay the passages of their friends."[68] After witnessing a large emigration from Knoydart in the 1780s, Mrs Macdonell of Glenmeddle, Morar, reckoned that the "people, when once they settle in Canada, will encourage others, as they are now encouraged by some friends before them. They will form a chain of emigration."[69] The "representations" of the New World sent back to Scotland by family and friends were clearly important in directing the emigrant flow. As one Cape Breton settler wrote in 1830 to a relative living in the congested township of Tong: "I wish you would still think of coming when I know it would be better for you than being at Tunk [Tong] or any other part of Lewis or Harris."[70] Such family ties were noted by Clan Ranald's factor in South Uist when he was preparing for the emigration of many of the estate's tenants: "The people from this country will all go to Cape Breton, and no where else if they can help it."[71] The pull of family and friends was often so strong that even those emigrants carried beyond Cape Breton by ships returning to Halifax or Saint John, New Brunswick, struggled back to the Island to settle with relatives.[72]

During the early emigrations to Cape Breton, there was little reference to destitution among the passengers; many still retained some capital to purchase land and supplies on the Island. Even in the later period, some immigrants were comparatively well off; in 1832, a newspaper reported that 568 Scottish passengers had been landed at Sydney and "appeared to be persons in comfortable circumstances."[73] But by then such arrivals must have been a rarity. After the passenger regulations were temporarily relaxed in 1827, emigrant ships were usually crowded, underprovisioned, and unsanitary; smallpox and ship-fever took their toll; and many of those in "great poverty & distress" were "thrown on shore ... incapable of procuring their own subsistence."[74] Some were supported by friends and relatives, others by government relief. Official expenditure on aid was so great that in 1832 the government instituted a head-tax on passengers to recoup some of its outlay and to dissuade people from emigrating to Nova Scotia.[75] Its main effect, however, was to exacerbate the poverty of the immigrants. Arguing for the repeal of the tax, one Cape Breton member of the provincial House of Assembly declared that he had seen "the bedding sold from under a poor woman, to raise the money to pay back to the shipmaster the amount of that tax – and he has seen poor children begging through the streets of Sydney for the means of paying that exaction to which they become liable, by venturing from one part of the Empire to another."[76] Conditions were so bad in Sydney that in 1842 local justices of the peace petitioned the government for aid "to erect a building ... for the relief of newly arrived emigrants, and ship-wrecked seamen and passengers."[77] Two years later, some 300 "poor emigrants from the Highlands of Scotland" who had arrived with no means of purchasing seed potatoes and oats, "without which their occupying wilderness lands, would be unavailing," also petitioned the government for assistance.[78] They were among the last such cases; the following year the potato crop failed and destitute immigrants from Scotland were directed elsewhere.

Almost all the Scottish emigrants to Cape Breton had been dislocated by the tremendous agricultural changes undertaken by Highland landlords in response to the growing economic demands of an industrializing Britain. A few emigrants left before these changes were carried through, hoping to preserve a threatened way of life in a new setting overseas, but most lacked sufficient means to exercise that choice. They experienced the trauma and dislocation of resettlement in the crofting townships, laboured in the kelp industry, and then suffered its collapse. No longer needed, they were among the first rural poor in Britain to be "shovelled out" to the New World,[79] their passages across the Atlantic frequently paid out of profits that landlords had made from sheep farming. Almost the first land sighted by returning timber ships, Cape Breton was a cheap destination for a destitute people. In 1829, just as the immigration of poverty-stricken Highlanders was at its peak, Thomas Haliburton concluded that Cape Breton was "a refuge for the poor."[80]

3 Agricultural Settlement in the Early Nineteenth Century

The mass immigration of Scottish settlers, combined with the natural growth of population, dramatically changed the population, settlement, economy, and society of Cape Breton during the early nineteenth century. From 2,500 in 1801, the population increased to nearly 19,000 in 1827–30. By 1838, it exceeded 35,000, and in 1851 reached almost 55,000.[1] Virtually all of these settlers were farmers, and they quickly occupied the vacant agricultural land on the Island. Settlement spread around the coasts, along the river valleys, and over the hillsides. Forest was pushed back; farms, fields, and roads were laid out. Scottish settlers enveloped the Loyalist communities at Baddeck River and Sydney and abutted the Acadian enclaves around Îsle Madame and along the Chéticamp shore. By the 1820s, Scots were the dominant ethnic group on the Island, and farming had displaced the fishery as the principal economic activity.

THE SPREAD OF SETTLEMENT

The early, relatively well-off Scottish tenant farmers and crofters who arrived in Cape Breton between 1802 and the mid-1820s had the choice of the best land and soon settled the accessible and fertile frontlands on the coast and along the major river valleys.[2] By 1820, Scots were settled along much of the northwest coast between the Acadian settlements at Chéticamp and Inhabitants Bay, and on the east coast among the Loyalist settlements around Sydney Harbour (Figure 3.1). A good deal of land in the Inhabitants, Mabou, Margaree, Middle, Baddeck, and Mira river valleys and at East Bay and

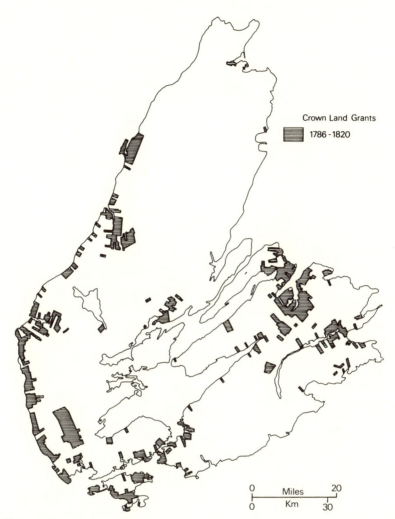

Crown Land Grants

1786-1820

Figure 3.1
Crown land grants on Cape Breton Island, 1786–1820
Source: Records of the Crown Lands Office, 1738 to 1962, RG 20/A/3, Public Archives of Nova Scotia, and the Crown Land Index Sheets 108–12, 114–33, and 135–40, Nova Scotia Department of Lands and Forests.

McNab's Cove on Bras d'Or Lake had also been granted. In the next decade, there were further grants to Scottish settlers along the northwest coast and in the Mabou, Margaree, and Middle River valleys. By 1830, much of the best land on the Island had been taken.

The later immigrants, consisting mainly of destitute crofters and cottars who arrived between the late 1820s and the early 1840s, occupied the remaining good land and large areas of poorer back-

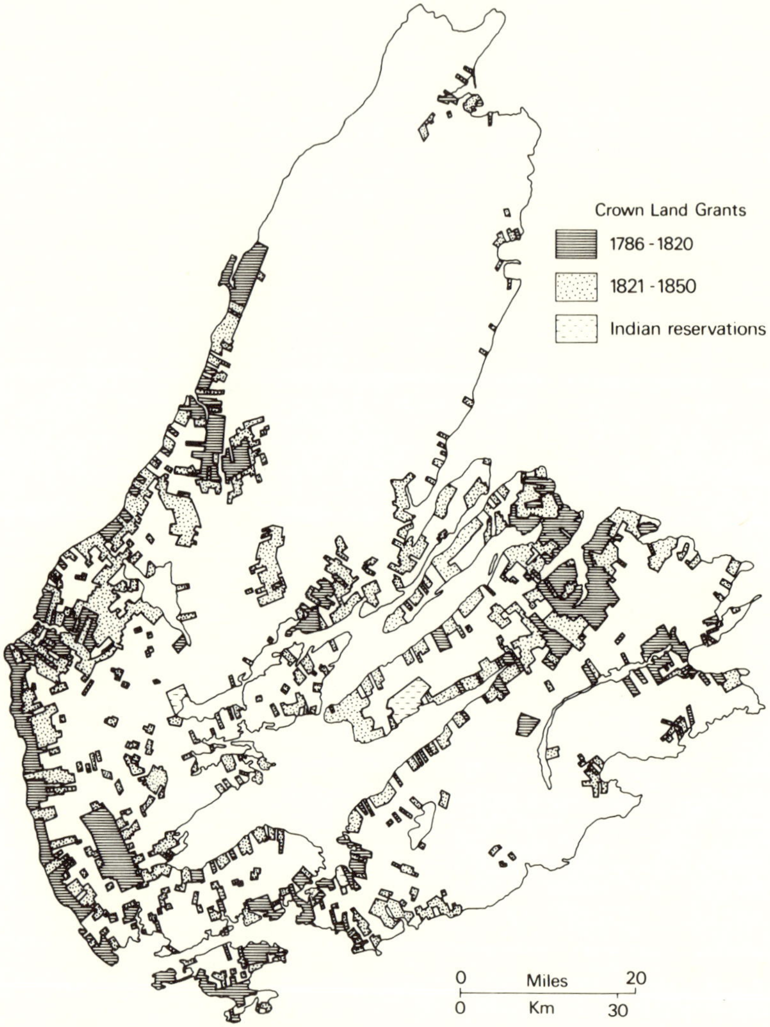

Figure 3.2
Crown land grants on Cape Breton Island, 1786–1850
Source: Records of the Crown Lands Office, 1738 to 1962, RG 20/A/3, Public Archives of Nova Scotia, and the Crown Land Index Sheets 108–12, 114–33, and 135–40, Nova Scotia Department of Lands and Forests.

land. The fertile tracts that were settled lay mainly around Bras d'Or Lake and along minor river valleys (Figure 3.2). At the west end of Bras d'Or Lake, land was granted at the head of West Bay, St George's Channel, Malagawatch, and along parts of River Denys Basin and Whycocomagh Bay. At the east end of the lake, grants were taken out along both sides of East Bay and St Andrew's Channel as well as at Grand Narrows, Washabuck Bridge, Baddeck, and Boularderie. Apart from some land along Grand Anse River at Pleasant Bay to the north of Chéticamp, there was little ungranted land left along the west coast. The east coast, however, was still relatively untouched, and land was granted around Aspy Bay at Cape North, Dundas Brook at Ingonish, and at North Shore, North River, St Anns, Bridgeport, and Port Morien. Along the south coast, much of the land was too rocky for agricultural settlement. Inland, settlers pushed into the farthest reaches of the intervales, taking up land at Kingross at the head of the Northeast Margaree and along the O'Law Brook, which flows into Middle River. Land was also granted along the intervales of Grand River and River Denys.

When these relatively fertile areas had been occupied, settlers moved onto backland behind the first range of lots. Much of this land was wretchedly bad. In the north of the Island, settlers had to contend with the rough terrain of the uplands, while in the south they faced rocky and wet lowlands. In both areas, soils are generally thin and stony and either erode quickly or are too wet to drain. Yet immigration was so great that most of the later settlers were on backland by mid-century. As many of these settlers were squatters, their holdings are not shown in Figure 3.2, but the main areas of settlement can be identified. In the east of the Island, backland settlements climbed the Boisdale and Coxheath hills overlooking Frenchvale Brook and straggled along Salmon River between Mira Lake and Lake Uist. In the south, backland settlements were scattered on the knobby, lake-strewn land behind Framboise, in the area between Red Islands and Loch Lomond, along the Lewis Cove Road, and on South Mountain. To the north, settlement took place on the thin strip of frontland between West Bay and North Mountain, on the Creignish Hills overlooking River Denys, along Skye Glen, around parts of Lake Ainslie, and at the head of Baddeck River. Elsewhere, there were other smaller patches of settlement, usually clustered along stream valleys where water and some alluvial soil were to be had.

ACQUISITION OF LAND

Although large numbers of immigrants began arriving in Cape Breton after 1802, the Colonial Office in London discouraged settlement until 1817. During that period, the restraining order on the granting of land, issued in 1790, remained in force: freehold grants could be made only to bona fide Loyalists and disbanded soldiers; others were limited to leases.[3] As Scottish settlers were generally unwilling to become tenants-at-will again, many who arrived on the Island soon moved on to the United States; those who stayed usually squatted illegally on Crown land. In 1814, some 315 squatters occupied more than 62,000 acres of Crown land.[4] Anxious to retain settlers in the colony, local government officers turned a blind eye on the squatting and lobbied the Colonial Office for a change in the regulations.[5]

Eventually, the Crown land regulations were loosened. With growing economic and social unrest in Britain after 1815, the British government looked to the colonies as a "safety-valve" for the country's surplus population and began to encourage emigration and overseas settlement.[6] In 1817, freehold grants in Cape Breton were allowed on generous terms.[7] After paying £3 to £5 to the Crown Lands Office for filing the grant and surveying the lot, a settler could acquire 100 acres subject to an annual quit-rent of 2s. per 100 acres, payable after two years of occupation. The settler also had to erect a house, clear and cultivate 3 of every 50 acres, and place three neat cattle on the land within three years. In 1820, when Nova Scotia resumed jurisdiction over Cape Breton, joint grants to three or more applicants were allowed in order to reduce the cost of survey and so make settlement "as easy as possible to poor settlers."[8] As quit-rents were never collected, a forested 100-acre lot was available for about £5 – equivalent to the annual rent of a 5-acre croft in the western Highlands and islands of Scotland.[9]

Many of the Scottish settlers already on the Island and a large number of relatively well-off immigrants who arrived after the end of the war quickly took out grants. By 1820, 541 grants comprising 229,220 acres had been issued, most of them on the best intervale land on the Island.[10] In Middle River, for example, 3 families had been granted or claimed 4,000 acres of prime intervale land by 1812, a landholding that stretched along four miles of the river. A further 24 families, who arrived in the early 1820s, were granted nearly 6,000 acres, effectively settling the rest of the intervale.[11] Fewer than 30 families had acquired nine miles of some of the best frontland in Cape Breton.

The later, destitute immigrants were much less fortunate. In 1827, just as Scottish emigration to Cape Breton was nearing its peak, the Crown land regulations were tightened.[12] In an attempt to standardize the dispersal of Crown land in the British colonies and to attract settlers with capital, the Colonial Office replaced the earlier system of free grants and quit-rents with a system of land sales at public auction. A reserve or upset price of between 2s. 3d. and 2s. 6d. per acre was set, pushing up the price of a 100-acre lot from

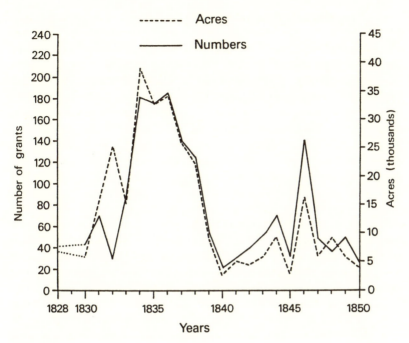

Figure 3.3
Number and acreage of Crown land grants on Cape Breton Island, 1828–50
Source: Annual Nova Scotia Blue Books and *Journals of the House of Assembly of Nova Scotia.*

about £5 to £12 10s. Payments could be made in four equal instalments, the first at the time of sale and the rest at yearly intervals, but even this inducement was removed in 1837 when the Colonial Office ordered that 10 percent of the purchase money had to be paid on the day of sale and the balance within 14 days.[13] Drawn up in Whitehall and modelled on regulations devised in New South Wales, the new system of land sales proved almost unworkable in Cape Breton. Many of the settlers were too poor to support themselves let alone purchase land at the new rate. As a result, H.W. Crawley, the surveyor general of Cape Breton, continued to allow settlement under the old regulations. It was not until 1832 that the Colonial Office caught up with the situation on the Island and ordered Crawley to comply with the 1827 directive.[14] Some grants were sold in the mid-1830s, but the number declined rapidly after the payment scheme was changed in 1837 (Figure 3.3). Fewer than 60 were made in 1839 and only 22 in the following year.[15]

The only alternative way of acquiring land was to purchase Crown land that had been alienated. This was usually more expensive than paying for a grant, especially if the land had been improved. In 1841, Crawley reckoned that unimproved land cost 7s. 6d. per acre, and partially improved and fenced land £3 per acre.[16] The 1851 census valued dyked or cleared intervale at £1 to £5 per acre.[17] During the 1830s partially improved frontland farms in Middle River were exchanging hands for between £100 and £200.[18] Obviously, any immigrant arriving after the best agricultural land had been granted needed considerable capital to settle in a frontland district.

As few, if any, of the later immigrants had such resources, the overwhelming majority became squatters. In 1837, Crawley estimated that 20,000 people, more than half the Island's population, were squatting on Crown land.[19] Seven years later, an army officer who was granted 500 acres could not find a suitable tract because the country was "overspread with persons who ha[d], without permission obtained ... or chosen for themselves all the vacant Crown Lands."[20] There was little the Crown Lands Office could do. The few sales of land hardly covered the salaries of the surveyors, and with the government unwilling to provide extra monies, Crown land lay practically unprotected. The regulations had foundered on the huge expense of policing vast areas of virtually worthless land. As a result, the law was flouted on a massive scale. "*Every* body is against protecting the Crown Lands," Crawley complained in 1844, "all being interested, in some way, in the plunder. The lawyers are no exception – Mr Dodd himself [the Island's chief justice] has openly advertised and sold lots of the Crown Lands, and I have no doubt has executed many a conveyance for persons whose only claim was illegal possession."[21] With the Island's law officers profiting from the illegal trade in Crown land, it was hardly surprising that "people learn to look upon the orders of the Govt. as mere matters of form, and conclude that they may do as they please, and that the surest way of obtaining land is to take it, without the delay of asking leave, and to plunder at pleasure."[22]

Crown surveyors were almost powerless to stop the scramble for land. In 1840, the surveyor for Richmond County, while marking out the boundaries of lot 9 at Red Islands for a new owner, was confronted with a squatter, "armed with a bludgeon," who warned that "the first person who would enter ... his fenced fields, for the purpose of making a survey, would never leave these fields alive." Earnestly advised by a gaggle of neighbours that the squatter had "fire arms concealed and a party ready to make use of them, and that a rencounter would certainly be attended with fatal consequences," the surveyor hastily withdrew to make his report.[23] The same surveyor had no more success a few years later when laying out lots at Aspy Bay, Victoria County. There, he encountered another squatter, who "made use of no ill language to me or any threats beyond respectfully yet firmly assuring me that nothing but physical force would enable me to make a survey."[24] Although the surveyor requested help from the local magistrates, they declined to assist, saying the dispute was beyond their jurisdiction.

With the forces of law and order reluctant or unable to intervene in matters as important as ownership of property, legitimate settlers often had no defence against trespassers. In many areas, Crawley observed, "the strongest helps himself and the weak takes what is left him."[25] The case of Samuel Campbell is illustrative. Born in 1754, probably in Skye, Campbell enlisted in the 76th Regiment of Foot when he was 21, and sailed for the Thirteen Colonies. There, he spent five and a half years fighting the Americans and a year and a half as a prisoner of war in Virginia. At the end of the war, he returned to Scotland and was discharged from the army. He probably spent his middle years crofting in Skye, for in 1830, when he was 76, he left the island with his family for Cape Breton. Given a letter of recommendation from the War Office authorizing a free grant of land, Campbell petitioned for 200 acres and settled along the Kempt Road in Richmond County. Three years elapsed before a Crown surveyor marked out the front of the lot and a small part of each side. Soon after, trespassers began to strip the lot of its valuable timber. First, one Alan McDonald with a gang of eight men logged the rear of the property; then one Murdoch McLeod with five men took away more timber. Another two men, Malcolm McDonald and Archibald McLelland, began preparing the stump-strewn land for cultivation. Although Campbell managed to warn off McDonald, McLelland stayed put, built a house, and was joined by "a tribe of ignorant Romancatholiks called the McCormicks cousins of his own." Faced with two families of squatters on his land, Campbell petitioned Lieutenant-Governor Campbell in August 1836 for a complete survey of his lot, and this was completed in April the following year. Within Campbell's lot, McLelland had fenced seven acres, while his wife's uncle, Dugald McFarland, held another parcel. Aged 83, Campbell felt, no doubt correctly, that the squatters were waiting for him to die and would then take possession of his lot. With land his only credit in a lawsuit, Campbell complained to the lieutenant-governor in June 1837 "that the inhabitants of this Island are more kept under by the quirk of lawyers and surveyors than by the frost and the decay in the potatoes," and that although he would employ a lawyer, he had "nothing to give him but one milk cow the only support I have to keep myself and my aged wife alive." He asked, therefore, for the government's consideration.[26]

Squatters, too, were often threatened by encroaching neighbours, as the situation of John McPherson of Inverness County makes clear. Born in Inverness-shire, Scotland, McPherson served as a private in the 51st Regiment of Foot and emigrated to Cape Breton in 1831. Arriving with "a weake and helpless family ... all lying in the small pox" and "being poor and destitute of money," McPherson squatted on backland near the head of the southeast branch of Mabou River. His 100-acre lot lay between the holdings of one Archibald Mac-Donald and his son, John. After four years labour, McPherson had improved about 15 acres, enough for himself and family to subsist on. Yet in 1835, John MacDonald, within months of getting married, began intimidating McPherson, "in the hopes," neighbours' conjectured, "of adding more to his lot." MacDonald began destroying "fine woods and fence polls" on McPherson's land, as well as planting crops. With "poor Mr McPherson and Family ... treated barbarously by the said John M[a]cDonald," the local magistrate, supported by several settlers, clearly regarded McPherson's claim worthier than that of MacDonald and asked the government for a grant to confirm McPherson's holding. The "moral economy" of the settlers was successful in imposing some order on a virtually lawless situation.[27]

Faced with widespread trespassing and sympathetic to the settler, who "ought to be encouraged, and not molested," the Nova Scotia legislature attempted to bring the land regulations closer to the realities of settlement in the province.[28] In 1840, the House of Assembly moved to reduce the minimum price of land, but its suggestion of 1s. per acre was rejected by the Colonial Office in London, which insisted on 2s.6d.[29] By early the following year, no one had applied for land in Cape Breton, and only 44 applications had been made in the rest of Nova Scotia.[30] It was becoming increasingly clear that the regulations were unworkable, and in 1842 the lieutenant-governor proposed to the Colonial Office that sale by auction should be dispensed with, the upset price fixed at 1s. 9d. per acre, and payment made at time of sale.[31] Acceptance of these proposals by the Imperial Government marked the beginning of the transfer of power to Nova Scotia, culminating in the winning of responsible government in 1848.[32]

The size and shape of lots granted in Cape Breton varied considerably (Figure 3.4). According to a schedule received by Crawley in 1820, single men were allowed 100-acre lots, married men 200-acre lots, and retired army officers 500-acre lots – the maximum per-

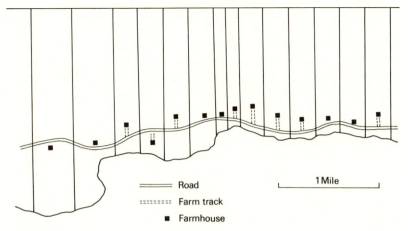

Figure 3.4
Hypothetical pattern of frontland settlement on Cape Breton Island in the early
nineteenth century

mitted amount.[33] Virtually all the lots surveyed in frontland areas
were rectangular (usually with a ratio of width to length of 1:5) and
fronted a coastline, lakeshore, river, or road. Where a road did not
exist, a reservation was left alongside a river or shoreline. Very few
lots had been surveyed in backland areas by 1850, and most holdings
were extremely irregular. Some settlers had hired unofficial surveyors to mark out their holdings, blazing illegal markers on boundary
trees in the hope of deterring trespassers and impressing Crown
surveyors, but such ruses were usually ineffectual.[34] The cadastral
pattern in backland areas only became clearer with extensive surveying in the late nineteenth century.

ESTABLISHING A FARM

After the settler had aquired some land, he faced the laborious and
expensive task of establishing a farm. Land had to be cleared, buildings erected, and seed and livestock purchased. Although much of
the clearing was done by the settler and his family, sometimes with
the help of friends and neighbours, some capital was needed. Without family labour, it cost £3 to hire a man to clear an acre and a
further £14 for a yoke of oxen to help with the clearing and to bring
the land into cultivation. In 1840, a simple log hut was estimated to
cost about £5; a more substantial frame dwelling, £40; and a barn
and stable, another £20. An alternative estimate put the cost of a
house, barn, and stable for three horses as high as £120.[35] Those

settlers who cleared the land and erected buildings themselves needed some basic tools (a couple of axes, four hoes, one saw, one or two planes, an adze, 20–30 pounds of nails) and possibly some household utensils (pots, tea mugs, a kettle, frying-pan, gridiron, and earthenware), which would cost a further £10.[36] Given these expenses, settlers were advised to bring as much as possible from Scotland. In 1830, Donald Campbell, a settler on the north side of Bras d'Or Lake, wrote to a relative in Lewis, telling him that "the first year we came here [Cape Breton] we came through many hardships for want of provisions for our support," and recommending that "if you come, mind, bring with you good store of wool, clothes, leather, herring nets and lines, big saw, and every other article you can."[37] More money was needed to buy seed and livestock: perhaps 15s. for wheat, barley, oat, and potato seed; £5 for a milch cow; £2 for a breeding sow; and £10 to £15 for 20 sheep. Eventually, the settler would need to purchase a plough (£3 to £4) and a harrow (£1 10s.).[38] There was also the cost of supporting the family for at least the first year. In 1829, a family of five persons was recommended to have 50 bushels of potatoes, 2 barrels of flour, 1 barrel of oatmeal, 2 barrels of pickled fish, a half barrel of beef, 5 gallons of molasses, 3 gallons of rum, 3 pounds of tea, and 12 pounds of sugar. All together that might cost £13 to £14.[39] Exclusive of the cost of land, a settler needed £50 to £60 to begin farming in Cape Breton – a sum the vast majority of settlers did not bring from Scotland.[40]

At least some settlers met these expenses by selling timber to local merchants for export and shipbuilding. In 1818, the first shipment of timber from Cape Breton to Liverpool, England, was recorded, and within a few years, 20–30 vessels were calling each year at harbours around Bras d'Or Lake to load cargoes of squared timber for the British market.[41] Lumber, deals, and shingles were also exported to St John's, Newfoundland.[42] Moreover, a considerable amount of lumber was used to build the numerous vessels launched each year from Island shipyards. Although some settlers sold timber from their own land, much of it was stripped off Crown land. In 1837, Crawley reported that "the depredations on the Crown Lands and timber are openly carried on to an extent that threatens shortly to leave nothing to plunder."[43] Even settlers with grants found it difficult to guard their trees; one complaint from L'Ardoise in 1851, which can stand for many made to the Crown Lands Office, spoke of "persons ... every day trespassing ... and destroying all the wood."[44] Few people were ever convicted of theft, for once the timber had been cut and removed, it was virtually impossible to identify where the logs had come from.[45] Income from the sale of lumber to Island merchants allowed settlers to hire a man to clear a few extra acres, purchase stock for the farm, or build a barn.[46]

Settlers also sold their labour. Some farmers employed men to clear land, while those on frontland frequently hired labour at harvest time. In the early 1840s, a farm labourer might expect an average wage of 2s. 9d. per day in the spring and 3s. 6d. in the fall, when labour was most in demand, or 2s. and 3s. respectively if board and lodging were included.[47] These payments were usually made in barter at cash prices. There was also some work available in the Island's staple industries. Although the Cape Breton fishery had probably only a handful of jobs for deck-hands on coasting and fishing vessels, visiting American schooners took on men for the summer mackerel fishery in the Gulf of St Lawrence.[48] The coal mines also provided summer labouring work for about 100 men. In the late 1830s, a labourer could earn from 3s. to 4s. per day without room and board.[49] Alternatively, immigrants could become full-time miners in the hope of saving enough money for a farm. In 1815, Michael Doyle, a native of Ireland, petitioned for land along the northwest arm of Sydney Harbour after working at the mines for seven years. Four years later, James Fitzgerald, another Irishman, requested a lot on the north side of Cape North after serving "faithfully at the Coal Mines" for nearly ten years.[50] Such strategies helped settlers become established on the land, but long-term success greatly depended upon access to agricultural markets.

AGRICULTURAL MARKETS

Situated almost midway between Halifax and St John's, the two major towns in Atlantic Canada, Cape Breton was well placed to supply agricultural produce to these urban markets and to provide foodstuffs for the cod fishery – the region's leading staple. Although Halifax was closer, most of Cape Breton's agricultural exports – cattle, sheep, and livestock products – were shipped to St John's (Table 3.1). Backing into rock and hundreds of miles from the best agricultural land in Newfoundland, St John's was heavily dependent upon imported foodstuffs. Until the Napoleonic Wars, the town had received most of its provisions from southern Ireland and, to a lesser extent, the English West Country. But during the war, Irish exports were increasingly diverted to England and the Newfoundland provisions trade contracted. By the first decade of the nineteenth century, butter and pork exports were greatly reduced and beef exports had virtually disappeared.[51] Farmers in Cape Breton, eastern Nova

Table 3.1
Exports of agricultural produce outside Nova Scotia, 1843 and 1853
(in pounds sterling)

1843	Britain	W. Indies	BNA[a]	USA	Other[b]
Cattle			13,955		
Sheep			1,256		18
Horses			156		
Beef	4		239		
Butter	10		3,693	48	
Bread			125		
Oats			167		
Potatoes			211		41

1853	Britain	W. Indies	BNA	USA	Other
Cattle			3,188		965
Sheep			655		222
Horses			185	375	
Beef & Pork		999	1,716	4	360
Butter		23	6,457	15	501
Bread			47		
Oats		7	634	11	18
Potatoes			51		
Other			294		36

Source: Annual Nova Scotia Blue Books and *Journals of the House of Assembly of Nova Scotia.*
[a]BNA = Newfoundland
[b]Other = St Pierre and Miquelon

Scotia, and Prince Edward Island stepped in to fill the gap. In 1814, the last year for which complete export data are available, 232 cattle, 95 sheep, 8 horses, 400 bushels of oats, and 500 bushels of potatoes were exported from Cape Breton to St John's.[52] By the late 1820s, trade had greatly increased, particularly in the export of cattle, sheep, and butter (Table 3.2). Between 1842 and 1848, an average of almost 1,500 cattle and nearly 1,400 sheep, as well as a "considerable quantity" of salted beef and pork, were exported to St John's each year (Table 3.3).[53] Despite this growth in exports, however, Cape Breton farmers faced stiff competition. In the vital cattle trade, Cape Breton competed with exports from Antigonish, Nova Scotia, and from Prince Edward Island.[54] When several boatloads of cattle arrived in St John's at the same time, as they often did during July and August, the price collapsed and Cape Breton merchants found it difficult to cover their costs.[55] Moreover, shipping live cattle across 500 miles of open ocean was hazardous; some arrived so weak that they had to be pastured on farms around St John's before they were fit for sale.[56] In the butter trade, the Newfoundland market was

Table 3.2
Exports of agricultural produce to St John's, Newfoundland, 1828–39

Year	Cattle (head)	Sheep (head)	Horses (head)	Butter (tubs)	Oats (bus.)	Potatoes (bus.)
1828	928	704	16	296	600	3,200
1830	594	600	15	329 +40 kegs	731	18,950
1832	486	587	6	200 +101 kegs +23 casks	71	899
1834	1,277	1,014	–	102 +15 kegs	800	160
1837	1,141	906	15	421 +37 kegs	450	–
1839	954	871	4	708	–	–

Source: *Newfoundlander*, 1828–39.

dominated by imports from Copenhagen and Hamburg; butter imports from Cape Breton and Nova Scotia were much smaller, more
expensive, and most likely of poorer quality.[57] In the market for
oats and potatoes, Prince Edward Island farmers were so competitive
that Cape Breton producers were effectively squeezed out.[58]

A lesser outlet for Cape Breton produce, particularly livestock
products and root and grain crops, was Halifax, the principal market
in Nova Scotia. In 1814, for example, 7 barrels of beef and pork,
43 kegs and 1,000 pounds of butter, 1,050 bushels of potatoes, and
585 bushels of oats and barley were shipped from Cape Breton to
Halifax, the only agricultural exports that year to the mainland.[59]
After 1820, exports to Halifax were no longer recorded, but shipments of crops and livestock products (salted beef and pork, butter)
continued.[60] It is unlikely that live cattle exports were ever important. Farmers in Cape Breton could not compete against large cattle
farmers in Colchester and Cumberland counties who drove their
stock overland to Halifax. The only other external markets were the
tiny French islands of St Pierre and Miquelon off the south coast of
Newfoundland, small markets mostly for cattle.

The lack of data for the Halifax trade seriously hinders any attempt at estimating the value of Cape Breton's total agricultural
exports and their importance to the Island's economy. Moreover,
the Customs House records of exports outside Nova Scotia are most
likely not completely accurate. Consequently, only rough estimates
of the value of agricultural exports can be made. In 1843, a buoyant
year judging by the trade returns, the total value of agricultural
exports outside Nova Scotia was £21,613 14s. 6d. sterling. If the same

Table 3.3
Exports of cattle, sheep, and butter outside Nova Scotia, 1842–48

		£ sterling					
	Quantity	Great Britain	W. Indies	BNA*a*	Other colonies	USA	Other*b*
Cattle (head)							
1842	750			4,850			96
1843	2,416			13,955			
1844	2,111			8,714			150
1845	1,206			5,556			125
1846	1,290			5,940			413
1847	1,303			6,274			150
1848	1,246			4,983			303
Sheep (head)							
1842	663			358			30
1843	1,966			1,256			18
1844	1,781			975			26
1845	1,126			654			10
1846	1,599			788			66
1847	1,587			756			31
1848	1,004			456			
Butter (tubs)							
1842	715	36		1,617			
1843	1,894	10		3,693		48	
1844	2,653			5,261	50		
1845	2,887	12	5	5,685	60		9
1846	3,725	19		7,204	34		36
1847	1,665			3,265	46		
1848	1,615			3,011	49		60

Source: Annual Nova Scotia Blue Books.
*a*BNA = Newfoundland
*b*Other = St Pierre and Miquelon

value of salted beef and pork, butter, oats, and potatoes shipped to
St John's was applied to the trade to Halifax – a not unreasonable
assumption – the total value of the Island's agricultural exports
would have been about £26,000 sterling. A few years later, between
1846 and 1848, the average annual value of agricultural exports
outside Nova Scotia had declined to £12,340 sterling and the total
value, including estimated trade to Halifax, to £17,666 sterling.[61]
Given that there were nearly 6,000 farmers on the Island at mid-
century, agricultural exports by volume and value were relatively
small. They were also worth much less than the exports of the Is-

land's two staple industries. Between 1846 and 1848, the average value of fish products exported outside Nova Scotia was £19,064 sterling, while the average value of coal exports was £20,092 sterling.[62] Neither of these sums includes the very valuable Halifax trade. While only a fraction of agricultural production entered regional markets, the bulk of production in the fishery and coal industry was exported.

Within Cape Breton, the fishing villages were probably the most important local market. Although only a few vessels were provisioned for long voyages to the banks, the fishing population provided a market for salted beef and pork, butter, lard, oatmeal, and potatoes. In 1842, the Richmond Agricultural Society reported that demand was "more than our farmers can furnish, so that a comparatively large amount of flour, pork, etc is annually imported by our merchants – also many cargoes of potatoes etc from Prince E[dward] Island are sold every season in Arichat and the adjacent fishing stations."[63] During winter, farmers in Richmond County sold several sleigh loads of produce in the streets of Arichat. There was also some demand from the approximately 1,500 inhabitants of Sydney, North Sydney, and Baddeck, the principal towns on the Island, and from the many backland farmers who often needed to purchase extra supplies of hay, potatoes, oats, and livestock.

FRONTLAND FARMING

Like many farms in northwestern Europe and northeastern North America, the typical frontland farm in Cape Breton was a mixed operation, combining arable and pastoral farming.[64] Arable production tended to be for domestic consumption, while livestock rearing was for the market. Given the demands of the farm family, market conditions in Atlantic Canada, and environmental limitations on large-scale cereal cultivation, this was the logical form of agriculture for Cape Breton. Moreover, mixed farming was familiar to the Scottish settlers. In the western Highlands and islands of Scotland, the oat and potato crops supported the tenant farmer and his family, while the cow or stirk (steer) paid the rent.

At mid-century, there were perhaps 1,500 farmers on frontland in Cape Breton. After a generation of back-breaking labour, many had made substantial improvements. In Mabou, Broad Cove, Margaree, and East and West Lake Ainslie in Inverness County, for example, improvements along the intervales and lakeshores were probably at least 37.5 acres in extent (figures 3.5 and 3.6).[65] Similar-sized improvements most likely existed on intervales elsewhere on

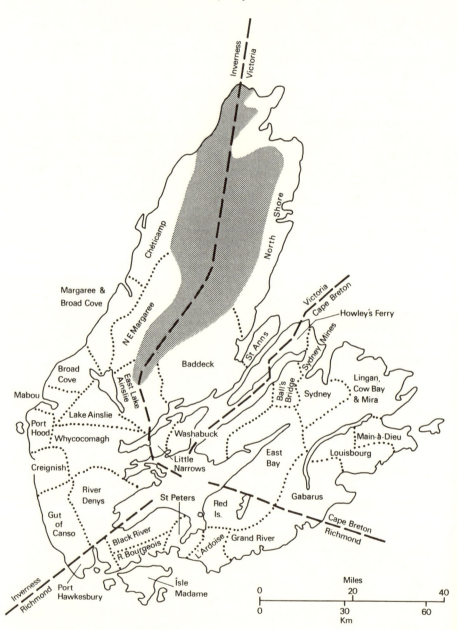

Figure 3.5
Census subdistricts on Cape Breton Island, 1851
Source: Public Archives of Nova Scotia.

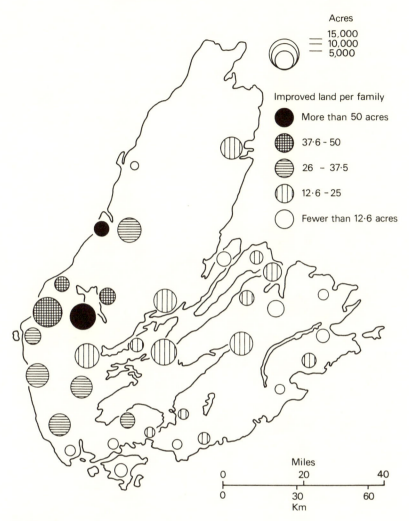

Figure 3.6
Improved land on Cape Breton Island, 1851
Source: Census of 1851, RG 1/453, Public Archives of Nova Scotia.

the Island. The principal cash items were livestock and livestock products. Farmers on the intervale land of Inverness County in 1851 almost certainly had more than the 8 cattle and 10 sheep that were the average for their districts (Figure 3.7). Indeed, as early as 1811, a handful of Scottish farmers in River Inhabitants, Richmond County, had 40–50 cattle and 20–30 sheep each.[66] Most of the livestock on frontland farms would have been "scrub" animals, un-

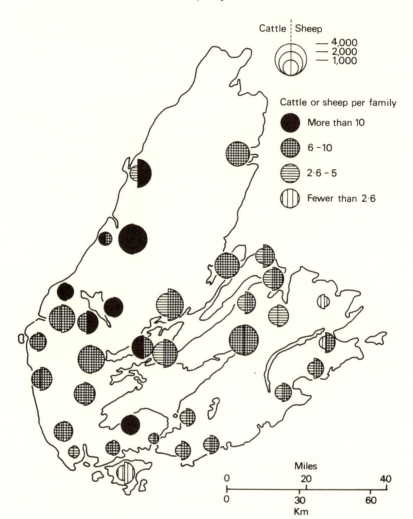

Figure 3.7
Distribution of livestock on Cape Breton Island, 1851
Source: Census of 1851, RG 1/453, Public Archives of Nova Scotia.

derweight and of mixed breed. Shortages of winter fodder and common pasturing of animals on rough land made it difficult to raise better stock. Only in the 1840s, when the government provided subsidies, were improved breeds imported from Prince Edward Island and the Canadas and crossed with local livestock.[67] In 1841, the Cape Breton Agricultural Society imported three South Down rams and three large New Leicester rams, crossed them with the best of the local variety to produce a "a very fine stock," and pronounced the suitability of "the *South Downs* and *Cheviots* for Upland Pastures, and the *New* Leicesters, for the rich Intervales – The two former are by nature hardy, can thrive well upon short herbage and travel far for Food, yielding a superior description of wool and finely flavoured meat – The Leicesters produce an immense carcass, and a heavy (Long Wool'd) Fleece – but require a rich bite, always close at hand –."[68] In 1845, the agricultural society at Broad Cove reported that "the off spring of the [imported] durham bull the size and beauty of the yearling steers & heifers showed the benefit of the change of stock."[69] Yet these initiatives were limited and failed to produce a rapid and substantial increase in the quality of stock.

Milk, butter, and cheese were the other main cash products. All of them entered the local market, and some butter was exported to Newfoundland. The most important dairy areas were around Lake Ainslie and along the intervales of Broad Cove, Mabou, and Margaree valleys (Figure 3.8). Probably most frontland farms produced less than 1,000 pounds of butter, and quality varied enormously.[70] Few merchants paid according to quality, and butter was usually left unsorted; tubs were often sent to market containing a variety of grades. Other livestock products included hides, tallow, and wool. These materials were usually used by the farm family for making leather, candles, and clothing (homespun).

At least two-thirds of the improved land on frontland farms was given over to pasture and grass for the support of livestock. Indeed, hay was the most important crop grown on frontland farms, often determining the number of animals that could be supported through the Island's six-month winter.[71] Timothy and red and white clovers were sown, and salt marsh and wild meadow grasses were cut for hay. An acre of intervale produced three to four tons of hay, sufficient to feed three cattle during the winter.[72] Although many intervale farms produced enough hay to support their livestock, a late spring could lead to shortages. The Nova Scotia Board of Agriculture considered it "an axiom that ... surplus hay will be required every fourth or fifth year," and warned farmers about stocking too many cattle.[73] The principal grain crop was oats ("the main prop of the people in the Island of Cape Breton"), but many farmers also grew barley and spring wheat.[74] During the 1820s, John Young, the leading advocate of agricultural improvement in Nova Scotia, urged farmers to cultivate wheat so that dependence on imported American flour could be lessened.[75] In that decade, wheat was exported from Cape Breton.[76] But early frosts, inclement harvest weather, and the depredations of the midge soon tempered enthusiasm for wheat.[77] The main root crops were potatoes and turnips, which

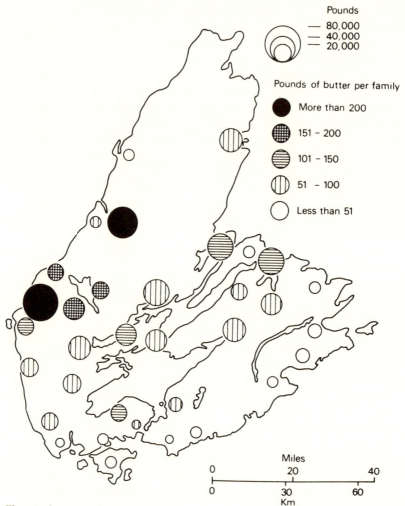

Figure 3.8
Distribution of butter production on Cape Breton Island, 1851
Source: Census of 1851, RG 1/453, Public Archives of Nova Scotia.

sometimes supplemented hay as livestock fodder during long winters. At least some frontland farmers also grew a variety of vegetables
(peas, beans, cabbage, carrots, parsnips, beets, and onions), planted
apple trees on favourable sites, picked berries, made maple sugar,
hunted game, and fished.[78]

Although the crops and livestock raised on frontland farms were
mostly the same as those raised in the western Highlands and islands
of Scotland, the system of farming was radically different. As farmers

in Cape Breton had a relative abundance of land and relied heavily upon family labour, the intensive use of land, labour, and fertilizer that characterized crofting agriculture was abandoned. Farming became much more individualistic and extensive. Instead of employing a communal system of grazing, farmers enclosed their fields and pastured livestock on their own farms. Instead of laboriously cultivating fields, farmers applied their labour to clearing the forest. Arable land was initially cropped for two or three years until yields declined, and was then seeded down to hay or turned over to rough pasture.[79] In the meantime, new land was made ready for cultivation. As the fertility of the soil was initially very high, manure was not collected and ploughed in, while lime, needed to counteract the natural acidity of the soil, was rarely applied. In 1822, the Agricultural Society of Sydney offered a prize of £2 10s. to encourage the use of lime, but discontinued the award two years later "principally because [it] had excited little or no competition."[80] A prize for summer fallow was also withdrawn. Yet by the 1840s more intensive practices began to be introduced. According to Hiram Blanchard, secretary of the Port Hood Agricultural Society, farmers had noted the "advantages to be derived from a judicious rotation of crops, particularly the now frequent ploughing of grass lands, which were formerly mowed as long as any hay could be obtained from them, frequently for 14 or 15 years successively."[81] The rotation of grains, grasses, and roots became more common; lime began to be applied; and some intervale farmers drained wet land to provide "fertile fields yielding best of crops & hay."[82]

Similar advances marked the use of agricultural implements. In the early years of settlement, agricultural tools were rudimentary. Locally made spades, forks, hoes, sickles, scythes, and flails were ubiquitous, some of them perhaps based on Scottish models. After the stumps had been cleared, wooden ploughs with iron-plated mould boards, such as Small's Plough, were probably also used. But as farmers accumulated capital and the use of improved agricultural implements became widespread in other parts of Nova Scotia, new tools were introduced. During the 1840s, forks and scythes were imported from Pictou, Nova Scotia, and more sophisticated implements, such as cast-iron, double-mould-board ploughs, winnowing machines, and harrows, were shipped in from Boston.[83] Although only a handful of improved implements were imported, they often served as prototypes for the fabrication of duplicates by local craftsmen.[84] Some implements were also shared among farmers, and their increasing use had considerable impact on farming practices. The cast-iron plough, for example, reduced the time and effort of ploughing; one yoke of oxen could do the equivalent work of two or three with a wooden plough. More importantly, it made practical the rotation of grass and clover with cultivated crops.[85] The import of revolving horse-rakes (as early as 1844) also reduced the amount of labour needed for haying; a revolving rake could do the work of five to ten men with hand rakes.[86] Few, if any, crofters in Scotland owned such improved implements.

In spite of the gradual introduction of the horse-drawn rake, much of the labour on frontland farms during the early nineteenth century was done by hand. Seed was broadcast, roots were planted by hand, cereals were harvested with sickles, and grass was mown with scythes. Many of these tasks were done by the farmer and his family, but on large farms, where more than 10–12 acres of grain or grass had to be harvested quickly, extra hands were needed.[87] Few farmers employed labour year-round, but hands were hired in May for planting potatoes and in July, August, and September for the harvest.[88]

In general, frontland farmers enjoyed a far higher standard of living than they had known in Scotland. They owned their own land and lived in much better conditions. The ready availability of wood allowed construction of farmhouses that were considerably more substantial and comfortable than the crofter's blackhouse. The first house – a rough, quickly made log shanty – was soon replaced by a larger and more commodious dwelling. The house was usually of one and a half stories, made from squared logs dovetailed at the corners, and covered with a shingled gable roof. Inside, there might be two or three rooms with boarded floors and an attic. By mid-century, many frontland settlers had built a more finished house that was similar to the Cape Cod house type in New England.[89] It, too, was of one and a half stories, but it was built from battens covered with clapboard or shingles. Its rooms were disposed around a large, central chimney; at the front were two living-rooms, while at the back were two or three rooms comprising a kitchen and bedrooms. A tight box staircase beside the chimney gave access to the attic, which was usually divided between a storeroom and another bedroom. A later variant of this house type that appeared in the 1840s had a chimney placed on either side wall and a central corridor running from the front to the back of the house. A dormer window was frequently inserted into the roof to open up the attic. Most houses also had a cellar for storing root crops. Typical furnishings included tables, chairs, settle, dresser, trunks, box-beds, and spinning-wheel, perhaps brought from Scotland. Livestock, hay, and agricultural implements – housed under the same roof as the crofter's family in western Scotland – were accommodated in a separate building. This was commonly a two-bay or "English" barn.[90] Built from round logs notched at the corners or from sawn lumber and shingles, the two-bay barn was rectangular, with central doors at the front and back large enough to take carts. Inside, there were bays on either side of a central threshing floor that were used for storing hay, grain, implements, and livestock. Animal pens were usually built against a partition separating the bays from the threshing floor, and these were accessible by a small door in the corner of the barn. On farms with large herds of cattle, the two-bay barn was often extended by one or more bays to provide extra accommodation.

Frontland farmers also enjoyed a much better diet. Although potatoes and oatmeal remained dietary staples, many frontland farmers ate wheat bread made from imported American and Canadian flour. In 1843, wheat flour was the second-largest import into Cape Breton from outside Nova Scotia.[91] Red meat was less of a luxury than in Highland Scotland and was supplemented by salted cod and herring. Barley was used in soups, and a wide range of vegetables were consumed. Settlers also purchased imported sugar, molasses, rum, and tea.

Although Gaelic songs composed on the Island frequently lamented the break with Scotland, successful frontland farmers were well aware of their improved standard of living in Cape Breton. "Thank God I am well pleased for coming to this country," declared Donald Campbell, "as I find myself quite easy, having occupied land called my own free from all burdens whatsoever." Freehold ownership of land and the creation of a family farm ensured a modest independence for many frontland settlers. "I did not envy *even* your larger *possessions* at home," wrote one Captain McNeil to his brother in North Uist, "as my property was improving apace, all my own, and to pass to my kin and successors for ever; such was my consolation, with a living, in comfort, tho' no in luxury."[92]

BACKLAND FARMING

On the backlands, most of the farmers in Cape Breton eked out livings from small, subsistence farms. According to the 1851 census, many backland settlers had cleared 10–20 acres. An average of 14 acres had been improved on the slopes of the Boisdale Hills in the Ball's Bridge district near North Sydney; 11 acres on the hillside farms around St Anns Harbour; and 14 acres in the rocky Red Islands district of Richmond County (Figure 3.6).[93] With sparse pasture and poor hay crops, such farms supported only a handful of livestock. In 1851, the average holdings were four cattle and seven sheep at Ball's Bridge; nine cattle and seven sheep at St Anns; and four cattle and seven sheep at Red Islands (Figure 3.7). Grazed on rocky pastures during the summer and barely kept alive in the winter by scanty feeds of hay, straw, and potatoes, backland livestock were usually small and undernourished. The main cereal crop was oats; in upland areas, it was the only cereal that could be grown with much success. Potatoes were a dietary staple and the most important root crop – "the only article," according to settlers from the uplands behind Little Narrows, "on which a poor man and family have to live upon for years on new back land farms in the Island of Cape Breton."[94] Essentially, backland farmers were subsisting on the same crops as those grown in the western Highlands and islands of Scotland.

Agricultural techniques and technology were unsophisticated. Like many frontland farmers, backland settlers practised extensive farming. Crops were not rotated, manure not applied, and fields not left in fallow. Oats and potatoes were grown on the same patches of land until yields declined, and then new clearings were planted. Improved agricultural techniques were rarely, if ever, practised. On each farm there were a few basic tools: a spade for cultivating potatoes, a sickle and flail for cutting and threshing oats, and a scythe for mowing hay. There might also be a primitive wooden plough for scratching the stony soil. Improved implements, such as those found on frontland farms, were virtually unknown. "Such a thing as a good harrow, plough, cart, etc ... is not to be seen," observed the Victoria County surveyor in 1844 at the backland settlement of St Patricks Channel, "whilst a drill machine, horse hoe, double moulded plough, and the implements of the most obvious utility, are not even known by name."[95] Almost all the labour on these small, subsistence farms was provided by the farmer and his family, with help from neighbours at harvest.

Such subsistence farming rarely produced a marketable surplus, and to purchase extra foodstuffs, manufactured goods, and Crown land, many backland settlers had to look for supplementary employment. In large part, they were able to find it locally. Frontland farmers needed labour, particularly at planting and harvest time, and usually paid for it in the form of barter. The transactions of John Belcher Moore, a frontland farmer near North Sydney, clearly reveal the workings of this local labour market. In 1856, Moore sold surplus produce to numerous farmers, and three, listed as coming from "back land," paid partly in cash and partly by work on the farm. In May, Neil McKay purchased 4 hundredweight of straw, 23 bushels of potatoes, and 2 bushels of oats, paying mostly by work. For several days in June and early September, Murdoch Ferguson worked to pay off 9s. 9d., the value of 57 pounds of barley flour, while John Beaton laboured to pay off 8s. 9d., the cost of a quarter barrel of oatmeal and 2 dozen herring.[96] Local merchants also needed men for fencing and shipbuilding, loading timber, processing fish, and ploughing fields. Such work was usually credited against the labourer's store account. John Ferguson, for example, a backland farmer at Little Lake near L'Archeveque, Richmond County, worked for John McKay, a local merchant, in return for store credit. In February 1844, Ferguson did five days' labouring at 1s. 3d. and two days' at 1s. 8d. The following month, he worked for two days at 2s. His next dealing with McKay came in August, when he sold codfish and cod oil, as well as 12 pounds of potatoes and a wooden block. He also laboured for a day at 2s. along with his son Angus, who earned 3s. Another son, John, shipped timber for four days, with Ferguson himself hauling three tons. Ferguson finished the month by working for two and a half days splitting and salting haddock. Although Ferguson still owed McKay £7 15s. 5¼d. at the end of the year, such intermittent employment helped him subsist on a rocky backland farm.[97]

Farther afield, there was limited work in the Island's staple trades. The fishing stations hired seasonal labourers and fishermen each summer, and many farmers close to the coast built their own boats and fished the inshore waters. After the failure of the potato crop in the late 1840s, the Crown surveyor in Richmond County thought it "very doubtful whether a settler on a new woodland farm could possibly exist, particularly at any distance from the sea."[98] There were also seasonal jobs in the coal mines: hauling coal to the heaps and shipping wharves and, at busy times, hewing underground. Even so, the staple trades could not have generated more than 200 seasonal jobs, and many settlers were forced to look beyond Cape Breton for work. In 1831, Lieutenant-Governor Maitland, in an attempt to dissuade the Colonial Office from directing more destitute immigrants to Nova Scotia, explained that "considerable numbers" of immigrants were "continually leaving the Province in search of employment, which they cannot find here."[99]

Although travellers to Cape Breton chastised settlers for their "mixed employment of agriculture, fishing, and lumbering," which relegated farming to "a secondary place,"[100] the need for additional work was a measure of the economic insecurity of backland families. Even with extra employment, the annual income of many farmers must have been paltry; most of them likely saw no cash from one year to the next. Debt was widespread, and many families lived a miserable existence. At mid-century, few backland settlers owned their land, and many still lived in shanties. These were usually built from round logs cross-notched at the corners, caulked with clay and dry moss, and roofed with rafters and stringers covered with birch or spruce bark.[101] The chimney was built from locally available field-stone. The one-room interior was small and spartan; there was a dirt floor, perhaps a window to let in some light, and a few rough-hewn furnishings. A shanty hardly provided better accommodation than the crofter's blackhouse. A few backland settlers had larger, more comfortable dwellings. These were built from squared rather than round logs, caulked with clay, and had a gable roof covered with shingles. The interior was most likely divided by a partition between living and sleeping quarters. Close to the farmhouse was a separate shanty for housing livestock and a root cellar for storing potatoes. The diet of backland settlers was meagre. At best, they ate oatmeal, potatoes, fish, game, and some red meat; often, they had much less. In 1834, a missionary at West Bay, Inverness County reported that he had lived on nothing but alewives and potatoes for a week, but considered himself fortunate, for a week earlier the family he was staying with "could have offered me only milk." Elsewhere, the missionary had "seen dwellings where six or eight of a family lived for five weeks on the milk of a cow, without any other food."[102]

Settled on some of the worst agricultural land in Maritime Canada and with little or no capital, backland farmers were extremely vulnerable. Within a few years of the great surge of settlement in the late 1820s, crop failures had reduced many recently arrived settlers to starvation. In 1829, a group of emigrants arrived "destitute of money or clothing ... from Scotland" and settled in a "remote place" about four miles from St Patricks Channel on Bras d'Or Lake. After "many things to encounter in supporting [them]selves," they managed to raise a few crops only to see them wither in the fall of 1833, leaving at least 20 families "poor and indigent without means of subsistence."[103] The government distributed relief supplies and money to some parts of Cape Breton that year.[104] A few years later, in July 1836, a severe frost almost completely destroyed the potato and grain crops in backland areas, reducing settlers to just a few supplies for the coming winter.[105] By the following spring, there was widespread distress; James Frazer, a missionary who had spent time in some of the most congested crofting townships, reckoned that he had "never witnessed such destitution in any part of Scotland."[106]

RURAL SOCIETY

Compared to the polarized society of the western Highlands and islands of Scotland, rural society in Cape Breton was much less stratified. The availability of land in Cape Breton and the lack of a highly commercial agricultural staple trade discouraged large landowners as much as they encouraged small family farms. The great estates and landlords of Scotland had no counterpart on the Island. No longer bound by the rents and dues of the Scottish feudal system, settlers relished their greater independence. "I go out and in [my house] at my pleasure," explained Donald Campbell to his relative in Lewis. "No soul living forces me to do a turn against my will, no laird, no factor, having no rent, nor any toilsome work but what I do myself." When the provincial government attempted to collect quit-rents in the 1820s, the lieutenant-governor reported that "the people are so *unaccustomed to pay rents of any kind or even the most-trifling taxes*, that ... the collection of the Quit Rents will occasion endless litigation and a great irritation."[107] The social release from the oppressive estate structure was palpable.

Although the estate system had been left behind, the lower levels of Highland society had been transferred to Cape Breton and their differences preserved. The relatively well-off tenant farmers and crofters who settled the frontlands eventually created substantial farms. In the 1830s, some of these farms were changing hands for £100 to £200. These farmers participated in a commercial economy, selling produce, buying land, and hiring labour. They formed a small, relatively prosperous yeoman class. The later immigrants, mostly poverty-stricken crofters and cottars, had been squeezed onto the backlands where they continued their struggle to make ends meet. In 1835, a backland farmer in Middle River mortgaged his property for £5 13s. 4d. worth of supplies.[108] With little produce to sell, backland settlers participated in the local agricultural economy by selling their labour. The relationship between frontland and backland farmers in Cape Breton was remarkably similar to that between tenant farmers and cottars in the western Highlands and islands of Scotland. Previous circumstances, the timing and scale of immigration, and Cape Breton's starkly differentiated terrain had combined to perpetuate at least part of the Old World order.

Family connections in the western Highlands and islands also had been transferred to Cape Breton. Although the overwhelming majority of households comprised individual nuclear families, kin usually lived close by. Many related families had left Scotland together and settled side by side where land was available in Cape Breton. In

1817, John Mathewson, Farquhar Mathewson, William Corbet, David Corbet, and Robert McCoy petitioned for 300 acres each along Grand River so "that Petitioners having left Scotland together and wishing to settle near one another would be tempted to endeavour to make a good settlement in said place."[109] Settlers sent back letters to Scotland to encourage relatives to join them. Donald Campbell, for example, regretted that his relative in Lewis had not accompanied him to Cape Breton, "as you would have lands near me but now occupied by others." He offered part of his lot as an inducement to emigrate: "If you come I will give you a house and part of what I have till you find a place to your wish or should you stop upon my land for ever you are quite welcome."[110] Where related families settled together, highly distinctive clusterings emerged. In the late 1820s, the settlement along the Southwest Margaree of Gillises, MacLellans, and MacDonalds, all Roman Catholics from Morar and Moidart, produced a series of related kin groups (Figure 3.9). Even where related settlers had not managed to occupy contiguous lots, they often settled nearby. Between McKinnon's Point and Judique in Inverness County, for example, 27 percent of Scottish families in 1818 had the most common surname (McDonald), and 68 percent had one of the seven most common surnames. Farther along the coast at Broad Cove, 32.5 percent had the most common surname (McIsaac), and 70 percent one of the three most common surnames. Similar high figures occurred at McNab's Cove on Bras d'Or Lake. None of these settlements were more than a generation old, and some settlers had been on the Island less than a year.[111]

The successful transfer of kin groups to Cape Breton, the lack of major immigration by other ethnic groups, and the relative isolation of the rural areas helped maintain the Gaelic language and culture. Although English was the language of government, education, and business, Gaelic was used in the home and on the farm and frequently in the store and at church. In some parts of the Island, the clustering of settlers from particular areas of western Scotland was so marked that regional dialects, as well as the language, were preserved. So long as Gaelic remained a functioning language, the rich body of folklore the immigrants brought with them survived. As Dr Johnson observed on his travels through the Hebrides in 1773, Scottish emigration to North America was "no longer exile" because the settler "that goes ... accompanied, carries with him all that makes life pleasant. He sits down in a better climate, surrounded by his kindred and his friends: they carry with them their language, their opinions, their popular songs, and hereditary merriment: they change nothing but the place of their abode; and of that change

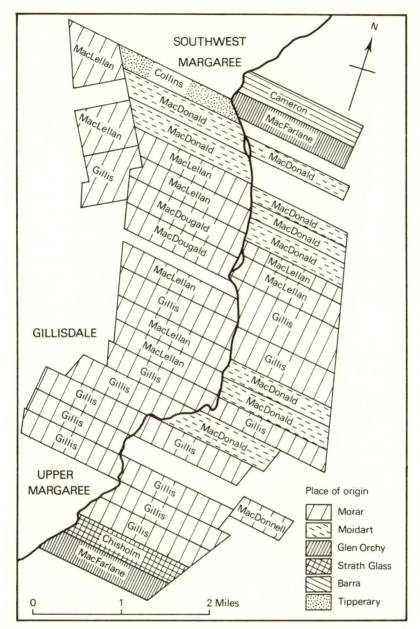

Figure 3.9
Settlement along the Southwest Margaree River, Inverness County, showing the
location of grants, 1831–36, and the name and place of origin of the settlers
Source: Records of the Crown Lands Office, 1738 to 1962, RG 20/A/3, Public Archives of Nova
Scotia; Crown Land Index Sheets 114–15, Nova Scotia, Department of Lands and Forests; and
J.L. MacDougall, *History of Inverness County Nova Scotia* (Truro, NS, 1922), 385–420.

they perceive the benefit."[112] Only increasing ties with the outside English-speaking world threatened this Highland culture.

Initially, at least, there were few social institutions in rural Cape Breton. Scottish institutions – the township constable and estate structure – had been left behind, while institutions in Cape Breton – local government and the church – were either very weak or entirely absent. One missionary, sent to Cape Breton in 1837 by the Glasgow Colonial Society, reported meeting "many persons grown up to be men and women who never saw the face of a clergyman before. Multitudes even of adults unbaptized, and thousands to whom the sacred rite had been administered sunk in the most deplorable state."[113] With few formal institutions to turn to, settlers formed their own compensating groups. Farmers got together at a work "bee" or "frolic" to help one another clear land or put up buildings. One missionary observed that "when a house was erected, trees to fell and burn, the neighbours collected to assist, and would have a frolic before parting ... dancing and drinking rum being the entertainment."[114] There were also "spinning" and "tucking" frolics, where women met to spin thread, beat cloth, and swap gossip, as well as informal "house churches," where families congregated to worship, sing psalms, and read scripture.[115]

The formal organizations that developed reflected the social and economic order that had been created in rural Cape Breton. With no gentry to support the established church, the Church of Scotland had little sway on the Island. Instead, the churches that flourished were those that had provided spiritual support to many tenant farmers and crofters in the Highlands of Scotland. Roman Catholicism was successfully transferred to Cape Breton; so, too, was evangelical Presbyterianism. Some settlers had experienced the evangelical revivals in the western Highlands and islands during the 1820s and 1830s, while others, after the material hardships of pioneering, were perhaps attracted by the aceticism of Calvinism. Certainly, the evangelical church took hold.[116] By the late 1830s and early 1840s, open-air services conducted by missionaries were attracting thousands of people, and in 1843, when the split between the Church of Scotland and evangelicals occurred, most Presbyterians in Cape Breton joined the Free Church. By 1850, there were five Presbyterian ministers on the Island, each with several churches to attend to.[117]

Agricultural societies emerged in response to initiatives and grants from the Board of Agriculture. In the 1820s, small groups of farmers in Sydney, Arichat, Judique, Port Hood, and Mabou clubbed together to form societies.[118] Although they collapsed in 1825 when government support was withdrawn, many reformed in the 1840s when the Board of Agriculture was revived. By 1850, there were societies at the Gut of Canso, Port Hood, Broad Cove, Margaree, Middle River, and Baddeck. To qualify for the government grant, each society had to put up £10 per annum, usually collected from membership subscriptions. Such charges could be afforded by only the wealthier farmers, and the societies soon became the preserve of the affluent. As the secretary of the Arichat branch of the Richmond Agricultural Society explained in 1841, "many of the most influential farmers, throughout the Country, were among the first to become members and Office Bearers of this Society, and their example and influence has been felt and appreciated."[119] Among the society's vice-presidents were several of the most prominent merchants in Arichat: DeCarteret, Janvrin, Belam, and Brymer. Such societies were probably the first institutions in Cape Breton that reflected the growing differentiation in wealth between frontland and backland settlers.

RURAL MANUFACTURING AND TRADE

The relative weakness of the rural economy and the nature of the agricultural export trade seriously hindered the development of industry in Cape Breton. The leading sector of the agricultural economy was the cattle trade, but this generated few linkages to other parts of the rural economy. As the trade was principally in live cattle that were driven overland to the ports for shipment, there was no need for carters and wagons and the concomitant investment in well-maintained roads, horses, wagon-works, blacksmiths, and taverns. There was also little demand for specialized slaughterhouses and meat-packing establishments. When cattle were slaughtered for export, the operation was most likely done on the farm. The processing of hides, however, was a specialized business and did support a handful of tanneries. Of the 14 tanneries on the Island in 1851, 3 were in Sydney Mines, probably supplying boots, jackets, and leather pulleys to the local coal mines; 2 served Sydney; 3 were in the Margaree Valley, one of the principal cattle-raising districts on the Island; and the rest were distributed among the Gut of Canso, Port Hood, Mabou, and the North Shore (Table 3.4). In total, these establishments employed 23 men. Sheep were also an important part of the livestock economy, but much of their wool was consumed domestically. In 1851, one out of every three houses had a hand-loom.[120] The six weaving and carding mills on the Island employed

Table 3.4
Manufacturing establishments in Cape Breton, 1851

	Number	Value £	Hands employed
Tanneries	14	1,576	23
Grist mills	75	12,012	107
Weaving and carding mills	6	900	7
Sawmills	30	2,741	70
Foundries	1	3,500	5
Other factories	6	976	19

Source: Census of 1851, RG 1/453, Public Archives of Nova Scotia.

only seven men. In sum, the trade in livestock did not contribute much to the development of rural industry.

Although many farmers grew cereal crops, few had sufficient capital until the late 1820s to invest in grist mills. In 1824, the inhabitants of Sydney petitioned the government for aid to build grist mills, stating "that throughout the ... County [Island of Cape Breton] much inconvenience is experienced from the want of grist mills, there being many settlements where the inhabitants are obliged to transport their grain, the quantity of which is every year increasing, a distance of fifty miles, or more ... to the mill, where also, in consequence of the quantities of grain brought, and the insufficiency of the ... miller, the people are kept waiting an unreasonable time, to their great loss and injury."[121] The petition claimed that after the destruction of a mill by flood waters, "there [was] not a single grist mill in operation ... in a circuit of about two hundred miles" around Bras d'Or Lake. Nevertheless, attempts were being made to build mills, even by "persons whose limited resources ... prevented their completion," and the government was lobbied for financial assistance. In 1824, James Doyle, secretary of the Mabou Agricultural Society, wrote to John Young, secretary of the Central Board of Agriculture in Halifax, explaining that "nothing would facilitate our agricultural pursuits more than the erection of oat mills ... and till we can manufacture oats it is in vain to encourage the growth of that useful grain."[122] A similar letter was sent to Young from the Port Hood Society, pointing out that farmers "instead of selling [oats and wheat] for one shilling per bushel to traders here" could get their grain "converted into flour, and sold in Arichat, which would in part prevent the French from drawing so much of the same article from Halifax."[123] In 1824, the House of Assembly, bowing to such pressure, granted £20 to each county for the erection of oat mills, and a couple of years later, two were being built in Cape Breton.[124] Further government aid was provided in the late 1840s, when the potato blight forced many settlers to grow more oats. The sum of £30 was granted to each county for the building of oat mills and kilns, and from government accounts it appears that much of this money was spent in frontland districts.[125] Among the areas to benefit were Broad Cove, River Denys, River Inhabitants, and the northeast branches of the Mabou and Margaree rivers in Inverness County; Middle River and Baddeck in Victoria County; and Cow Bay and Mira River in Cape Breton County. By 1851, there were 75 grist mills on the Island – one for every 80 farmers – grinding grain primarily for domestic consumption.[126]

Among the other rural industries on the Island were 30 small sawmills which handled the day-to-day requirements of settlers for boards, shingles, and clapboard and also processed lumber into deals for export. Six other factories listed in the 1851 census made agricultural implements, carriages, furniture, soap, and candles. Most settlements would have also supported craft shops belonging to saddlers, wheelwrights, coopers, carpenters, blacksmiths, weavers, and tailors. The greatest single capital investment in manufacturing was the foundry at Lingan, which supplied ironwork to the coal mines. The restricted market and competition from overseas manufacturers hardly encouraged more diverse consumer industries.

All these various establishments were small, employing few men, making only a limited number of items, and attracting little capital investment. Most were family-owned businesses, usually set up by a frontland farmer with spare capital or by a merchant, and few were capitalized at more than £200. In Middle River, for example, Charles MacKenzie, son of a prominent frontland family, mortgaged his farm for £107 in the 1830s to raise capital to build a grist mill; in 1850, Angus McDonald, grandson of another frontland settler, mortgaged his farm for £125 and invested the money in a fulling and dressing mill and dying establishment.[127] Such businesses were no more valuable than an improved frontland farm and not always as good an investment. By 1854, McDonald was in difficulties over his mortgage payments and had to petition the House of Assembly for financial assistance.[128] The largest manufacturing enterprise on the Island was a sawmill at St. Peters, Richmond County, which employed 20 men and was valued at £850 – a business considerably smaller than the Jersey fishing stations on nearby Île Madame.

Other businesses employed far fewer men, usually a father and one or two grown sons and a couple of hired hands. Even then, employment was intermittent, tied to the seasons and market demand. Grist mills and sawmills, for example, depended upon water-power and were shut down during the winter freeze. Many enterprises only worked when they had specific orders or sufficient material. Production runs were extremely small and sensitive to local demand.

Rural trade was handled by the farmers themselves and by country storekeepers. Some farmers clubbed together and chartered vessels to take their produce either to a Cape Breton merchant for forwarding or straight to market in Halifax and St John's. Along exposed parts of the coast, shipping was particularly complex. With the chartered vessel standing offshore, the smaller export produce – bags of wool, tubs of butter, geese, pigs, sheep, lambs – were loaded onto small boats and ferried out to the waiting vessel. Cattle and horses, however, were too big to be transhipped and had to be strapped with ropes and towed out to the vessel, hoisted aboard, and lowered into the hold.[129] More prosperous frontland farmers also invested in the carrying trade, purchasing shares in vessels and investing in shipbuilding. Two well-established Middle River farmers, for example, financed the construction of the 76-ton schooner *Rory MacKenzie* in 1854.[130]

Merchants and country storekeepers organized the rest of the trade. They imported goods to be retailed to the settlers and exported produce to be wholesaled in Halifax and St John's. As the trade in any one commodity was small and intermittent, they sold a wide range of goods and purchased a variety of country produce. The stock of a typical country store included clothes, millinery, bedlinen, haberdashery, hardware, drugs, dry goods, and groceries. The merchant collected the small agricultural surpluses (a bushel of oats or potatoes, a tub of butter, a cow, a couple of sheep), quantities of wood (spars and lumber), and fish (a barrel of pickled fish, a half quintal of dried cod). Although some transactions were in cash, shortage of specie made barter the most acceptable form of payment. Most of the produce came from the area within a half day's overland journey to the store, although water transport often expanded a merchant's hinterland. Some produce was consumed locally, particularly if the store was close to a town or fishing settlement, but much was shipped by sea to a main centre of demand. There, it was consigned to the merchant's wholesale supplier or to a commission agent. Country storekeepers also acted as bankers for the surrounding farmers and invested in local manufacturing and services. In a frequently marginal trading environment, their interests had to be varied and general.

With an extensive coastline and Bras d'Or Lake accessible from the sea, the Island's import-export trade was divided among many small shipping places. The fragmentation of trade and involvement of farmers in shipping meant that it was impossible for merchants to funnel trade through one or two ports and thereby capture much of the business (as occurred, for example, in New Brunswick where much of the province's timber and agricultural trade flowed down the Saint John Valley to merchants in Saint John). As a result, rural hinterlands of Island merchants were comparatively small and profits from trade were limited. In 1829, Thomas Haliburton reckoned that the annual incomes of Cape Breton merchants – "in general the most affluent class" – averaged no more than £200.[131] With limited income from country trade, merchants found it difficult to diversify much beyond small local industries and services.

The weakness of the rural economy limited urban development on the Island. In 1850, perhaps 3,000 people, 5 percent of the total population, lived in towns. The principal urban places were Sydney, North Sydney, Arichat, Baddeck, Port Hawkesbury, Port Hood, Mabou, Margaree Harbour, and Chéticamp. All of these places were engaged in import-export trade, shipping, shipbuilding, and fishing. In addition, some had basic manufacturing (grist mills, sawmills, tanneries, carriage works) and limited services (schools and churches). Sydney, Baddeck, Arichat, and Port Hood were also county seats and had administrative functions. Although Sydney was the largest town, with some 600 inhabitants in 1850,[132] it did not dominate the Island's economy. The fragmentation of trade ensured that no town captured all the Island's import-export business. Fish were exported from Arichat, coal from the General Mining Association's (GMA's) wharves at Sydney Mines, and agricultural produce from Sydney, North Sydney, Baddeck, Port Hawkesbury, Port Hood, Mabou, and Margaree Harbour. The towns that dominated the Island's economy were located elsewhere: Halifax, St Helier in Jersey, and London.

For the thousands of Scottish settlers who poured into Cape Breton during the early nineteenth century, the Island was a meagre patch of New World land. A handful of relatively well-off tenant farmers and crofters who left Scotland in the early 1800s found in the frontlands of Cape Breton an agricultural niche in which to re-create their traditional independent life on the land. The application of limited capital and massive amounts of labour eventually yielded a farm. Sales of livestock to local and regional markets provided a comfortable income as well as some capital to invest in land, manufacturing, or services. Yet once the small amount of fertile land had been taken, agricultural opportunities for new settlers were drastically curtailed. After the trauma of the Clearances, the destitute immigrants who came later found that they had exchanged landlords and bailiffs for acidic soils and six-month winters. Although they often squatted illegally on Crown land and at least enjoyed the prospect of improvement, the realities of farming such marginal land quickly became apparent. Few could support themselves from farming alone, and many turned to whatever additional employment was available. Even with supplementary employment, however, many found it difficult to subsist; in particularly bad years, subsistence quickly turned to starvation. For these Highland crofters, a transatlantic migration had scarcely improved their situation; they still faced rural poverty and migration. The meagre land of Cape Breton also provided a niche for the reassembly of Highland families and communities disrupted during the Clearances. The relative economic backwardness and isolation of the Island allowed Gaelic culture to become established. A new regional culture had been implanted in British North America.

Although Cape Breton provided a niche for destitute Scots, the weakness of the Island's agricultural sector and fragmentation of trade hindered capital accumulation among the Island's merchant class and slowed urban development. Unlike early nineteenth-century Ontario, where the wheat staple generated profits that were reinvested in developing and diversifying the economy, as well as in stimulating widespread urban growth,[133] Cape Breton's relatively small and fragmented cattle trade had not produced much economic spin-off. Agriculture was not an engine of rapid economic development. For impoverished Scottish settlers, the niche was indeed limited.

4 The Staple Industries in the Early Nineteenth Century

Despite the massive expansion of agricultural settlement in Cape Breton during the early nineteenth century, the staple industries and shipping continued to play important roles in shaping the Island's settlement, economy, and culture. Both of the Island's staples continued to attract external capital, and more than a quarter of its workforce were still employed in fishing and mining at mid-century (Table 4.1). Although the fishery remained a classic commercial staple, organized by merchants, tied to distant foreign markets, and dependent upon intensive labour and pre-industrial technologies, the mining industry underwent considerable change. In the late 1820s, the local mercantile capital that had been involved in the mines gave way to British industrial capital. Among the earliest industrial enterprises in British North America and the largest industrial development at that time in Nova Scotia, the Cape Breton mines were restructured through the use of new technologies, working patterns, and the investment of industrial capitalism. By the third decade of the century, industrial coal mining was firmly established alongside the old commercial staple of the cod fishery and an extensive agricultural economy of family farms.

THE COD FISHERY

During the early nineteenth century, the fishery continued to be concentrated in the southwest corner of the Island at Île Madame, River Bourgeois, and L'Ardoise; along the south coast at Gabarus,

Table 4.1
Occupational structure of the Cape Breton workforce, 1851

Occupation	Number	%
Farmers	5,884	53.3
Fishermen	2,669	24.2
Lumberers	74	0.7
Mechanics	1,046	9.5
	(approx. 500 = miners)	
Registered seamen	79	0.7
Men employed at sea	975	8.7
Clergymen and ministers	34	0.3
Doctors	13	0.1
Merchants and traders	259	2.3
Total	11,033	

Source: Census of 1851, RG 1/453, Public Archives of Nova Scotia.

Louisbourg, and Main-à-Dieu; and on the northwest coast at Ché-ticamp. Elsewhere, new outports were established. Along the east coast, a few fishermen were scattered around Mira Bay, Glace Bay, Indian Bay (Lingan), Sydney Harbour, and the North Shore, particularly at Ingonish. There was also a large concentration of fishermen at Howley's Ferry on Little Bras d'Or Lake. On the northwest coast, there was some expansion at Margaree Harbour, Port Hood, and along the Gut of Canso. A considerable number of farmers on Bras d'Or Lake, particularly at Baddeck, were also involved in small-scale fishing (Figure 4.1).

Although the Napoleonic Wars ended the migratory fishery from southwestern England to Newfoundland, most of the Channel Island companies in Cape Breton and around the Gulf of St Lawrence managed to weather the war and maintain their grip on the fishery.[1] The only casualty in Cape Breton was Remon & Co., which pulled out of Sydney in 1797, but the Robin and Janvrin companies stayed in business.[2] They were joined on Île Madame by DeCarteret & LeVesconte, another Jersey firm, which opened establishments at Arichat, D'Escousse, and River Bourgeois in the early 1800s.[3] By mid-century, the company was probably second only to Philip Robin & Co. as an exporter of dried fish. Thoume Moullin & Co., a Guernsey firm, also operated in the Île Madame area during the early 1830s, but it sold out to a Cape Breton merchant in 1836.[4] In addition, Robertson, Forsyth & Co., from Greenock, Scotland, appears to have had a fishing station at Arichat during the second decade of the century.[5] These companies continued to outfit resident fish-

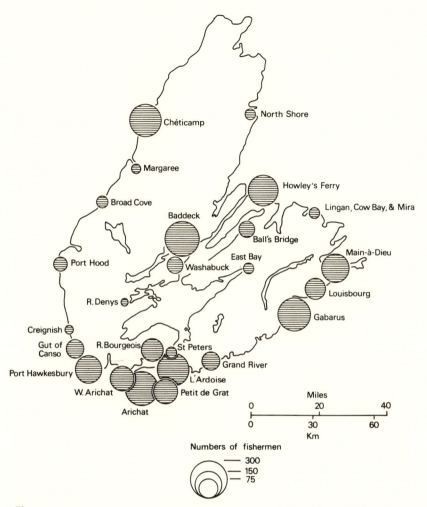

Figure 4.1
Distribution of fishermen on Cape Breton Island, 1851
Source: Census of 1851, RG 1/453, Public Archives of Nova Scotia.

ermen and to receive fish in return. In 1814, the last year for which complete export data are available, the three British companies (Janvrin, Robin, and Forsyth, Robertson & Co.) exported 57 percent of Cape Breton's dried fish: 16,589 quintals to Spain and 300 to Jersey.[6]

The well-established trading patterns of the Channel Island merchants hardly changed during the early nineteenth century. The companies still sent supplies, capital, and skilled labour to their fishing stations on the Island each year and exported dried fish directly to markets in southern Europe, the Caribbean, and, from the 1820s, Brazil.[7] Links were also developed with Halifax and Montreal. Dried and pickled fish were exported to both places in return for flour and other items that were cheaper to buy in North America than in Europe.

This pattern of trade is well exemplified by the dealings of DeCarteret & LeVesconte. Each spring, Peter LeVesconte, resident in Jersey, sent a supply vessel laden with salt, provisions, iron, nails, cordage, and crockery to his partner, Peter DeCarteret, in Arichat, for the outfit of local fishermen.[8] Further supplies – dry goods, clothing, and provisions – were purchased from Creighton & Grassie, a wholesaling firm in Halifax with Channel Island connections. On 22 April 1842, for example, DeCarteret ordered "30 Kegs Hogslard, 1 Hhd. Rice, 1 Dz. oiled Jackets & Trousers, 2 Dz. Common Southwester Hats for fishermen, 2 dz. Wool Cards, 25 Pepper, 1 Hhd. lime, 6 dz. Tin Pints, 2 Keg Tobacco, 2 Chest Tea ... to supply forty or fifty Shallops to go a fishing."[9] In return, he promised 500–600 quintals of dried cod. At the same time, DeCarteret dealt with Donald Frazer, a commission agent in Montreal, sending him cargoes of pickled fish in summer and fall to pay for shipments of fine flour received in spring.[10] DeCarteret also traded with local merchants, such as Nicholas Paint and Joseph Wilson at Port Hawkesbury, buying fish for export and timber for shipbuilding.[11]

DeCarteret & LeVesconte's main commerce, however, was with the Caribbean, South America, and southern Europe. Every fall, one or two vessels loaded with the season's dried and pickled fish were dispatched to each of these markets, hopefully arriving before the influx of fish from Halifax, St John's, and the Gaspé lowered prices. At each port, the firm dealt with a commission agent who arranged to sell the fish and find a return freight. During the 1840s, these agents included McCulmot & Co. in Pernambuco; Muller & Co. in Bahia and Rio de Janeiro; Aguire & Borando in Bilbao; Arnot & Co. in Barbados; and Graham & Taylor in Liverpool.[12] In the West Indies and South America, the vessels were loaded with sugar, molasses, and rum for either the European market or Cape Breton. In southern Europe, they took on cargoes of salt or sailed in ballast to Jersey, where they picked up supplies for Cape Breton.[13] Such transatlantic movements had to be carefully synchronized to ensure that at least one vessel was at Arichat by late August in order to carry the first fish to market.[14]

The rest of the fishery continued to be organized by local merchants dependent upon larger Halifax houses for their supplies and market connection. Dried and pickled fish, sealskins, country produce, and the occasional vessel were all shipped to Halifax to pay for salt, flour, provisions, and manufactured goods. Such trade is well illustrated by the commerce of Joseph Wilson, a Port Hawkesbury merchant. After an unsuccessful business partnership in Halifax, Wilson moved to Cape Breton in 1836 and settled at Port Hawkesbury, probably purchasing a fishing station from the Guernsey merchants, Thoume Moullin & Co.[15] Situated halfway along the Strait of Canso, Wilson was well placed to supply fishermen on both sides of the strait, as well as American schooners passing through the strait to fish in the Gulf of St Lawrence. Certainly, he dealt with fishermen who lived as far away as Cape Mabou, while beyond the Island he traded with merchant-wholesalers in Halifax and St John's.

Wilson's main dealings were with William Pryor & Sons, a wholesaling firm in Halifax. They supplied him with provisions (flour, meal, molasses, sugar, rum, and tea), dry merchandise (earthenware, glass, and cloth), fishing gear (hooks, lines, and nets), and shipbuilding materials (putty, turpentine, pitch, pumps, and rigging).[16] Pryor & Sons also acted as an underwriter – insuring Wilson's cargoes, fishing vessels, and vessels under construction – and his principal creditor.[17] Merchandise was shipped to Wilson in the spring on the credit of fall fish, and cash was provided for Wilson's shipbuilding ventures.[18] In return, Wilson sent dried and pickled fish, fish oil, lumber, and vessels to be sold in Halifax.[19] Wilson also dealt with Stewart & Co., a St John's firm, sending them shipments of cattle and butter.[20] Locally, he fitted out fishermen for the boat and vessel fisheries (in August 1842 he had the 40-ton pink-sterned vessel *Perseverance* insured for a two-month fishing voyage in the gulf) and received fish in return.[21] With his country trade and his shipbuilding interests, Wilson had a busy and varied business, pivotal to the commerce of the area and typical of many outport merchants in Cape Breton.

The technology of the cod fishery remained traditional. More than three-quarters of all fishermen on the Island fished from boats in inshore waters; the rest crewed schooners used in inshore fishing and coastal trading (Table 4.2).[22] Hand-lines were still used, and most of the catch came from around Île Madame and off Chéticamp, with smaller hauls at Gabarus, Louisbourg, and Howley's Ferry (Figure 4.2). There was also a minor cod fishery in Bras d'Or Lake. After the catch was landed, the fish were headed, gutted, lightly salted, and dried on flakes for several days until they were hard and dry. Some of the leading merchants – Robin and

Table 4.2
Boats and vessels in the Cape Breton fishery, 1851

County	Boats		Vessels		
	No.	Men	No.	Tonnage	Men
Richmond	522	860	99	2,197	456
Inverness	247	379	74	1,007	264
Cape Breton and Victoria	654	1,298	21	463	83
Total	1,423	2,537	194	3,667	803

Source: Census of 1851, RG 1/453, Public Archives of Nova Scotia.

DeCarteret – also outfitted a few vessels for the small bank fishery in the Gulf of St Lawrence. Most of the fishing took place around the Magdalen Islands, off Anticosti Island, and along the north shore of the gulf, with occasional voyages through the Strait of Belle Isle to Labrador.[23] Such trips had only mixed success. J.W. Robin reported in 1853 that "the deep sea fishery on the coast of Cape Breton is not flourishing, we keep two decked shallops at Chetican more to collect our fish than the good they do a fishing."[24] On banking trips, the fish were processed on board and heavily salted to preserve them until the vessel docked. They were then thoroughly washed and laid out to dry.

Channel Island and Cape Breton merchants were still involved in the herring and mackerel fishery (Figure 4.2). Some herring were caught around the Magdalen Islands and in St George's Bay on the southwest coast of Newfoundland,[25] while around Cape Breton the largest catches of herring and mackerel were taken along the Strait of Canso and off eastern Cape Breton, where the fish trimmed the coast as they migrated to deep water. A small fishery for herring and mackerel was also prosecuted in Bras d'Or Lake. Salmon continued to be caught by boat fishermen using nets, and the largest hauls were at Margaree Harbour, Main-à-Dieu, and Gabarus.[26] Channel Island merchants exported most of their pickled herring and mackerel to the Caribbean and, increasingly, to Montreal for the expanding domestic market.[27] Cape Breton merchants sent their pickled fish, including salmon, to Halifax for re-export.

Sealing, too, continued to attract interest, particularly during the 1830s and 1840s when it was encouraged by government bounties.[28] Most of the investment came from merchants and planters resident at Chéticamp and Margaree Harbour, although some merchants at

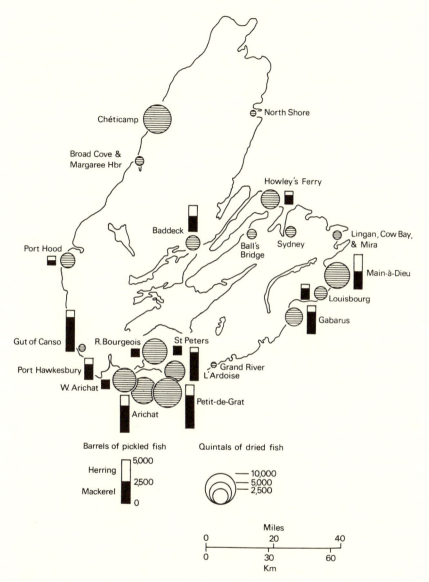

Figure 4.2
Distribution of dried- and pickled-fish production in Cape Breton, 1851
Source: Census of 1851, RG 1/453, Public Archives of Nova Scotia.

Arichat and Sydney were also involved. Sealing vessels were usually small, less than 40 tons, and used in the summer for the cod fishery. In 1835, 15 Cape Breton vessels, ranging in size from 26 to 43 tons (average 36 tons), received £269 in bounties. In 1842, a Sydney merchant outfitted a vessel on the "Newfoundland scale" and made £14,000 from a three-week voyage. Encouraged by his success, 22 vessels went to the ice the following year and caught nearly 10,000 seals, an ample return. By 1845, 25 vessels, with 4 over 50 tons, were pursuing the seal hunt. Thereafter, the seal fishery, dogged by disasters at sea, the high cost of outfit, and the withdrawal of the bounty, gradually contracted.

Many fishermen also turned to the American fishery for supplies and employment. American schooners had been fishing close to Nova Scotia since the eighteenth century, and their numbers increased dramatically as the mackerel fishery developed in the Gulf of St Lawrence in the early 1830s.[29] By 1843, it was estimated that there were between 700 and 800 American vessels in the gulf, many manned by fishermen from Cape Breton.[30] In late June 1836, William Crichton, a merchant at Little Arichat, found "much difficulty in getting a crew of eight good fishermen to man a vessel for a mackerel jigging voyage." Although he searched the "Gut of Canso from one end to the other, most of the best fishermen were either already gone with the Americans, or engaged and waiting their arrival."[31] In 1851, there were upwards of 200 fishermen from the Strait of Canso alone crewing American vessels. Many more traded bait, fish, barrels, salt, and vegetables with the Americans for tobacco, spirits, clothing, boots and shoes, and sometimes money.[32] Such smuggling helped Cape Breton fishermen and their families to subsist.

Fishermen also relied on the domestic economy for support. Many kept small gardens in which they grew hay, oats, and potatoes – the staple crop. On rough ground, they pastured a handful of sheep and cattle (Figure 3.7).[33] The 30 families, mostly dependent on the fishery, living at Main-à-Dieu in 1818 were reported to keep "large stocks of cattle," which were supported through the winter on salt-marsh hay cut from the offshore island of Scaterie. Farther around the coast at Louisbourg, fishermen practised a form of transhumance. About the first of May, they moved from their winter quarters in the woods to their fishing rooms and gardens along the shore. There, they spent the summer fishing. In November, they moved back to their winter houses, about two or three miles inland, where wood was available for fuel, furze could be cut for cattle fodder, and the woods provided livestock with protection from winter storms.[34]

The forest also provided game, berries, and building materials. As the men spent most of their time fishing, much of the tending of vegetables and livestock was done by their wives and families – a sexual division of labour imposed by the demands of the fishery.[35]

Labour for the fishery remained overwhelmingly residential (Figure 4.1). With the great increase in the Island's population during the early nineteenth century, merchants had no shortage of men to outfit for the fishery; in 1851, there were some 2,700 fishermen in Cape Breton. Assuming that each fisherman had four dependents (probably an underestimate), the fishery supported some 13,500 people.[36] The Acadian populations at Chéticamp, River Bourgeois, and Île Madame provided much of the labour, but Scots were increasingly involved in the fishery, particularly along the northwest coast and around Bras d'Or Lake. The Channel Island merchants also continued to import seasonal labour from Jersey; in 1837, there were 180 migrant workers at Arichat and Chéticamp employed in fishing, processing, and shipbuilding.[37]

The outports were still dominated by the merchant premises. Channel Island companies retained their large establishments on Île Madame and at Chéticamp, while Cape Breton merchants had similar, though smaller, stations. Typical of a medium-sized Channel Island fishing station was the property belonging to Thoume Moullin & Co. at Port Hawkesbury. This "valuable fishing establishment" consisted of a two-storey residence, a three-storey dry fish store, a two-storey dry goods store, a cooper shop, a one-and-a-half-storey cookhouse, a blacksmith's forge and stable, a 120-foot-long wharf, flakes covering an acre of land, and a shipyard. The whole establishment stood on six acres of enclosed pasture land. More typical of the smaller fishing premises was a property sold at River Bourgeois that comprised a three-and-a-half-storey store (divided into areas for storing dry fish and goods), an 80-foot-long wharf, and an acre of fish flakes.[38] The rest of an outport consisted of a loose collection of fishermen's homes, outbuildings, wharves, flakes, and gardens.

Economic stratification in the outports remained marked. The Channel Island merchants continued to hold sway in the Île Madame area and along the Chéticamp coast. With their considerable capital, they could ride out the periodic depressions in trade and continue to extend credit to fishermen. The small, local merchants had insufficient capital to carry such a burden and frequently withdrew credit in a downturn.[39] In 1842, DeCarteret reported to his partner in Jersey that the fishermen "in these bad times ... cannot go to any other person for supplies so that they have to come to us." At that time, DeCarteret & LeVesconte were "the only house [at

D'Escousse] that have to supply the fisherman in full."[40] Left in a monopoly position, the Channel Island companies controlled much of the fish trade. After spending two months at Arichat in 1839, one traveller noted that of the £80,000 worth of business done there each year, "a considerable part ... is drawn away to be spent elsewhere, by merchants residing in Jersey, who arrive in the spring and depart in the fall with the fruit of the fisherman's labour."[41] Charged high prices for their supplies and paid low prices for their fish, many fishermen were left indebted and poverty-stricken. Lorenzo Sabine, one of the most knowledgable commentators on the American east coast fishery, considered Cape Breton to be "the poorest part of British America"; he knew American captains who had seen families "covered with scurvy, applying for medicine, and although they obtained it, were informed by the doctor that it was fresh and wholesome provisions they wanted most; at which time one of the parties admitted that his stock was reduced to some herrings and a few potatoes." Such destitution, Sabine reckoned, was "*general* among the fishermen of Cape Breton."[42]

Despite the influx of Scots, the older ethnic distribution in the outports had not been disturbed.[43] Acadians continued to dominate Îsle Madame, River Bourgeois, L'Ardoise, and Chéticamp, while people of Irish and New England descent were still a significant part of the populations of Gabarus, Louisbourg, and Main-à-Dieu. Elsewhere, Scots were the major ethnic group. In places such as the Gut of Canso, Creignish, Port Hood, Broad Cove, North Shore, Howley's Ferry, Sydney, and around Bras d'Or Lake, Scots were the overwhelming majority. By mid-century, the Acadians, New Englanders, and Irish had been in Cape Breton for three generations or more, and many of the Scots for at least a generation. With immigration largely over by the 1830s, there was little new blood coming into the fishing villages and most families were becoming increasingly interrelated.

As the population increased, many outports were able to support a resident priest or minister and build a church. Catholic churches served the Acadian populations at Arichat, River Bourgeois, L'Ardoise, and Chéticamp, and the Highland Scots at Creignish, Port Hood, Broad Cove, and Margaree. The Free Church was well entrenched among the Presbyterian Scots at Grand River, Howley's Ferry, North Shore, and Gabarus. Catholic, Presbyterian, and Anglican churches served the more diverse populations at Main-à-Dieu and Louisbourg. Clergy were often community leaders and sometimes arbitrated local disputes; in 1829, Father Courteau, the Catholic priest at Chéticamp, intervened on behalf of fishermen who had fished "on shares" with planters but had been deprived of their share of the government bounty on cod.[44] With friends and relatives, the clergy offered some support to fishermen in economic need.

THE ESTABLISHMENT OF AN INDUSTRIAL STAPLE: COAL MINING, 1827-57

Until the late 1820s, there was little change in the mining operation at Sydney Mines.[45] Local entrepreneurs continued to run the mine on short leases, investing sufficient capital to keep the diggings going but not to develop them further. No more than 13,000 tons of coal were raised in any one year, and apart from one or two annual shipments to New England, exports remained limited to Halifax and St John's. No attempt was made to mine the other seams that outcropped between Sydney Harbour and Mira Bay, although fishermen and farmers dug small amounts for domestic use and for sale to American traders. Mining remained pre-industrial and small scale: simple pick-and-shovel operations with horses turning winding-gear and pulling wagons to the shipping wharf. Fewer than 100 miners were employed each summer, many of them Irish, the rest Loyalist descendants and Highland Scots. Mostly young and single, the men continued to be accommodated in dilapidated bunkhouses.

In 1827, the coalfield entered a new phase of development.[46] The lease of the mine and rights to exploit the rest of the coalfield were taken over by a British-based company, the General Mining Association. Within a few years and after massive capital investment, production at Sydney Mines was greatly expanded, a new mine opened at Bridgeport, railways and wharves constructed, a mining village laid out, a larger, highly skilled workforce recruited from Britain, and steam power introduced. The new technologies, production processes, and working practices of the industrial revolution had come to Cape Breton, a portent of future developments on the Island.

Although the GMA was the largest industrial company in Nova Scotia during the early nineteenth century, the involvement of British industrial capital in the coal mines of Cape Breton was somewhat inadvertent. In 1788, George III, by royal prerogative, gave his favourite son, the duke of York, a 60-year lease on all unworked mineral resources in Nova Scotia. The lease was not taken up until 1825, when the duke, hard-pressed by his creditors, sublet the rights to the London jewellery firm of Rundell, Bridge, & Rundell. With some experience of mining in South America, the firm held on to the lease and began prospecting in Nova Scotia. After the nature and extent of the mineral resources had been established, the firm set up a joint-stock company, the General Mining Association, to develop the extensive coal reserves. As some of the best seams were already being worked and thus not included in the duke's grant, the GMA had to purchase the leases as they came up for renewal. By 1828, these leases had been purchased, leaving the association with a monopoly of all mineral development in Nova Scotia. To oversee the development and operation of the mines, experienced British managers were hired and sent out to Nova Scotia. Richard Smith, the GMA agent in Nova Scotia, supervised the development of the coalfield in Pictou County, while Richard Brown, a young mining engineer, reorganized Sydney Mines.[47] After Smith's return to England in 1834, Samuel Cunard, rising merchant-prince of the Maritimes and a failed bidder for the coal leases, was appointed provincial agent and a company director. By 1846, the GMA had spent some £300,000 developing the mines in Cape Breton and those at Pictou on the mainland.[48]

The "chief object" of the GMA was to develop an extensive trade with the United States.[49] Sydney's bituminous coal was best suited for household use, and Boston, New York, and Philadelphia were easily accessible by sea. Nevertheless, as the GMA began to develop its mines, American tariffs were introduced to cancel out the cost advantage of water transport and protect the emerging coal industry in Pennsylvania. Although the GMA attempted to circumvent the tariffs by price cutting, it suffered considerable losses. Market demand, too, was lessening as consumers switched from the smoky bituminous coal from Cape Breton to the cleaner, longer-burning anthracite from Pennsylvania. As a result, between 1830 and 1854, only about a third of exports went to the American market, with annual shipments averaging 22,000 tons (Figure 4.3). Although exports increased after the Reciprocity Treaty was signed in 1854, shipments were mainly of gas-coal for use by city gas manufacturers, rather than bituminous coal for domestic consumption.

The failure to penetrate the American market successfully forced the company to sell to small, local markets, principally in Nova Scotia and Newfoundland.[50] Most of the coal went to Halifax and St John's for use by householders, small industries, and the garrisons. Prices were kept low to stimulate demand, and with the populations of both cities rising rapidly in the 1830s and 1840s, shipments increased markedly (Figure 4.3). Even so, supply far outstripped demand; with the unremunerative trade to the United States, the GMA barely covered its costs. In 1842, Samuel Cunard, while lobbying the govern-

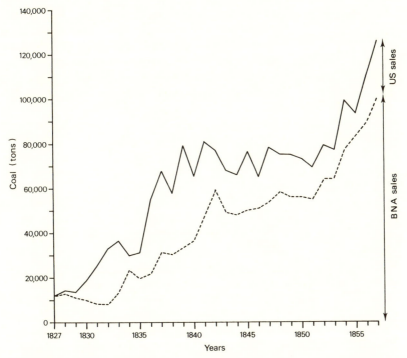

Figure 4.3
Production and export of coal from Cape Breton, 1827–57
Source: R. Brown, *The Coal Fields and Coal Trade of the Island of Cape Breton* (London: Sampson, Low, Marston, Low, and Searle, 1869), 76.

ment for a reduction in the royalties charged on coal sales, stated that "no interest or return has ever yet been paid."[51] By the late 1840s, the company shares were trading at 65 percent of their original value,[52] and in 1853, before a select committee on the coal industry, Richard Brown reported that "the association have expended an enormous sum of money, and have reaped no adequate return, in consequence of the demand never having as yet been nearly equal to their ability to supply."[53]

With the development of the mines in the late 1820s and 1830s, output rose from 12,000 tons in 1827 to 68,000 tons in 1837 (Figure 4.3). Over the next 16 years, annual production remained roughly stable at around 70,000 tons, but when the Reciprocity Treaty opened the American market, production picked up again and reached 126,000 tons in 1857. Much of the output during those years came from Sydney Mines, the focus of most investment

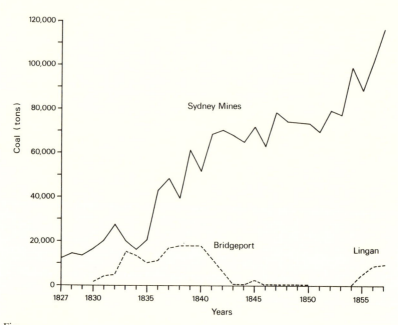

Figure 4.4
Coal production at the principal mines on Cape Breton Island, 1827–57
Source: R. Brown, *The Coal Fields and Coal Trade of the Island of Cape Breton* (London: Sampson, Low, Marston, Low, and Searle, 1869), 76.

(Figure 4.4). Between 1827 and 1829, the triennial average annual output of Sydney Mines was 13,425 tons. By 1837–39, it was 49,700 tons, and by 1847–49, 75,493 tons. The GMA also opened four other mines: the works at Little Bras d'Or and Point Aconi were exploratory and only produced a few hundred tons of coal each year; Bridgeport, a mine near Indian Bay, was considerably more productive and during the 1830s and early 1840s was the GMA's other major mine on the Island; Lingan, a gas-coal mine that was opened in 1854 in anticipation of free trade, supplied all the gas-coal the GMA exported to the United States (figures 4.4 and 4.5).[54]

After the GMA took over Sydney Mines, the old adits, shafts, and levels were rationalized. A series of new shafts were sunk at progressively greater depths: 200 feet in 1830, 320 feet in 1834, and 400 feet in 1854.[55] At the bottom of each shaft, a pair of levels were driven in either direction along the seam's dip, one for haulage and the other for miners' access.[56] Every 60 to 200 yards, the levels were connected by horse roads driven at right angles. The blocks of coal were then mined on the upside of the road, creating a worked-out

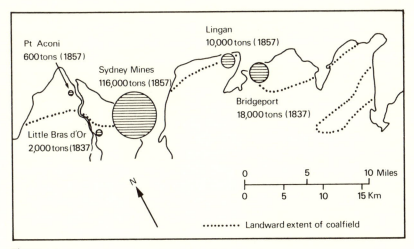

Figure 4.5
Distribution of coal mines on Cape Breton Island and their maximum output, 1827–57
Source: R. Brown, *The Coal Fields and Coal Trade of the Island of Cape Breton* (London: Sampson, Low, Marston, Low, and Searle, 1869), 76.

space (a bord). Although pillar and bord mining had been used in the earlier diggings, it was more organized and probably safer in the GMA pits.

As underground workings became deeper and more extensive, more efficient methods of drainage, ventilation, and haulage were needed. Steam engines were installed at Sydney Mines and Lingan for pumping and winding, although the small Bridgeport mine was drained by an adit.[57] Ventilation was assisted by furnaces. Positioned at the base of an upcast shaft, the furnace drew air from the downcast shaft and around the levels.[58] Partitions of sackcloth stretched over wooden frames (bratticing) deflected the air into the work spaces. Ponies were introduced underground to haul tubs along the levels, while on the surface, tramways linked mines to wharves. Horses continued to haul the coal wagons until 1853, when they were replaced by two steam locomotives.[59] Coal wharves, too, were improved. In 1835, a new wharf was built at North Bar to serve Sydney Mines with facilities for direct loading into the ships' holds.[60] Similar wharves were built at Bridgeport and Lingan.[61] The quality of the coal was also improved. As the bituminous coal mined from Sydney Mines was friable (easily crumbled), the GMA introduced grading of the coal underground and screening at the pit-head. The screens consisted of iron gratings set at half-inch widths that separated out small coal or slack from large or round coal. Large coal was stored or "banked" ready for sale, while slack was divided into nut coal for the miners' domestic use and dust, which was carried to the "duff heap" and allowed to take fire spontaneously.[62]

Virtually all the sophisticated technology used at the mines was made in Britain. Steam pumps, winches, boilers, locomotives, as well as general goods and materials, were all imported from England. They were brought out on a supply vessel each year.[63] Apart from the foundry at Lingan, which handled basic manufacturing, there was no development of any manufacturing industry on the Island to supply the mines. The mines were simply too small to justify such investment. There was also no spin-off from the building of the railways and shipping wharves to the rest of the Cape Breton economy. The railways did not extend into farming areas, while the wharves were unsuitable for agricultural exports.

As coal mining was still unmechanized and heavily labour intensive, increased production depended upon a larger workforce. In 1832, the GMA employed 174 men at Sydney Mines;[64] by September 1838, there were 372 men and 37 boys at Sydney Mines and 143 men and 13 boys at Bridgeport.[65] With the steady trade, the workforce remained roughly the same size for the next 20 years; in December 1858, there were 323 men and 70 boys at Sydney Mines and about 50 men during the summer at Lingan.[66] These were by far the largest individual workforces in Cape Breton.

The GMA also ensured more efficient production by imposing a highly specialized division of labour (Table 4.3). An underground hierarchy was formed with about half the workers serving the face-workers, the hewers or colliers. A hewer and his mate were assigned to each bord and left responsible for cutting and grading coal. Loaders or fillers transferred the coal to tubs, which were then pulled along the roads to the main levels by haulers and their ponies. There, the tubs were collected by drivers and their horses and taken to the shaft bottom where they were loaded into the cage by onsetters. Door-keepers operated the ventilation doors between the roads and levels as the drivers and their ponies passed through. Boys as young as nine or ten were employed as door-keepers, and teenagers worked as haulers and drivers. Timbering and throughways were maintained by road makers, while ventilation was looked after by wastemen. On the surface, the workforce was divided between unskilled labourers and mechanics or "wise men."[67] Most labourers were employed hauling and storing coal, filling the coal wagons, and doing odd jobs around the coal yard. At the pit-head, banksmen operated the winding-gear and off-loaded coal tubs from the cage. A company official

Table 4.3
Workforce employed at Sydney Mines and Bridgeport, September 1838

Description	Sydney Mines	Bridgeport
Colliers	112	69
Coal fillers and haulers	57	10
Horse drivers (boys)	28	13
Door keepers (boys)	9	
Road makers and wastemen	12	4
On-setters	4	
Labourers	123	45
Banksmen	6	
Wharf builders	6	
Lightermen	7	
Blacksmiths	7	3
Carpenters	10	3
Sawyers	2	2
Masons	4	
Iron moulders	2	
Engineers	10	
Ostlers	2	2
Pilots		2
Clerks	2	
Overseers	4	2
Resident agent	1	1

Source: "Statement of Men, Horses, and Machinery, employed at Sydney Mines and Bridgeport Mines in September 1838," RG 1/463/32–3, Public Archives of Nova Scotia.

weighed the tubs and entered the amount against each miner's tally, an operation that in the late nineteenth century (and possibly earlier) was supervised by a check weigher employed by the miners to ensure fair play.[68] Before the introduction of steam traction, drivers took the horse-hauled wagons to the wharf where lightermen or trimmers loaded the vessels. The "wise men" included carpenters, sawyers, masons, blacksmiths, and iron moulders, who were responsible for the maintenance of the pit, tramways, wagons, wharves, and buildings. There were also engineers, who looked after the pumps and winches, and ostlers, who stabled the ponies and horses. Supervising the workforce and ensuring the efficient running of the colliery was the management, the overseers and deputies who were responsible to Richard Brown, the company agent.

As few, if any, Cape Breton miners before 1827 were particularly skilled, the GMA had to recruit experienced miners in Britain. Men from the coalfields of northern England and South Wales were brought out to Cape Breton to form a cadre of skilled miners.[69] During the 1830s, more men were hired from the "distressed districts" of England, although later immigrants came from Scotland.[70] By 1850, the majority of miners were from Scotland, some from the north of England, and a few from other parts of Britain. By then, the immigration of skilled men had been reduced to a trickle. "A few emigrants are understood to arrive each year from Great Britain," reported an American mining engineer, "but I did not learn that much effort was made by the Association to introduce them."[71] There was little need to continue importing miners when surplus labour was readily available from rural Cape Breton. Initially, at least, the recruitment of skilled men from Britain must have lessened the ties between the mines and the surrounding countryside. Settlers could no longer expect to combine part-time farming with hewing, as many had done in the earlier workings. But as British miners drifted away to mining jobs in the United States, the GMA took on more local men and the close ties between farm and mine were re-established.

Although the ice blockade of the shipping wharves from January to May imposed a seasonal regime on the export of coal, the mines continued to operate, albeit at a reduced level, during the winter months. As Table 4.4 shows, most colliers were employed from January to April. The GMA was keen to provide winter employment in order to retain the skilled miners imported from Britain; it also wanted coal banked in readiness for the opening of navigation in late May. The greatest expansion of the labouring workforce, however, was during the summer when extra hands were hired to cope with shipping and to attend to jobs neglected during the winter.[72]

When the mines were fully operational, men worked five or six days a week, and the GMA expected the men to work regular hours to ensure uninterrupted production. Irregular working hours and unscheduled stoppages were discouraged. After the GMA took over the mines, it found that the Irish Catholic miners were accustomed to taking time off for religious holidays. On 16 March 1830, for example, an overseer at Sydney Mines reported that coal was raised "from Pillar and Gin pits until 3 o'clock – when the men left off on account of the morrow being St. Patricks." On the following day, "none of the men [were] at work except the sawyers and some of the carpenters." By the day after, "the greater part of the colliers and all the mechanics" were back at work. Faced with further stoppages for other saint's days as well as Christmas until the "twelfth day," Easter Day, and Ascension Day, the GMA threatened miners

Table 4.4
Monthly employment of colliers and labourers at Sydney Mines, Queen Pit, 1839 and 1857

1839	J	F	M	A	M	J	J	A	S	O	N	D
Colliers	94	89	92	92	79	80	71	73	70	72	71	67
Surface labourers	43	35	25	18	45	72	72	118	115	79	30	26
Total workforce	301	277	260	260	256	275	269	326	299	262	223	190
1857	J	F	M	A	M	J	J	A	S	O	N	D
Colliers	181	187	186	186	174	163	160	153	153	153	154	182
Surface labourers	49	50	49	55	57	57	66	63	62	63	77	65
Total workforce	318	317	315	322	317	300	301	292	286	290	303	332

Source: Workmen's Time and Pay Books, Sydney Mines, 1839, MG 14/19/A.1, Beaton Institute, and Workmen's Time and Pay Books, Sydney Mines, Queen Pit, 1857, MG 14/19/A.6, Beaton Institute.

with dismissal. On 16 August 1830, "R. B[rown] being informed that Saturday next would be kept as a holy day by the men informed them that every man who did not attend his work on the day should be discharged. August 27 Monday. Several of the men having been idle on Saturday contrary to orders 9 diggers and 4 haulers were discharged this morning but 2 of the latter were allowed to go to work on account of having reasonable excuses for absence."[73] The imposition of work discipline went hand in hand with the introduction of the new productive system.[74]

The mining villages at Sydney Mines, Bridgeport, and Lingan were larger, more elaborate settlements than the earlier work camp. The GMA provided relatively comfortable accommodation at the mines to help retain the skilled labour and to exercise a measure of control over the workforce. In the event of a strike, the company could bring pressure on the miners by evicting them from company housing.[75] Although laid out by the GMA on company land, the villages had no formal plan (Figure 4.6). Rows of houses were built either along a road leading to the mine or by the side of the colliery railway (Figure 4.7). The availability of land allowed the rows to be more dispersed than was common among the pit villages in Britain, although the plan and construction of the houses followed British practice. Probably because Richard Brown and the imported craftsmen had no experience of timber-frame construction, the houses were built in brick and laid out in rows, exactly as they would have been in England.[76] The exteriors were uniformly plain; the interiors were small, usually including one room and a kitchen, perhaps two or three rooms, a kitchen, and sleeping space in the attic.[77] Most

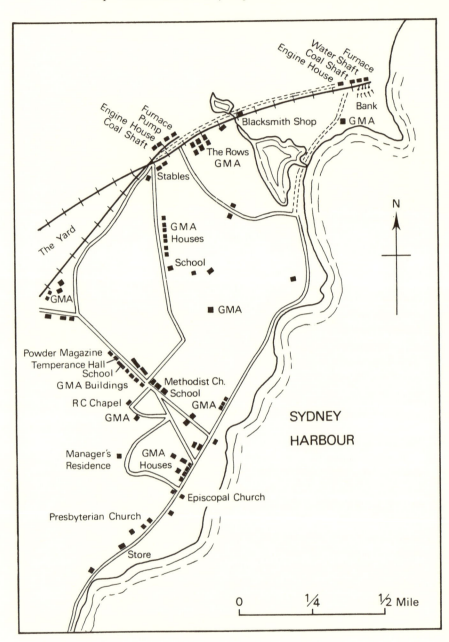

Figure 4.6
The GMA's village and pits at Sydney Mines, Cape Breton County, 1877
Source: A.F. Church, *Topographical Township Map of Cape Breton County Nova Scotia* (Bedford, NS: A.F. Church & Co., 1877).

Figure 4.7
GMA housing, Sydney Mines
Source: National Archives of Canada, PA 120434.

houses had an earth closet and a garden attached at the back. The rest of a mining village consisted of service buildings for the mine or for the mining population. Around the pit-head clustered the furnace shaft and chimney, pump and winding engine-houses, stables, foreman's office, and blacksmith's shop. Elsewhere, the company had a powder magazine and a retail store. There was also a schoolhouse, Roman Catholic and Presbyterian churches for the Irish and Scottish miners, and a Methodist chapel for nonconformists from northern England and South Wales. For all intents and purposes, the mining settlements were company towns.

The population of the villages appears to have been more balanced than in the earlier work camp. At least some of the men recruited from Britain had families; others were single and had no family ties in the area.[78] By mid-century, there were 321 families and a total population of 2,116 at Sydney Mines, although not all of these people lived in the GMA village.[79] With people drawn from Cornwall, South Wales, northern England, and the Lowlands of Scotland, as well as from Cape Breton and Newfoundland, there was considerable ethnic variety. Miners spoke Gaelic and various dialects of English. Most likely, they observed different mining traditions and ways of work. Such diversity and the apparent transiency of many miners must have hindered the development of a common mining culture. There was probably little of the cultural homogeneity found in other parts of Cape Breton.

In an industry where most miners were full-time employees, economic differences between masters and men were clearly drawn.[80]

In 1850, it was reported that a former agent of the GMA had been paid a salary of £800 sterling; most likely Richard Brown drew such a salary. Overseers could expect about £144 sterling, including a house and fuel; while overmen were paid about £72 sterling with the same additional benefits. Miners were paid piece wages, but an average daily wage was about 5s. sterling (but could be as much as 8s.), making their annual gross earnings about £50 sterling. Charges for lights, powder, doctors, and schooling reduced that sum to about £40 sterling, but fuel and housing were free. Compared to wages in the Lanarkshire coalfield in Lowland Scotland, the average earnings in Cape Breton were at least half as much again, a reflection of the shortage of skilled men on the Island.[81] Labourers could expect about 2s. 6d. sterling per day, making their seasonal earnings about £11 or £12 – a useful supplement for subsistence farmers.

Although wages were higher in Cape Breton than in Scotland, the cost of living probably made up the difference. Most of the miner's staple foodstuffs had to be imported and were sold through the company store on credit, usually at high prices. Some miners fell into arrears and were effectively tied to the company until their debts were repaid.[82] Others earned enough to get by; in 1835, one miner declared: "Our wages have been tolerable; and we have a well stored house with flour, beef, bacon, sugar, and other victualling commodities."[83] Some of these items would have been drawn from the miner's well-tended garden, where a cow, chickens, a pig, and potatoes were raised.

Working in a large group in a sharply stratified industry and faced with the dominance of the GMA, many miners turned to collective action to improve their conditions. "We met with cross looks and angry words from the Master," one miner wrote in 1835, "and he told us plainly that he believed we were all combined against him. He also told us that the greater part of the men on the concern was in debt ... This has made a great complaining among the men."[84] Strikes occasionally took place. In 1830, Richard Brown reported that "several of the cutters remained idle owing to their being charged with rent & fuel." A year later, all the miners "except sinkers, smiths in new forge and two sawyers at the whf." stood out for an increase in wages, but although the strike lasted for 23 weeks, it was broken by contractors with "scab" labour.[85] In 1849, one observer reported that "'strikes' and other irregularities, have sometimes occurred" at the mines.[86]

Emigration was the miner's more effective recourse. In a time book for 1832, a GMA official recorded the emigration of Newfoundland Irish, writing terse comments alongside names such as Cahilly,

Conway, Donovan, Maghan, and Nowlan: "left the mines," "absent the whole month," "gone to Halifax."[87] Some men absconded, leaving debts at the company store and risking arrest. In 1832, the GMA agent at Halifax was instructed to look out for three Welsh miners, Thomas Jones, David Lewis, and James Davis, who had left debts of £38 19s. 1d.[88] These men were later spotted "on the land," but most – born to a life of mining – looked for similar work in the United States. This is well illustrated by a letter written by a hewer at Sydney Mines in 1835 to his brother-in-law who had just moved to Pennsylvania:

It made our hearts glad to hear you were doing so well in the mines, and that times were so prosperous about Pittsville [Pottsville?] and vicinity. – Since I last wrote severall have left this place for the United States ... Indeed the Mines is thin of people to what it used to be. There is only about 12 houses that pay rent occupied. And some of the shantees are deserted. Letters has been recived from most of them, and they all send good accounts. Peppet and Wilson has both gone to Boston. Most of the others went to Boston. James Andrews and Richard Richards is working at a tunnel 6 miles from New York at 1 dollar and half per day and 30 more men is wanted. A letter has been recieved from Isaac Brown he is at a place called Semples Landing in Ohio 1d[ollar] 1/4 per day. John Hay is at Pittsburgh, also David Flowers John Davies and Bason and John James. Henry Anderson is gone to the Messouree Territory. – You will persieve from these things that great changes has taken place at Sydney Mines. And it is likely that numbers more will leave in the spring. Mr. Brown is growing a hard master, he is pinching of at every end.[89]

In 1850, a visiting American mining engineer was asked "several times ... by laboring men, miners, and others, if ... working people could get a 'chance' now 'in the States,' meaning of course *good wages*."[90] Another observer reported that "of a number of families that were recently brought to the mines at the cost of the Association only a few have remained in the country. The greater number embarked for the United States."[91] Few miners ever returned to Cape Breton.

SHIPPING AND SHIPBUILDING

The expansion of fishing, coal mining, and agriculture in Cape Breton during the early nineteenth century led to a considerable increase in the Island's coasting and oceanic trade. Dried and pickled fish were shipped along the coast to Halifax, as well as to the Caribbean,

South America, and the Mediterranean. Coal was regularly exported to Halifax and St John's and less frequently to Saint John, New Brunswick, and Charlottetown, Prince Edward Island. Farther afield, shipments were sent to Portland, Boston, New York, and Philadelphia.[92] Agricultural produce, too, was shipped to Halifax and St John's as well as to St Pierre and Miquelon. Although agricultural exports became increasingly important, the two staple trades generated much of the carrying trade. In 1814, for instance, cargoes of fish and coal accounted for 241 (80 percent) of the 301 clearances from Arichat and Sydney. Shipments of coal alone accounted for 183 (61 percent) clearances.[93] Even in the trade to St John's, the principal market for Cape Breton's agricultural produce, coal was the dominant cargo. Of the 152 vessels carrying goods from Cape Breton to St John's in 1837, 83 (55 percent) were loaded with coal.[94] Without the two staples, much of the Island's shipping would have been idle.

The shipping industry continued to be an important employer on the Island; in 1851, more than 1,000 men were either registered seamen or employed at sea, the third-largest occupation in Cape Breton (Table 4.1). Most of the sea captains and crew were based at Arichat, Petit-de-Grat, and River Bourgeois; the rest were distributed among the Gut of Canso, Louisbourg, Main-à-Dieu, and Sydney Mines. Many of the crews were family members and divided the profits from coasting "mutually ... amongst them."[95]

Shipping and fishing were also a major stimulus to the Island's shipbuilding industry. In the early nineteenth century, several hundred schooners, brigs, brigantines, and barques were built in Cape Breton. In the late 1820s, one observer estimated that some 1,500 vessels and boats were built on the Island each year and that 50 of the vessels were square-riggers.[96] In 1851, 216 vessels were on the stocks, totalling 14,316 tons.[97] Although shipyards could be found on many creeks and inlets, the industry was concentrated overwhelmingly on Île Madame and the Gut of Canso; in 1851, shipyards in the area were building 73 percent of the tonnage under construction in Cape Breton. Arichat was clearly the centre of the Island's maritime trade. The investment in shipbuilding came from both the Channel Island and Cape Breton merchants, sometimes in close cooperation. In the spring of 1840, for example, Peter DeCarteret began building the 149-ton brig *Lady Falkland*, contracting with Joseph Wilson of Port Hawkesbury for the timber.[98] Trees were cut from the forests around River Inhabitants, sawn into deals and shipped across to DeCarteret's shipyard at D'Escousse on Île Madame. The keel was laid in August 1841, and with four carpenters at work, DeCarteret expected to have the vessel ready for the following fall. In a letter to his partner, Peter LeVesconte in Jersey, he reckoned that "she will answer us for the West Indies trade."[99] Like many vessels built by the Channel Island companies, this one was later transferred to Jersey.[100]Although shipbuilding gave work to lumberers, sawmillers, carpenters, and shipwrights, the industry did not lay the basis for further manufacturing activity on the Island. Much of the outfit – pumps, winches, rigging, deck irons – used on vessels were not manufactured in Cape Breton but imported from Britain via Halifax or Jersey. Cape Breton provided wood and labour for the industry, but little else. As a result, the backward linkage from the staples to shipbuilding, while important in terms of local employment and merchant profits, did not lead to much economic diversification.[101]

By mid-century, the early pattern of the staple trades in Cape Breton was well established. British mercantile capital continued to dominate the cod fishery, while British industrial capital had a firm grip on the coal industry. Lines of control stretched from Cape Breton across the Atlantic to Jersey and London, tying the colonial periphery to the imperial centre. The staple economies remained overwelmingly dependent upon foreign markets, and as the fluctuations in the coal trade revealed, they were vulnerable to changes in international demand. The staples played a crucial role in the expansion of shipping and the growth of the shipbuilding industry. Shipbuilding provided a local market for timber, which helped settlers get established on the land. The staples also provided a market for agricultural produce and gave employment to a few hundred seasonal labourers. Linkages from the staples reached quite far into the rural economy. Nevertheless, the staples were not large enough to employ the thousands of poverty-stricken settlers squatting on Crown land or to provide a market for manufacturing industry. Mining and fishing were no longer the central pillars of the Cape Breton economy.

Apart from the growth of shipbuilding and the coasting trade, the outports and mining villages remained completely dependent upon their respective staples. They were still specialized, single-industry settlements. Within these settlements, the wealth generated by the staples was distributed highly unequally. The smuggling and occupational pluralism of the fishermen testified to their poverty, while the strikes and transiency of the miners were marks of their economic weakness. Although poverty was widespread, there was little sense of a unified working class. The dispersal of the communities, the differences in work, and the great variation in language, culture, and religion all mitigated against coherent action by the staple work-forces. Feeding into a North Atlantic economy and drawing upon British capital thousands of miles away, the staple economies and workforces in Cape Breton were still highly fragmented.

5 The Potato Famine, 1845–1849

By the mid-1840s, the tide of Scottish emigration was ebbing away from Cape Breton and the rest of the Maritimes towards the Canadas and Australia. An open frontier for settlement at the beginning of the century was now virtually closed. The best land in Cape Breton had long been taken and was becoming increasingly difficult to buy as land prices rose. Most farmers were struggling to survive on back-land at the very margin of arable cultivation; the crop failures of the 1830s had already shown how precarious such farming could be. The potato blight that began in 1845 would reduce many farmers to a level of destitution that, ironically, had its closest parallel in western Scotland, and would start, this time from Cape Breton, another round of emigration.

First observed in 1843, potato blight (phytophthora infestans) is one of the most serious plant diseases in the Northern Hemisphere. Now recognized as a fungus, it can spread rapidly, especially in the right weather conditions. Warm, moist breezes can disperse spores over fields of potato plants in minutes; the first tell-tale signs of the disease appear as dark brown-black stains on the leaves and stems.[1] If the tops of the plants are cut and burnt, the spread of the disease may be checked, leaving the tubers unharmed. But once the fungus has taken hold, the potatoes turn mushy and brown, usually rotting in the ground before they are raised. A notable effect of the disease is the overpowering stench; fields of rotting plants in Cape Breton produced a smell so "sickening" that many commented on it.[2]

Potato blight appeared on the Island in late August 1845. In the humid days of late summer, the disease spread quickly from the Gut of Canso, the nearest point to the mainland, along the coasts and into the interior.[3] At Port Hood, on the northeast coast, the potato crop suffered severely; farther along the coast at Broad Cove, it was a total failure; while in Margaree, three-quarters of the crop was lost.[4] Yet to the east, in Cape Breton County, much of the crop was raised unharmed.[5] No one had much idea about the cause of the blight. One farmer observed: "The richer the ground the worst – Highlands not as bad as Intervale."[6] Others thought that the disease "cannot be accounted for by any reference to the description of seed – peculiarity of the soil or nature of cultivation – all where the disease had made its appearance having suffered alike."[7] Some even saw it as the "direct interference of the Almighty ... a punishment inflicted upon man for his presumption in attempting to introduce disorder into the economy of Nature by giving undue prominence to the potato."[8]

Frontland farmers weathered such "punishment" lightly. Apart from the loss of their potatoes, they enjoyed a relatively good harvest. In Margaree, there was an average crop of oats and an above average crop of hay; at Port Hood, the harvest was "uncommonly good."[9] Cattle, the staple product of frontland farms, were unaffected by the disease, although some died in Margaree after they had been fed diseased potatoes.[10] The fall sales of stock to Newfoundland left frontland farmers well prepared for winter, and a few, "happily for themselves removed above the consequences" of the blight, bought up sound potatoes to sell at high prices in the spring.[11]

Fishermen and backland farmers, who depended almost completely upon potatoes and would bear the brunt of any speculation in the crop, were in far more difficult straits. They unsuccessfully petitioned the government for an embargo on potato exports and soon were struggling to find enough to eat.[12] They had few other crops and little money to buy potato seed and provisions. After the failure of the summer herring and fall mackerel fisheries, fishermen at St Peters and Red Islands had no income at all.[13] Few had land grants that could be offered to merchants as security for winter credit, and many were loath to part with their cattle, virtually their last resource.

As fall turned to winter and the January snows fell, backland settlers rapidly ran out of food. In Broad Cove, those in the "poorer class" were reported to be in "a deplorable condition," while on the south side of St Patricks Channel, settlers expected to be starving by summer.[14] In response to petitions for aid, the government made money available for relief.[15] Largely drawn from each county's annual road grant, the money was placed in the hands of specially appointed commissioners, usually local clergy and magistrates, who purchased rye flour and cornmeal for distribution to needy settlers. The recipients were expected to repay the government by working on the roads during the summer. In 1846, Inverness County drew £500, the largest provincial share; Cape Breton County, £486; and Richmond County, £233. Relief saved many from starvation, and although it provided only a meagre subsistence, many settlers and government officials were optimistic that the blight was over and that further relief would not be needed.

Such was not to be. Later that year, brown smudges appeared on the potato plants and within days entire fields were destroyed. In Broad Cove, the crop was a total failure; in Margaree, the potatoes rotted in the ground, not even yielding the seed; in Middle River, the crop was completely lost; while around Sydney, only half a crop was raised.[16] Not all the potatoes were blighted, however, and "considerable quantities" were exported from Sydney and other ports to Halifax. Other crops were also good. In Cape Breton County, there was an average crop of hay, an above average crop of oats, and a very large crop of wheat. In Middle River, the "crops of grain [were] as good as usual."[17] Frontland farmers again avoided the full brunt of the disease, which fell, as before, on backland farmers.

By the end of the year, many backland settlers had run out of food. In late January 1847, 110 families at the front and rear of St Patricks Channel required aid.[18] In early February, 28 families – "all new settlers on woodland farms" – along the new road from Little Narrows to Lake Ainslie complained that they had missed the previous season's allocation of provisions and were now in a "deplorable state."[19] Later that month, settlers around Loch Lomond expected to be destitute by spring and had no seed potatoes or grain of any kind to put in the ground.[20]

The situation of backland settlers would grow worse as the winter dragged on. At L'Ardoise, Arthur Brymer, MPP for Richmond County, reported on 8 April that "the winter has been so severe that the oldest inhabitants does not recollect even to have seen the winter so severe and long. There is still three feet of snow on the ground."[21] By the first week of May, two feet of snow still remained on the uplands.[22] Cattle, usually half starved by that time of year, could not be put out to forage and were only being kept alive by feeding on the last seed potatoes; many were to die before summer. At Whycocomagh, River Denys, and Malagawatch, "great numbers of the beasts" starved to death; while at the south end of Lake Ainslie, "a considerable number of sheep and cattle" were also lost.[23] By the second week of May, some 500 cattle had died at Whycocomagh, Lake Ainslie, and Skye Glen, wiping out the capital of many farmers.[24]

Without cattle as security, farmers could not obtain credit from merchants for winter supplies, and consequently, many faced starvation. At L'Ardoise, some 200 families were destitute of food and seed potatoes, while another 200 had seed but nothing to eat.[25] At Whycocomagh, River Denys, and Malagawatch, justices of the peace, freeholders, and other inhabitants met in late April to petition the government for relief "to avert the calamity of a threatened famine."[26] Some 300 families required seed, and 100 were "literally suffering in a state of gradual starvation." Around Lake Ainslie, a survey carried out in early May by merchants, magistrates, and other inhabitants found 300 families completely destitute. Relief was needed immediately "to avert the progress of actual starvation, of which ... one *death*, at least, has already been the effect."[27] At Arichat, the magistrates, headed by leading fish merchant John Janvrin, unanimously resolved to spend the monies allocated by the government for road and bridge repair on provisions and seed. "Altho this will give assistance, it will only be scantily," explained Janvrin to the provincial secretary, "the distress is very great and the calls are most urgent, many families are in a state of starvation, their accounts of their sufferings are indescribable, daily the back land settlers arrive here in numbers of 20 and more, demanding assistance ... you may suppose the distress must be great, when these poor individuals travel from their homes the distance of 40 to 50 miles to obtain ¼ or ½ barrel flour."[28] In the second week of May, justices of the peace in Inverness County also petitioned for aid. "In many of the new settlements," they declared, "the people are now without provisions or seed their cattle dying and no prospect by which they can be sustained."[29] Among the areas in greatest need were the back settlements of the Strait of Canso, the River Denys Road, the country around New Canada and Campbell Mountain, Skye Glen, Whycocomagh, Lake Ainslie, Broad Cove, the head of the southeast branch of the Mabou River, Cape Mabou, and the back settlements of Margaree River. After receiving reports from the "leading men" of Inverness County, William Young, MPP, wrote to Lieutenant-Governor Harvey in support of the petitions, "convinced that the picture of absolute destitution both of provisions and seed, though it may appear at ... distance to be highly coloured, is not overcharged."[30] "The people must not be allowed to starve," he continued, adding that "seed ought at all hazards to be provided for the ensuing crop."

In Halifax, the provincial government was becoming increasingly concerned. Meeting in March, the Committee for the Relief of Distressed Settlers was in no doubt that destitution and suffering were widespread in the province, but the committee members, concerned about the cost of relief, felt they could not recommend aid except "where distress had pervaded the whole settlement, where it prevails to an extent almost universal, and in a manner that renders the ordinary modes of relief ineffective."[31] Such conditions were judged to exist in Cape Breton, and the committee proposed that £600 should be set aside for relief in Cape Breton County, £350 for Inverness County, and £300 for Richmond County.

In Cape Breton, the commissioners began ordering relief supplies from Halifax. Late in April, the magistrates at Arichat ordered 200 barrels of cornmeal from Messrs Fairbanks and Alison to be "forwarded immediately," and soon requested a further 50 barrels of rye flour.[32] When the supplies arrived in May, "so eager and so urgent [were] the wants of the poor," reported Janvrin, that "we had to use force to prevent their seizing forceably upon it."[33] Such provisions were soon exhausted. At Loch Lomond, most of the oats and Indian meal sent from Arichat in late May were gone by the second week of June, and many families were subsisting on the few potatoes set aside for seed. "They cannot now plant these potatoes," the settlers declared, "without plunging themselves into a state of immediate and hopeless destitution." They were thus reduced to "choosing between the horrors of immediate want, or the appaling and almost certain prospect of starvation during the rigours of a Cape Breton winter."[34] As potatoes could be planted up to the first week of July, they petitioned for Indian meal or other food so that the potatoes could be used for seed. Elsewhere, supplies were also running out. By mid-June, the 200 barrels of flour and meal supplied to settlers at Whycocomagh, River Denys, Malagawatch, Indian Rear, and Skye Glen were exhausted. Each family had received only a quarter of a barrel (49 pounds) of meal, which was soon consumed. As they looked forward "to the length of time before us, ere we receive succour for the fruit of our toils," they could see "nothing but death awfully staring us in the face." Most cattle and sheep had died and the few surviving livestock were in "such a feeble state, as to yield ... little or no milk, nor is it likely they will do so this season." With only one scanty meal a day, the settlers petitioned the government for aid, stating that they "would be most thankful to receive any thing eatable."[35]

In late summer, the potato blight struck again. In Margaree, much of the crop was lost; around Sydney, only potatoes sown on new burnt land survived; while in Middle River, the crop was far below average, and with the rot spreading through the stored potatoes, there was insufficient to last until the spring.[36] Moreover, other crops had been damaged by heavy rain: wheat had been flattened; the yields of oats, grown from seed issued as relief, were very light; and barley had not matured on poor upland soils.

Hopes were dashed and the government was forced to admit that "poverty, wretchedness and misery have spread through the Island of Cape Breton ... to an alarming degree."[37] In late November, the magistrates and minister of Middle River reported that the "failure is more extensive & some of the poor people settled on rear lots have not a bushel of potatoes in their possession at this time ... We called a meeting of those who were really in need last week where forty five heads of families came forward some declaring that they had no potatoes at all – others only a few bushels & the rest not so much as would keep their families alive till May. These dear Sir are chiefly new settlers who have very little grain & neither cash nor produce nor credit to procure provisions otherwise."[38] Their petition for aid joined many others. Three hundred families were in need at Grand Narrows, upwards of 100 families at Cape North, 49 families at Ingonish, and 48 families at Gabarus and Grand Mira.[39]

More government aid was made available.[40] In addition to the sums already granted, Inverness County drew £3,879 and Richmond County £1,800, while Cape Breton County made do with the £600 previously provided. Among the supplies ordered, 850 barrels of meal – enough for between 1,700 and 3,400 families – were distributed at St Anns, Boularderie, Grand Narrows, Little Narrows, Baddeck, Middle River, East Bay, and Sydney. Yet the Committee for Distressed Settlers was becoming increasingly concerned about repayment. No returns of labour performed on the roads had been submitted, leading the committee to deprecate a system of free welfare.

In Cape Breton, Charles Harrington, MPP for Richmond County, held a similar view.[41] In December, he reported to the provincial secretary "that the vigilant charity of the Government was last season abused shamefully ... many individuals sought and obtained the public relief, who had abundance at home." During the summer and fall, he had taken it upon himself to warn people that they had to help themselves rather than rely on the government. He went on to suggest that two competent individuals be appointed to inspect the homes of those claiming relief and make a return, verifying the number of people, livestock, and provisions. This task was not to be entrusted to the magistrates or John Janvrin, who, he advised, should not again control public funds or provisions. He further proposed that no relief should be distributed before the first of March or April, a potentially disastrous suggestion. Later that December, Harrington travelled through the greatest part of the county to ascertain the situation. In some areas, he "discouraged to [the] upmost any application for provisions," believing that several districts that had received government relief would now get by, "altho' by partial suffering." Yet in spite of his zeal in stopping the "infamous villainy" of people who had applied for unneeded relief, Harrington had to admit that destitution existed, particularly in the lower part of St Peters, the backlands of Bras d'Or Lake, and the Îsle Petabe settlement on Îsle Madame. These areas required "immediate relief." In the family of one Edward Carter at St Peters, a 20-year-old daughter had died of the "effects of privation," while the inhabitants of Îsle Petabe, in several instances, "had to kill their dogs and eat them – others have lived for some time past on fresh codfish *only* – without bread or potatoe." Harrington went on to request that 300 barrels of Indian meal be warehoused and distributed to the needy, after "the strictest enquiry" by three justices of the peace (Peter DeCarteret, Simon Donovan, and Hector McDonald).[42] The large number of barrels ordered – enough for between 600 and 1,200 families (35 to 70 percent of the population of the county) – suggests that the extent of destitution was far greater than Harrington was at first prepared to admit.

As the new year arrived and winter intensified, requests for aid continued to descend on Halifax. In late January 1848, the freeholders and other inhabitants of the east side of Lake Ainslie reported that 36 families, most of them on rear lots, were destitute. Many of them had subsisted on government relief since the fall and needed further aid to carry them through till spring. The petitioners pointed out that "had we money we could procure in mills and among thriving farmers what would prevent starvation till summer" and, in a letter accompanying the petition, blessed Providence "that the majority of us who reside on the first concession of lots of the east side are not so badly of this year ... as the surrounding people."[43] Clearly, the blight affected settlers on backland much more than those on frontland.

By late February, the 100 barrels of meal distributed to the destitute settlers around Baddeck had been exhausted and further relief, particularly oat, wheat, and potato seed, was needed.[44] Just over three weeks later, in mid-March, Alexander Farquharson, the minister of Middle River, and James Frazer, the minister of Boularderie, reported that the "poor people ... having consumed all the provision they could get, have now almost or altogether slaughtered their cattle & sheep. Starvation stares them in the face ... and, what is to be done in the meantime, to bring them through till the summer breaks in, we cannot tell." They went on to plead for more supplies: "The existing destitution imperatively calls for *immediate* & *extraordinary* exertions; without which, famine & pestilence will have done their last work."[45] At St Anns, the Rev. Norman McLeod complained to Lieutenant-Governor Harvey that the 50 barrels of Indian meal sent as relief had been insufficient and that without further supplies many newcomers, as well as more established settlers, would face "dismal suffering and starvation."[46] At Little Baddeck, the secretary of the local agricultural society reported in mid-April: "Times are very dull in this quarter – moreso than I have ever known them before star-vation is stareing many in the face."[47] Farther north in Margaree, an area that had not previously petitioned for assistance, the local Baptist minister, at the request of some of the inhabitants, reported that many families were without food and that provisions as well as oat, barley, wheat, and potato seed were required. "If there is not something done," he concluded, "death must be the consequence as their neighbours cannot supply them."[48]

In April, the government moved to avert a disaster.[49] It placed at the disposal of Lieutenant-Governor Harvey a sum of £1,700 to be distributed in £100 amounts to each county for the purchase of seed. It also appropriated any agricultural monies in the Treasury or in the Central Board and placed them with Harvey "to be at once expended in the purchase of seed, to be distributed among distressed settlers." Richmond and Inverness Counties drew £41 13s. 6d. and £50 respectively from the agricultural grant for the purchase of seed.

In August 1848, the blight reappeared for the fourth consecutive year. In Margaree, the potatoes appeared sound at digging time but soon started to rot in the root cellars; at Baddeck, the crop was a complete failure; while at Middle River, the disease attacked the potatoes very early and destroyed much of the crop. Other crops were affected by poor weather and disease: wheat was damaged by rust, oats were slight, hay was about average, and green crops were very indifferent.[50]

The government appears to have been prepared for this failure, for only one petition for aid arrived in Halifax from Cape Breton. In early January 1849, the clergy, magistrates, and other "respectable inhabitants" of St Andrew's (Grand Narrows) requested relief sup-plies for 77 destitute families.[51] Elsewhere, supplies must have been getting through and certainly large sums were still being spent on provisions. The government renewed the special grant of £1,700, appropriated the agricultural grant, and set aside half the annual school grant for the three Cape Breton counties.[52] During 1849, each county spent £150 drawn from the special and agricultural grants, while Inverness and Cape Breton counties also spent £438 10s. and £250 respectively from the school grant. Such relief tided settlers over until harvest, when, for the first time in five years, the potatoes were reported free from disease. Some areas were still affected but generally the crop was sound. The Central Board of Agriculture concluded in its annual report that "confidence in the potato crop is sufficiently restored to induce a speedy return to extended culture."[53] Although small outbreaks of the disease reoccurred in the early 1850s, the blight was effectively over.[54]

Contemporaries likened the famine in Cape Breton to that in Ireland, but it was much less severe and very few people had died. The government had acted swiftly, despite reservations about large-scale relief funding, and had provided sufficient food to prevent mass starvation and death. In addition, settlers had scratched enough food to keep themselves alive. Along the coasts, families had fished, scoured beaches for shellfish, and probably hunted birds and collected eggs.[55] A few cod, combined with vegetables, at least provided some nutrition. Inland, settlers were worse off. There was some game and a few freshwater fish, but an occasional rabbit and trout were hardly enough.[56] It was from the backlands that most petitions for aid were sent and where relief was most needed.

Undoubtedly the impact of the famine had been selective. Front-land farmers had emerged from the crisis relatively unscathed – no petitions were ever sent from intervale settlements – and no doubt many profited from rising grain prices. But on the backlands, the limits of arable agriculture had been starkly exposed, not only by the inhabitants' overwhelming reliance on the potato, but also by their failure to raise other crops such as oats and barley. Despite grants to build oat mills (used more by frontland than backland farmers) and encouragements to grow more grain, harvests dependent on thin soils and a short growing season would always be precarious. Moreover, the blight had frequently wiped out the work of 10–20 years of pioneering. Livestock had died, land had been mortgaged, and many settlers struggled to pay off loans from merchants during the years of famine. One contemporary noted that they were often in debt "so deep that there lands have, or must go to liquidate them."[57] Between 1849 and 1852, William McKeen, principal merchant at Mabou, took over ten farms totalling 1,757 acres for outstanding debts.[58] For families cleared from the crofting townships of western Scotland, it was another crushing blow. As the commissioners organizing relief in Inverness County reflected in June 1847, "The prospects of emigrants [from Scotland] were that at last they should triumph and rest even in a foreign grave, thereafter their successors to reflect of the vast field held before them for industry and cultivation – Alas' they are now nearly discouraged – Times have failed."[59] After losing their land, there was little alternative but to emigrate once more.

6 Agricultural Settlement in the Late Nineteenth Century

Although the potato famine marked the beginning of extensive emigration from Cape Breton, the Island's population continued to increase during the late nineteenth century. From 55,000 people in 1851, it rose to 75,000 in 1871 and to 87,000 in 1891.[1] With immigration largely over by the mid-1840s, virtually all of this growth was accounted for by a high rate of natural increase, swelling the proportion of native-born people. By 1871, 87 percent of the Island's population had been born in Nova Scotia.[2] Although personal ties with Scotland had loosened, most of the population were of Scottish origin; the rest consisted of Acadians, Irish, and families of Loyalist descent (Figure 6.1). After nearly 50 years of immigration and settlement, the Scots occupied much of rural Cape Breton, particularly in Inverness and Victoria counties, where they comprised more than 75 percent of the population. They also formed the largest ethnic group in the towns and mining villages in eastern Cape Breton County. Most of the Acadians continued to be concentrated in the southwest corner of the Island at Île Madame, River Bourgeois, and L'Ardoise, as well as on the northwest coast at Chéticamp, Belle Côte, and the north side of Margaree Harbour. There were also a few Acadians at Little Bras d'Or and Sydney Mines. The Irish, although outnumbered by Scottish settlers at Main-à-Dieu, were still dominant at Louisbourg and had carved out niches among the Acadians, particularly at Rocky Bay on Île Madame, and among the Scots at Margaree Forks, East Lake Ainslie, and Port Hood. Important Irish settlements also existed at Ingonish and Neil's Harbour,

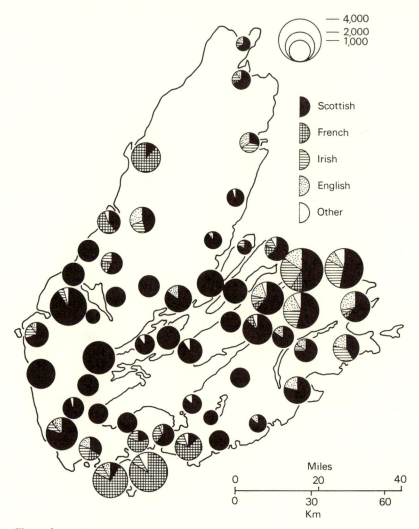

Figure 6.1
Origin of population of Cape Breton, 1870–71
Source: Census of Canada, 1870–1871, Canada, Department of Agriculture.

peopled by immigrants from Newfoundland. In the mining villages, the Irish formed the second-largest ethnic group after the Scots. Descendants of Loyalist families still lived at Sydney and Baddeck River. The patchwork pattern of different ethnic groups occupying relatively discrete areas of the Island that had been established in the early nineteenth century was now well entrenched.

Table 6.1
Principal occupations of the Cape Breton workforce,
1881

Occupation	Number
Farmers	14,536
Fishermen	3,190
Miners	1,043
Blacksmiths	313
Boot and shoe makers	155
Carders and weavers	79
Carpenters and joiners	648
Coopers	157
Dressmakers and milliners	68
Engineers and machinists	80
Millers	89
Shipbuilders	109
Stone masons	71
Tailors and clothiers	124
Clergymen	69
Commercial clerks	154
Dealers and traders	58
Government employees	95
Labourers	811
Mariners	1,357
Servants	1,243
Shopkeepers	116
Teachers	433
Teamsters and drivers	73

Source: *Census of Canada, 1881*, Canada, Department of
Agriculture.

THE SPREAD OF SETTLEMENT

The Island's population remained overwhelmingly rural and dependent upon farming. In 1881, some 14,000 people, 55 percent of the workforce, were farmers; several thousand more people were farm servants, labourers, and country tradesmen (Table 6.1). Despite the poverty of the soil, many settlers continued to take up land. The total area of occupied land increased from perhaps 1,000,000 acres in 1851 to nearly 1,128,000 acres in 1871 and to 1,184,000 acres in 1891.[3] Virtually all of this expansion occurred behind existing settlements (Figure 6.2). There were also some squatter settlements (not shown on Figure 6.2) along Mira River, behind East

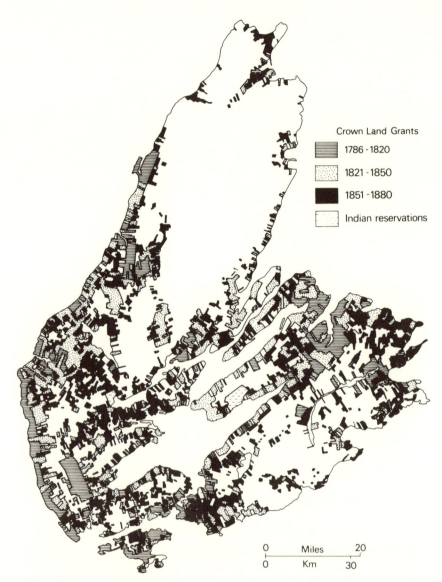

Figure 6.2
Crown land grants on Cape Breton Island, 1786–1880
Source: Records of the Crown Lands Office, 1738 to 1962, RG 20/A/3, Public Archives of Nova
Scotia, and the Crown Land Index Sheets 108–12, 114–33, and 135–40, Nova Scotia
Department of Lands and Forests.

Bay, around Loch Lomond and Lake Uist, and on South Mountain and the Creignish Hills.[4] The Cape Breton Highlands and the uplands between Lake Ainslie and Middle River, too high for agricultural settlement, were left largely untouched. In both frontland and backland areas, some farms were subdivided to accommodate new settlers. In Middle River, for example, the number of occupiers increased from 141 to 161 between 1871 and 1891, whereas the area of occupied land expanded by only 205 acres, enough for perhaps two farms.[5] Several farms must have been subdivided, causing the average farm size to fall from 208 to 184 acres. In Inverness County, the most important farming region in Cape Breton, the average farm size in most agricultural districts fell between 1871 and 1891. By 1891, 56 percent of holdings in the county were less than 100 acres, and 22 percent were less than 50 acres.[6] Nevertheless, the availability of backland and emigration from rural Cape Breton helped relieve pressure for land; the "Malthusian scissors" did not cut as deeply as in pre-industrial Europe or colonial America.[7]

Almost all of the newly settled land was extremely poor. As early as 1861, H.W. Crawley, retired from the Department of Crown Lands for over a decade but with a lifetime of experience of settlement in Cape Breton, reckoned that "little or no good land remains unoccupied."[8] Crown surveyors considered available land to be completely "barren."[9] It was thin soiled, rocky, and in places excessively wet. On high ground, these shortcomings were compounded by a very short growing season. Attempts to settle the uplands invariably failed. In the late 1880s, an attempt was made to colonize the plateau lying about 1,200 feet above sea level between St Anns and Margaree. Roads were driven into the area from either side and 200-acre lots laid off. "We may here state that the farmers both in Margaree and Baddeck are writing to there sons who are at present in the United States to return and build up our own country," wrote one official in 1888, "and the prospects are that a number of them will come back and occupy the fertile valleys of the Fielding Colony."[10] But by 1892, the realities of settlement had dissipated such optimism: "Many of those who were most enthusiastic a short time ago," explained the commissioner of Crown lands, "have grown weary of the effort and removed from the scene."[11] Agricultural settlement in Cape Breton had reached its physical limit.

ACQUISITION OF LAND

Many of these new settlers and a considerable number of earlier backland settlers were too poor to pay for a grant and squatted on

Crown land. In 1857, Crown surveyors reckoned that there were 752 squatter families in Inverness County (approximately a quarter of its population) and "not less than 1,500 families" squatting in Cape Breton County (about two-thirds of its population).[12] Most likely similar proportions existed in Richmond and Victoria counties as well. Three years later, in 1860, the Committee on Crown Property estimated that 500,000 acres – nearly half of all occupied land in Cape Breton – was held by squatters.[13] For government and squatter alike, the situation was hardly satisfactory. The government's legal authority was still being flouted on a massive scale, while the squatter, unprotected by law, had no defence against trespassers and could not legally bequeath his improvements to his successors. With little permanent stake on the Island, squatters were easily tempted to emigrate.[14]

After the winning of responsible government in 1848 and full control over the price of land in 1851, the Nova Scotia legislature began to tackle the squatter problem. In 1850, an act was passed confirming in fee simple all leases and other titles issued during the colonial regime in Cape Breton.[15] Four years later, another act was passed settling titles on the Island.[16] Settlers in possession of land who had applied for grants and paid the fees were entitled to grants without further charge for a survey. In 1859, the Department of Crown Lands was instructed to survey all the occupied holdings on the Island.[17] Commissioners were appointed in each county to assess claims to Crown land, settle lot lines, and refer all disputes to the commissioner of Crown lands for adjudication by the governor-in-council. After holdings had been surveyed, squatters were requested to take out grants at a price of 1s. 9d. per acre, payable within a year.

Yet even though many squatters were willing to pay for grants, few could find the full amount within the allotted time. Deposits were sent to Halifax, often accompanied by pathetic notes. "I am a very poor man," wrote Donald McDonald of Catalone in March 1867, "with a large and helpless family consisting of eight children nearly all girls and am at present unable to make up the price of the Grant. However I send enclosed eight dollars $8.oo, and in the spring as soon as some of my cattle are in order to dispose of, I will make up the difference. You will very much oblige me by accepting this sum at present, and I will be punctual to send the balance early next summer as possible, as, if I lose my land, myself and family will be utterly ruined. And I fear I will never again regain my loss."[18] Very often balances were never paid. In 1867, 2,075 people still owed $55,706 on their land.[19] Many had given up the payments entirely, while others, faced with "the utter hopelessness of being able to make

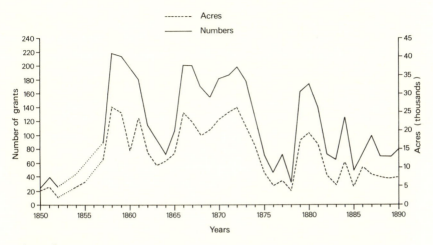

Figure 6.3
Number and acreage of Crown land grants on Cape Breton Island, 1850–90
Source: Journals of the House of Assembly of Nova Scotia.

the payments," made no effort at all, putting their faith, according to one Cape Breton surveyor, in "the exertions of their political friends to free them from any payments whatever."[20]

Such pressure soon began to tell. In 1870, an act was passed reducing the price of Crown land for a limited period.[21] Provided the land was purchased before 31 December 1871, the settler paid only 20 cents an acre, a considerable reduction on the regular price of 40 cents. After that date, the price rose progressively: 25 cents in 1872, 30 cents in 1873, 35 cents in 1874, and 40 cents thereafter. This tactic appears at first to have worked, for a large number of grants were made out between 1870 and 1872, although not as many as the Department of Crown Lands expected (Figure 6.3).[22] Yet after 1872, as the worldwide trade depression began to take hold in Cape Breton, the number of new grants plummeted and considerable sums remained outstanding. "Of the large sum ... due in the Island of Cape Breton," wrote Nova Scotia's attorney general in 1879, "it is impossible to make speedy collection; the claims are mostly of long standing – the settlers who owe these arrears are, in very many cases, poor, and in numerous instances the original applicants have died and left widows and children who occupy the land, but of whom it is useless to seek money."[23] That year another attempt was made to encourage squatters to take out grants. Provided the money was paid before 1 May 1880, land that had been occupied for more than 15 years could be purchased for 20 cents an acre.[24] This reduction, combined with the "energetic efforts which were used to induce the settlers to avail themselves of the provisions of the Act," led to another surge in applications and grants (Figure 6.3).[25] In 1880, the restriction on length of occupation was reduced to two years and the act was extended for a further year.[26] After the act lapsed in 1881, new regulations were introduced the following year whereby any settler who had occupied land for more than five years paid only 20 cents an acre.[27] But despite all these special inducements and the lowering of the price of land, the number of grants issued each year remained small (Figure 6.3). As the commissioner of Crown lands admitted in 1887, granting of land "is being accomplished very slowly, the people only seeking the patent or grant for their lands when some incident happens which puts their holdings in jeopardy."[28] The prevalence of squatting, even in the early 1890s, was a measure of the continuing poverty of much of rural Cape Breton.

With the surveying of lots after 1859, the pattern of backland settlement became clearer (Figure 6.4). Crown surveyors realized that the long lots laid out on frontland were unsuitable to the broken and rugged terrain of backland, and that the imposition of regular, uniform lots on the irregular holdings of the squatters would lead to endless dispute.[29] Instead, they followed the boundaries claimed by the squatters, and where disputes arose with neighbouring landowners, they referred the case to the county commissioner. Some holdings were never completely surveyed, leaving a legacy of claim and counter-claim to the present day. The end result of surveying the backlands was a patchwork cadastral pattern that contrasted markedly with the uniformity of frontland lots.

AGRICULTURAL MARKETS

The principal export markets for Cape Breton farmers remained Halifax, St John's, and St Pierre and Miquelon. Cattle, butter, sheep, swine, oats, and barley were shipped to these markets (Table 6.2). Within Cape Breton, the major markets were still the towns, the fishery, and backland settlers. The population of Arichat, Baddeck, Port Hawkesbury, Port Hood, the Sydneys, and the mining villages comprised some 16,000 people in 1891 and consumed quantities of dairy produce, oats, and vegetables.[30] Cattle were also driven overland from places as far away as Broad Cove and Christmas Island for sale in North Sydney or for shipment to the Newfoundland market.[31] Backland settlers needed hay and oats, while the fishery provided a market for butter, lard, and salted beef and pork. In

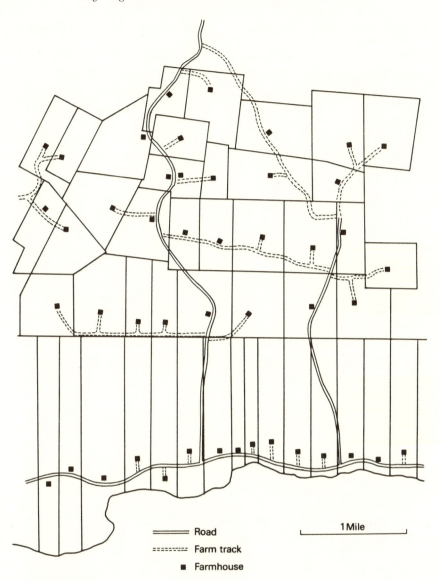

Figure 6.4
Hypothetical pattern of frontland and backland settlement on Cape Breton Island
in the late nineteenth century

Table 6.2
Principal agricultural exports outside Nova Scotia, 1864–65

Product	Year	NB	Nfld	St Pierre	Other
		$	$	$	$
Beef and	1864	106	4,044	20	350
pork	1865	130	3,040	22	202
Butter and	1864	6,103	50,542	615	240
lard	1865	320	33,827	200	4,610
Cattle	1864	5,916	37,741	2,928	
	1865	7,021	33,812	1,460	
Grain	1864	65	366	24	
	1865	58	1,360	85	1,200
Horses	1864		740		
	1865		436		
Potatoes and	1864	528	550	92	
turnips	1865	888	754	255	
Sheep and	1864	1,329	4,641		
swine	1865	1,045	6,022	570	

Source: Journals of the House of Assembly of Nova Scotia.

addition, farmers close to the Strait of Canso supplied the American mackerel fleet with fresh produce until the decline of the mackerel fishery in the late 1860s.[32] Even so, Cape Breton farmers still faced strong competition from farmers in other parts of Nova Scotia and in Prince Edward Island. Indeed, produce from Prince Edward Island was sold in Cape Breton markets. In spring 1883 and again in spring 1884, the *Port Hood Referee* reported the arrival of cargoes of potatoes from Prince Edward Island for sale in Port Hood.[33] Six years later, in 1889, the *Island Reporter* noted that "the P.E.I. produce people have made a 'dead set' on the Whycocomagh market and in a consequence potatoes and oats are selling very low. Two schooners and a Charlottetown steamer discharged cargoes this week. So much for spuds."[34] After the end of the American Civil War in 1865, Cape Breton farmers also competed with beef producers from the American West. Because beef was one of Cape Breton's two principal agricultural exports, this western competition was particularly disastrous. By 1890, cattle raising was reported "to be paralized by low prices," forcing farmers on the Island, like others in eastern North America, to specialize in dairying.[35] Although distance largely insulated Cape Breton from American butter and milk, Island markets for the local products were limited to the small urban population. All in all, the opening of the West and the increasing regional specialization of agriculture on the continent combined to squeeze the already restricted commercial sector of the Cape Breton agricultural economy. In 1893, one observer reported that "farmers are everywhere complaining that local markets are too small and unimportant for their products; and as a consequence, that industry is languishing all over the island – dragging out a dying existence."[36]

THE COMMERCIAL FRONTLANDS

The commercial farms were still concentrated on the intervales, favourable frontland along the coast, and good land close to the Sydneys, the most important local market. In these areas, at least one-third of the occupied land was cleared by 1891. Apart from the densely populated fishing settlements on Îsle Madame and the mining villages in eastern Cape Breton County, most clearance had taken place along the Mabou intervale, on the frontlands at Boularderie, New Campbellton, and Grand Narrows, and around the towns of Port Hood, Sydney, and North Sydney. At Grand Narrows, more than half of all occupied land had been cleared by 1891.[37] In these districts, the average clearance was at least 26 acres; in River Denys, Glencoe, Mabou, and Middle River, it was more than 50 acres (figures 6.5 and 6.6). A random sample of 156 farm households from the 1871 census reveals that 25 percent of farms – most likely all on frontland – had improvements of 51–300 acres (Table 6.3).[38] Much of the improved land continued to be in rough pasture and hay meadow; in Broad Cove, Northeast and Southwest Margaree, River Inhabitants, and Middle River, at least 80 percent of all improved land was in pasture or grass in 1891.[39]

Livestock were still the Island's main agricultural export and the major cash product of frontland farms. Most frontland farmers had at least 10 cattle, and some had much larger herds (Figure 6.7). The 1871 sample shows that 17 percent of farmers had 11–20 cattle, and 3 percent had 21–60 cattle (Table 6.3). Traditionally, these had been mainly beef cattle raised for the Newfoundland market, but in the last third of the century, American competition forced many farmers to switch to milch cows. This transition was most noticeable in eastern Cape Breton, where there was sufficient market demand to support dairy farming. More than 60 percent of cattle in this district were

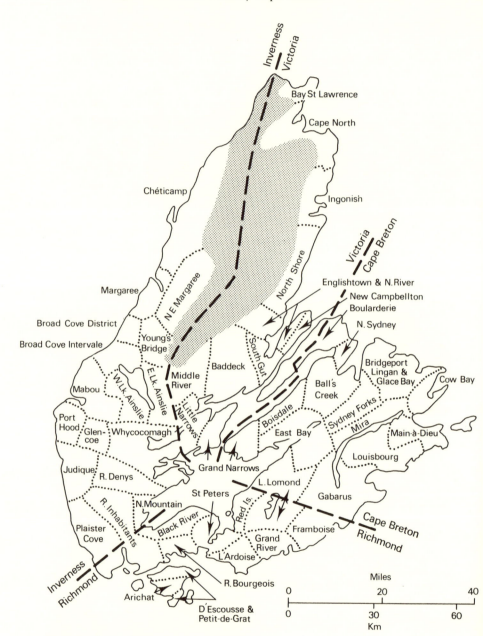

Figure 6.5
Census subdistricts on Cape Breton Island, 1891
Source: Public Archives of Nova Scotia.

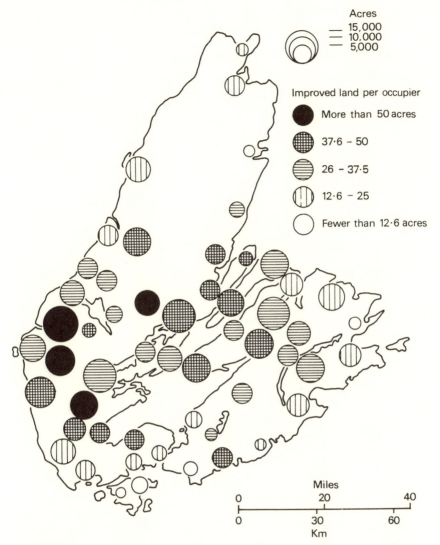

Figure 6.6
Improved land on Cape Breton Island, 1891
Source: Census of Canada, 1891, Canada, Department of Agriculture.

dairy animals in 1891.[40] In general, the quality of Island livestock remained poor. In 1892, there were only 143 registered thoroughbreds, mostly Shorthorns, Ayrshires, and Jerseys, on the Island.[41] Many of these animals had been imported by agricultural societies, usually with a considerable government subsidy.[42] Frontland farm-

Table 6.3
Distribution of farms by size, improved acreage, and livestock holdings, 1870–71

Acres	0–50		51–100		101–200		201–300		301–600		Total
	#	%	#	%	#	%	#	%	#	%	
Size	17	11	58	38	59	39	8	5	11	7	153

Acres	0–25		26–50		51–100		101–200		201–300		
	#	%	#	%	#	%	#	%	#	%	
Improved acreage	70	45	47	30	32	20	6	4	1	1	156

Head	0–5		6–10		11–20		21–30		31–60		
	#	%	#	%	#	%	#	%	#	%	
Cattle	79	50	47	30	27	17	4	2	2	1	159

Head	0–10		11–20		21–30		31–40		41–70		
	#	%	#	%	#	%	#	%	#	%	
Sheep	77	48	61	38	14	9	1	1	6	4	159

Source: Random sample of 300 households (159 cases were farms) from the *Census of Canada, 1870–1871.*

ers also continued to keep sheep (Figure 6.7). Flocks averaged 20–30 sheep, although some intervale farmers had as many as 60–70 animals. Like other livestock, few sheep were purebred; however, improved strains, such as New Leicesters, Cotswolds, Shropshires, and South Downs, were found on some farms.[43] Butter, the Island's other main agricultural export, was also in demand in eastern Cape Breton and was a particularly important product of intervale and frontland farms around Sydney (Figure 6.8). In these areas, farms produced on average at least 500 pounds of butter. Nevertheless, these quantities were small; by 1890, no one on the Island had invested in a creamery.[44] With little control over quality, much of the Island's butter was greasy and hardly fit for consumption.[45] Frontland farmers also cultivated oats, barley, spring wheat, potatoes, turnips, and vegetables, mostly for farm consumption and local sale.

Apart from the switch to dairying in some areas, the greatest change on frontland farms during the late nineteenth century was a move towards mechanization. Many commercial farmers, either

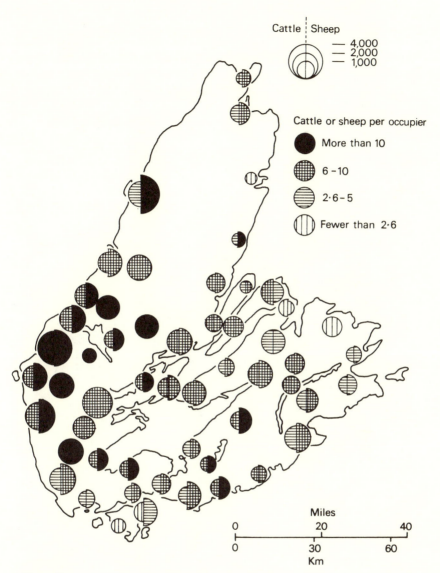

Figure 6.7
Distribution of livestock on Cape Breton Island, 1891
Source: Census of Canada, 1891, Canada, Department of Agriculture.

individually or in conjunction with their local agricultural society, invested in horse-drawn machinery to improve productivity. By 1871, there were 29 reapers and mowers and 123 horse-rakes on the Island.[46] The saving in labour was considerable. A horse-drawn mower, for example, could cut an acre of grass in four hours,

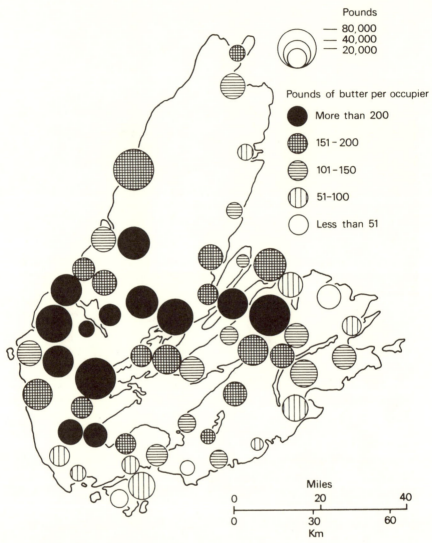

Figure 6.8
Distribution of butter production on Cape Breton Island, 1891
Source: Census of Canada, 1891, Canada, Department of Agriculture.

whereas a man took 21 hours.[47] As implements purchased by an agricultural society were passed from one member to another, a horse-rake, mower, or threshing machine could be used by as many as 50 farmers in a season.[48] Along the intervals, the "blythe sound of the scythe" was increasingly "superseded by the din and rattle of

Figure 6.9
Frontland settlement, Christmas Island, Bras d'Or Lake, late nineteenth century
Source: National Archives of Canada, PA 21554.

the Toronto Mower, Buck-eye, etc."[49] Fewer hands were needed for the frontland harvest, and the wages that frontland farmers saved were used to pay off the cost of the machine. An increasingly efficient harvest also allowed the commercial farmer to put much more land under grass.

For sons of the first and second generations of settlers who inherited the family farm, a comfortable living was still possible in Cape Breton, particularly if they lived close to the Island's growing urban markets (Figure 6.9). Many took over well-cleared and well-stocked farms which produced a modest income from sales of cattle, sheep, and dairy products. In Middle River in 1861, the wealthiest 20 percent of farmers – all located on frontland – produced 50 percent of the district's surplus livestock. From the sale of agricultural produce, some of these farmers had annual incomes of more than $200.[50] After purchasing everyday necessities, some capital was usually left over for investing in land, livestock, and agricultural machinery, as well as in local manufacturing.

The modest prosperity of frontland farmers was reflected in house styles. The "Maritime vernacular house" was widespread in the first half of the century and was still being built in the late nineteenth century, often with dormer windows inserted into the roof. The "temple" house, introduced into Nova Scotia from the United States in the late 1830s, was also becoming common. A rectangular, two-storey structure, its gable end or "temple-front" usually faced the road (Figure 6.9). On the ground floor was a hall, parlour, dining-room, and kitchen, while on the second floor were bedrooms. Like other houses on the Island, it was of balloon-frame construction covered with either shingles or clapboard. Few houses displayed Gothic gingerbread trim, a reflection of the local conservatism and relative poverty of the region.[51]

The benefits of inheriting a well-located frontland farm can be seen in the case of John Belcher Moore (1823–97), a third-generation farmer who lived two miles southwest of North Sydney on the north-west arm of Sydney Harbour.[52] When Moore took over the farm in 1853, the property had been in the family's possession for 60 years. Moore's grandfather, Adam, had come to the predominantly Loyalist farming community after emigrating from Aberdeenshire in the early 1790s. At that time, the settlement around Sydney Harbour was no more than a decade old, and with fewer than 800 people in the area, good, accessible land was still available. In 1794, Adam Moore was granted an 80-acre lot that faced southeast and ran back from the foreshore to Pottle Lake, about 100 feet above sea level. The farm's soil was a moderately stony, well-drained, sandy-loam till.[53] With the colony's capital across the harbour, Sydney Mines five miles along the coast, and neighbouring North Sydney destined to grow, the Island's principal markets were easily accessible. Com-bined with these locational and physical advantages was careful fam-ily management. When John Belcher inherited after his father's death, the lot, house, barn, and outbuildings were valued at £300, three times the Island average.[54] In addition, he received 50 acres of a 200-acre woodlot at Georges River, three miles away, and pur-chased the remainder from his four sisters. That lot was valued at £50. Personal property included livestock worth £64 14s., household furniture worth £40, farming implements worth £15, and black-smith's tools also worth £15. By this inheritance, Moore, then 30, acquired a relatively secure and independent living; it was a patri-mony that he considerably improved.

By 1871, Moore had added a further 70 acres to the home farm.[55] At that date, 50 acres were improved: 32 acres of pasture and 12 acres of hay land supported 7 milch cows, 5 neat cattle, 4 sheep, 2 horses, and a pig. The census also records that 2 cattle, 12 sheep, and 2 pigs had been slaughtered or sold for export. The rest of the improved land consisted of 1.5 acres in spring wheat, another

1.5 acres in potatoes, and the remaining 3 acres divided among barley, oats, and vegetables. Although the farm had a small arable component, the commercial orientation was clearly towards livestock. In 1871, the farm produced 600 pounds of butter, and no doubt much of it, along with milk and cheese, was sold in nearby North Sydney. Moore's cattle were sold to his relatives, the North Sydney merchants John and William Moore, who dealt in the Newfoundland trade. Small quantities of wheat, oats, oatmeal, barley, barley flour, turnips, potatoes, hay, straw, veal, and hides were also sold to numerous local farmers and tradesmen, including John and William Moore.[56]

Described by the local R.G. Dun agent as a "prudent man" and "very mean & saving," John Belcher Moore shrewdly invested his surplus income in mortgages and land speculation.[57] Ten years after taking over the farm, Moore had lent £380 to four mortgagees to be repaid with due interest within three to nine years; between 1862 and 1890, he lent a further $1,740 to five mortgagees. Although the interest payments provided a steady income, it was his land transactions that produced the greater profit. In 1866, for example, he paid one John Gibson $716 for land beside the road from North Sydney to Sydney Mines and sold it, nine years later, to Vooght Brothers, the North Sydney merchants, for $2,775. In 1858, Moore was reckoned to be worth £1,500; in 1862, a tax assessment recorded his total taxable wealth at $2,064 – double the average for North Sydney's number-one assessment district and fifth highest of 63 taxpayers.[58] Thirty-five years later, his real estate had increased in value from $1,400 to $2,550 and his personal property from $664 to $2,284.[59] At the time of his death, Moore owned the home farm, neighbouring land called "The Point," and two water lots in North Sydney. In monetary terms, he had more than doubled his patrimony. Clearly, John Belcher Moore was a man of consequence – "a man of standing" – in the local community.[60]

THE SUBSISTENT BACKLANDS

Behind the frontlands, much of the rural population continued to subsist on tiny forest-bound clearings (Figure 6.10). According to the 1871 census sample, some 30 percent of farmers on the Island had 26–50 acres improved and 45 percent had less than 25 acres improved. In Red Islands, a predominantly backland area, no farmer in 1871 had more than 50 acres of cleared land and 78 percent had fewer than 25 acres.[61] On the larger backland farms, there were 6–10 cattle, at least 10 sheep, a horse, 2–3 pigs, and fowl; on the smaller

Figure 6.10
Backland farm, Tarbert, Cape Breton Highlands, c. 1890. Note the boulder-strewn field and two large mounds of rocks.
Source: J.M. Gow, *Cape Breton Illustrated* (Toronto: W. Briggs, 1893).

farms, fewer than 6 cattle and 10 sheep, a horse, a pig, and fowl (Table 6.3). Livestock were mainly scrub animals, raised for domestic use and consumption. Most of the improved land was in hay and rough pasture, the rest in oats, potatoes, and vegetables. On high farms, oats would not ripen. Little or no attention was paid to rotations or manuring, and the thin, acidic soils were quickly exhausted. Apart from a plough, horse-drawn implements were rare, and most mowing, reaping, threshing, and winnowing were still done by hand.

As backland farms produced only small surpluses for sale, many farmers continued to rely on off-the-farm employment to make ends meet. In Middle River, for example, half the farmers in 1861 – 80 percent of them on backland – depended on supplementary work.[62] In the earlier part of the century, employment was available on frontland farms, planting crops and bringing in the harvest, but with the introduction of horse-drawn mowers and rakes in the 1860s and 1870s, such local work began to disappear. Mechanization of frontland agriculture knocked away one of the main buttresses of backland farming. Some backland farmers found other local work as carpenters and coopers, and a few worked in grist and saw mills. Most men had to look farther afield, which inevitably meant separation from wife and family and the costs of accommodation at the place of work.

The staple trades continued to provide alternative employment, creating what the *North Sydney Herald* called "a hybrid race – half farmer, half miner or half fishermen."[63] Such employment fluctuated with the external demand for the Island's staples. The coal trade expanded in the early 1860s, in 1871–72, and again in the 1880s, drawing men from the country to the mines. "The force of men employed now is larger than it was," reported a miner at the International Colliery in 1882. "Some folks say, that the whole of the Little Narrows' has removed to Bridgeport [Mine]."[64] The following year, at Reserve Mines, "the pit is crowded with men, all Mira, not to speak of the Grand Narrows, have left the peaceful shores of the 'Mira' and taken up their dwelling place (temporary) here."[65] Employed in unskilled, labouring jobs, these summer workers were paid 90 cents a day or about $100 for five months' work.[66] A large portion of that money was spent on room and board, but even $20 to $30 helped a family to survive on a subsistence farm. Settlers close to the coast continued to fish in inshore waters, and a few may have been hired on coasting vessels. The once large American mackerel fishery in the gulf was declining by the late 1860s and provided little employment.[67] There was also work available in shipbuilding, retailing, factories, and domestic service in Halifax and, more particularly, Boston. In 1857, the surveyor for Cape Breton County noted that "all the tradesmen and young men of the county go to the States for employment in the summer as there is no work for them at home." He continued, "Those who represent this class occupy in general, Crown lands as squatters, and by means of farming conducted by their wives and children, and going themselves during the summer season to distant parts of the province or to the United States, they eke out the means of a scanty subsistence."[68]

Women, too, left home to find work. Domestic service was the fourth-largest occupation in Cape Breton in 1881 (Table 6.1), and of the 1,243 servants listed, 1,019 (82 percent of the total) were female. Some of these domestic servants were employed in Sydney, but probably most found work in Halifax and especially in the leading New England cities. Earnings from "dutiful daughters" employed in service were an important source of income for backland families.[69] "I am sending you 3 dollars against the count," explained Betsey McKinnon of 27 Liberty Street, Gloucester, Massachusetts, in a note to merchant Malcolm McDougall of Christmas Island, Cape Breton, adding, "Let me know how is the Account write to me soon."[70] Whether or not Betsey was engaged in service is unknown, but the transfer of funds from New England to Cape Breton is clear. For many backland families, the household economy stretched way beyond the outer fields of their farms to include the mines in eastern Cape Breton, the vessels fishing around the Island, and the towns and cities of the northeast.

The produce of backland farming and the income from seasonal employment yielded a meagre living for backland families. Milk, butter, cheese, some red meat, salted fish, oatmeal, and potatoes made up much of the diet. White flour was probably not commonly used. Houses were small and spartan. Simple log structures still survived but were being replaced by small, one-storey frame houses covered with clapboard or shingles (Figure 6.10).[71] On the ground floor of such a house was a kitchen-parlour and two bedrooms, while under the gable roof the attic was used for storage and another bedroom. The old log house was often made over to a barn.

Typical of the better-off backland farmers was Donald Murray, who emigrated from Scotland to Cape Breton, possibly in the late 1840s, and settled at Oban near South Mountain, Richmond County, after purchasing 100 acres from a squatter. Murray's lot was situated between 100 and 200 feet above sea level on gently rolling land straddling a stream. Its soil, composed from glacial till, was poorly drained and sufficiently stony to make ploughing difficult. The land was best suited to rough pasture. Yet by 1849, Murray had "planted both oats and potatoes and fenced in about four acres." Two decades later, 31 acres had been improved: 20 were in pasture and grass, 8 in oats, 2 in potatoes, and 1 in other crops and vegetables. Although no neat cattle were recorded in the 1871 census, 5 milch cows produced 300 pounds of butter, and there were also 9 sheep, a pig, and 2 horses. Murray's mixed, semi-subsistence family farm produced small surpluses of butter, oats, potatoes, sheep, and fowl, which were probably sold at St Peters five miles distant. With insufficient income to purchase his land, Murray had to wait until 1973, when his son Duncan went "to Halifax at the Water Works for the express purpose of obtaining money to get out a Grant."[72]

James Ross, "newly come from the old country" in the early 1860s, who settled on Skye Mountain near Whycocomagh, was considerably poorer. His lot had fallen in such "an uncomfortable position" high on the mountain that it was almost impossible to farm. As he explained to the Department of Crown Lands, "In all low places the seed will be in the ground before we can hardly travel here with dry shod with snow melting & winter's frost and late sowing will always be late ripining." Although Ross had two sons whom he "kept about ... hoping that times would turn better," they "saw that there was no prospect of getting better ... [and] went away to work to a coal mine to Sidney." Apparently they would return only if Ross settled near the shore at Whycocomagh. Ross managed to find a lakeside lot of some 8–10 acres, but as he explained to the local surveyor, even for that amount of land "one thing sure, I could not pay it at once." Like other backland farmers, he depended on other sources of income, and he hoped that his sons "would make more eager in laying by their money" if he was granted the land.[73]

RURAL SOCIETY

One Scottish traveller to Cape Breton in 1879 thought that it was impossible to compare the position of farmers on the Island to "the descendants of those they left behind [for] they are, in comparison, princes on a small scale, each possessing his own lands, and all the comforts necessary to make him happy and contented."[74] Certainly, many frontland farmers were much better off than their distant relatives in Scotland. In the late nineteenth century, Scottish crofters were still struggling to secure their rights to land. The bitter land wars that crofters waged against landlords in the 1880s led to the Napier Commission. The commission looked into crofters' grievances and laid the basis for the Crofters' Holding Act of 1886, which guaranteed security of tenure to crofters.[75] A meagre independence was eventually won. For many frontland farmers in Cape Breton, such independence was a birthright. Moreover, a typical frontland farm produced a much higher standard of living than any croft in Scotland. On the backlands, however, conditions were much different and were probably not observed by travellers to the Island. With squatting still common, many backland farmers had no secure title to land and faced almost constant pressure from trespassers. Poverty was widespread, and many second- and third-generation settlers preferred seasonal migration to the mines or Boston over the task of clearing the rocks and forest off an upland farm. Their situation was little different from that of the crofters and cottars who sought work in the Lowlands of Scotland.[76] Both suffered insecurity of tenure, a low standard of living, and the travails of participating in spatial economies that stretched over considerable distances. The stratification that characterized the early settlement of Cape Breton remained marked.

By the late nineteenth century, rural Cape Breton was a thick weave of kith and kin. The settlement of related families from Scotland, the passing of first, second, and even third generations, and the lack of further immigration had produced close ties among families. Along the Southwest Margaree in 1871, three of the four main ethnic groups on the Island were present, and within each group many families were related. Of the 97 Scottish families, 19 were Gillises and 53 were either Gillises, McLellans, McDonalds, McDougalls, or McDonells. More than a quarter of the 34 Irish families were Coadys, and a third of the 45 Acadian families were Le Blancs (Whites). Of 12 Acadian surnames, 5 accounted for 82 percent of the Acadian population. In the backland district of Red Islands, 27 of the 104 Scottish families were MacDonalds and 82 were either MacDonalds, McNabs, Johnstons, Campbells, or McMullins. The 3 Irish families were all Cashes. Endogamous marriages helped preserve ethnic and religious identities. The Scottish and Acadian settlements were usually large enough to provide a pool of marriage partners, which helped maintain each group's separate identity. In two or three settlements, this was also true for the Irish, but in general, the Irish and Loyalist populations were so small and dispersed that intermarriage and assimilation into the larger ethnic groups became inevitable. Such unions usually followed religious lines: Catholic Irish married Catholic Scots or Acadians; Protestant Loyalists married Protestant Scots. The denominational divide between Catholic and Presbyterian Scots was also respected.[77] As a result, many communities were either completely Catholic or Protestant (Figure 6.11).

These rural communities were intensely local, even in the last decades of the century. The Intercolonial Railway did not reach the Island until the early 1890s, and it was a good day's journey by ferry and stagecoach from Port Hawkesbury to Halifax. Most Cape Bretoners did not make such a journey from one year to the next. For frontland farmers, the extent of their travels were occasional visits to the local market town – Arichat, Port Hood, Baddeck, the Sydneys – to sell produce and buy supplies; backland farmers travelled even less. While surveying the farms around Catalone Lake in eastern Cape Breton County, a Crown surveyor reported in 1863 that the farmers suffered "sad inconveniences" from want of roads.[78] The farms, settled since the late 1820s, were about a quarter of a mile apart and connected by bridle paths so narrow that they were impassable for carts. Overland communication was extremely difficult. In such isolated, close-knit communities, Gaelic was still widely used, and much oral tradition, folk medicine, and music from the Highlands flourished. Only when young sons and daughters, displaced from the land, emigrated to the mining villages or the "Boston States" were Gaelic language and culture threatened. For those families who had sons and daughters working away from home, horizons could be both very near and very far. "Where does that road go to ...?" asked an American traveller of a Cape Breton girl in 1885. "It goes

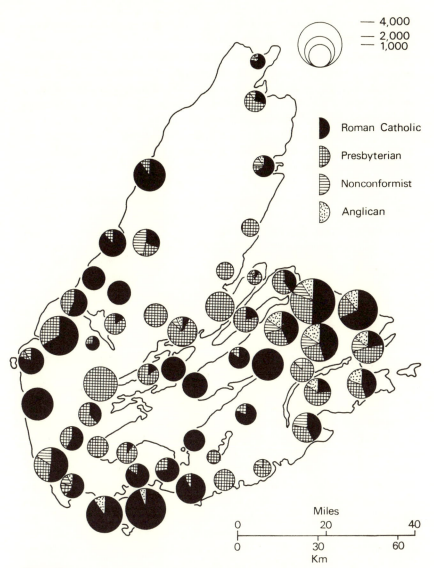

Figure 6.11
Religious denominations of the Cape Breton population, 1870–71
Source: Census of Canada, 1870–1871, Canada, Department of Agriculture.

to the Strait of Canso, sir, and on to Montana – that's where my brother John is workin' on a ranch – and I don't know where else it goes," she replied.[79]

Detached from the wider world, the lives of most inhabitants revolved around the everyday realities of family and farm, occasional business with the local storekeeper, and weekly or monthly meetings at the local church and agricultural society. Most frontland families had access to a church by the late nineteenth century, and religion played a large part in most lives. Many backland settlers were far removed from a church; James Ross on Skye Mountain complained that he had "no connection with any society of whatever character or denomination."[80] The occasional evangelical meeting at the local market town may have drawn such settlers from the mountains. In 1874, one visitor to the Island observed two to three thousand Presbyterians attending an open-air service at Baddeck to celebrate the annual Holy Communion.[81] Agricultural societies struggled on, scarcely attracting more members than they had in 1850. In 1890, there were 13 societies with 548 members, nearly all found in frontland settlements: Sydney, Sydney Mines, Margaree Forks, Strathlorne, Mabou, Port Hood, Middle River, Baddeck, and Arichat.[82]

RURAL MANUFACTURING AND TRADE

Rural industry expanded during the late nineteenth century (Table 6.4). Some 500 hands were employed in industry in 1851; 1,136 in 1871; and 2,385 in 1891.[83] In addition, there was a considerable seasonal workforce, not recorded in the census, employed in manufacturing. Little of this growth was due to Cape Breton's agricultural export trade. As this trade was still principally in live cattle, there was no need for a large meat-packing industry. The advent of canning in the 1870s, however, did encourage some investment in meat-packing. Between 1871 and 1891, the number of meat-packing establishments increased from 3 to 12 and the workforce from 35 to 64. Much of the industry was located in Inverness County, particularly at Port Hood, one of the principal cattle exporting ports. In the early 1880s, McLellan Brothers and D. MacDonald & Co. set up canning establishments in the town. These were seasonal businesses, operating from the beginning of September to the end of December; they processed cattle and sheep but also geese and rabbits ("an entirely new branch of the canning business here").[84] In 1883, MacDonald's processed 502 head of cattle and 900 head of sheep. The 2,200 cases – worth about $12,672 – were shipped, via Halifax, to the European market.[85] The canneries gave employment to some 60 men and women.[86] But the main growth in manufacturing employment was in small, labour-intensive trades: blacksmithing, carpentry and joinery, coopering, dressmaking, tailoring, and weaving. In part this reflected the growing demand for services from a larger

Table 6.4
Principal manufacturing establishments in Cape Breton, 1871 and 1891

Industry	Year	Number	Hands employed	Value of articles ($)
Blacksmithing	1871	149	221	79,191
	1891	206	276	132,274
Boots and shoes	1871	31	124	39,657
	1891	68	99	67,103
Carding and fulling	1871	–	–	–
	1891	21	36	48,820
Carpenters and joiners	1871	15	38	15,850
	1891	125	226	170,158
Carriage makers	1871	19	34	16,275
	1891	47	86	76,529
Cooperage	1871	9	11	2,435
	1891	92	120	38,968
Dressmaking	1871	1	2	1,000
	1891	62	95	41,041
Flour and grist mills	1871	74	107	188,567
	1891	40	55	50,530
Foundries and machine works	1871	1	2	1,740
	1891	7	53	63,600
Lime kilns	1871	14	22	1,670
	1891	33	75	27,395
Meat curing	1871	3	35	18,269
	1891	12	64	29,690
Sawmills	1871	85	130	37,505
	1891	140	228	169,861
Shingle making	1871	29	56	11,003
	1891	33	55	23,213
Tailors and clothiers	1871	15	34	12,941
	1891	50	131	91,445
Tanneries	1871	22	52	44,010
	1891	21	43	50,938
Weavers	1871	–	–	–
	1891	316	413	45,084
Woollen mills	1871	–	–	–
	1891	3	24	37,680

Source: *Census of Canada, 1870–1871* and *Census of Canada, 1891*, Canada, Department of Agriculture.

population, but also an increasing supply of people, unable to acquire land, who had taken up small trades. Most of these tradespeople required little capital to set up, and they often operated their businesses from a roadside house or store. There was also some growth in the larger industries. More sawmills were built to supply the grow-

Table 6.5
Capitalization and type of merchants in Cape Breton, 1870

	Capitalization ($)					
	50,000– 100,000	25,000– 50,000	10,000– 25,000	5,000– 10,000	2,000– 5,000	Less than 2,000
Dry goods			1	1	8	8
General store	2	1	8	13	41	107
Groceries			1		1	8
Merchant			1			11
Supplies				1	2	9
Trader				1	1	11

Source: Dun, Wiman & Co., The Mercantile Agency Reference Book, vol. 10 (Montreal, Toronto, and Halifax: Dun, Wiman & Co., July 1870).

ing demand for sawn lumber, particularly from the expanding towns and coal mines, and additional lime kilns were constructed to provide lime for frontland farmers. But other industries contracted. Flour milling declined, particularly between 1871 and 1891, as American and Canadian flour penetrated the local market.

Although the number and range of industries had increased, rural manufacturing and processing remained essentially small scale and pre-industrial. Apart from shipments of sawn lumber, manufactured items were not exported; production served limited local markets. Water provided the motive power, capital investment was restricted, and most, if not all, of these enterprises were family owned. Fathers and sons worked together in mills, tanneries, and coopering sheds; wives and daughters helped with weaving and provided much of the labour for dressmaking and millinery.

Country storekeepers continued to organize the collection of farm produce for export, retailing imported goods for the rural population and extending credit to local farmers. In 1870, there were 172 general merchants on the Island and a further 65 dry goods merchants, grocers, merchants, suppliers, and traders (Table 6.5). Most of these businessmen served the rural population, but some retailed goods to the mining, fishing, and urban populations. No business was capitalized at more than $100,000, and 90 percent of the merchants were capitalized at less than $2,000. Apart from the Channel Island fish merchants, the wealthiest merchant in Cape Breton was Charles J. Campbell of Baddeck, Victoria County. In 1858, his capital was estimated at £20,000. Much of this wealth had

been produced by "a large country bus.[ness]" and had been reinvested in property, shipbuilding, and a coal mine at Campbellton
on the Great Bras d'Or. By 1870, Campbell's wealth was reckoned
to be $50,000 to $100,000.[87] Another prosperous merchant was
Peter Smyth of Port Hood, who owned several stores in Inverness
County retailing groceries, dry goods, and liquor. Considered to be
"the principal bus.man" in the county, Smyth's estimated wealth in
1858 was £10,000.[88] More typical of the small country storekeeper
was Malcolom MacDougall, a merchant at Christmas Island, Bras
d'Or Lake, who had less than $2,000 invested in his business in
1870.[89] MacDougall entered business in the 1830s, at first retailing
goods supplied by merchants in Arichat and then later, when he was
established, dealing with Halifax wholesalers on his own account.
Much of his export trade, though, was to St John's. By 1880, he
described himself as an "Importer and Dealer of Flour and Meal,
Dry Goods, Groceries, Hardware, Stationery, Readymade Clothing,
Boots and Shoes, Hats and Caps, Crockeryware, Country Produce,
etc., etc." – the typical mix of trade of a country storekeeper. That
year, his ledger records $4,403 worth of purchases: $3,041.66 or 69
percent of it in barter, $787.81 or 18 percent in cash, and $574.33
or 13 percent in work. Of the bartered goods, 87 percent consisted
of livestock or livestock products (horned cattle, steers, milch cows,
and heifers made up 79 percent of the livestock total, followed by
horses and foals, sheep, butter, and pork); much of the rest consisted
of hay, the most important fodder crop. Among the jobs done for
MacDougall were hauling, repairing a barn, butchering, shoemak-
ing, ploughing, and driving cattle to North Sydney. Most of the
produce came from around Christmas Island, although water transport allowed farmers to ship from other parts of Bras d'Or Lake,
particularly from Malagawatch and East Bay (Figure 6.12). From
Christmas Island, the produce was forwarded either to Cape Breton
towns or to St John's.

With the growth of rural manufacturing and services, the urban
centres in Cape Breton increased in size during the late nineteenth
century. The principal centres were still Sydney, North Sydney, Baddeck, Port Hawkesbury, Port Hood, and Mabou. In 1891, their total
population was about 6,500 people; Sydney, the largest settlement,
had some 2,400 inhabitants.[90] In the larger centres – Sydney, North
Sydney, Baddeck, and Port Hawkesbury – a wide array of services
was available: general stores, dry goods stores, grocers and liquor
shops, drugstores, blacksmiths, tanners, shoemakers, tailors, hotels,
livery stables, saddlers, as well as schools and churches.[91] In smaller

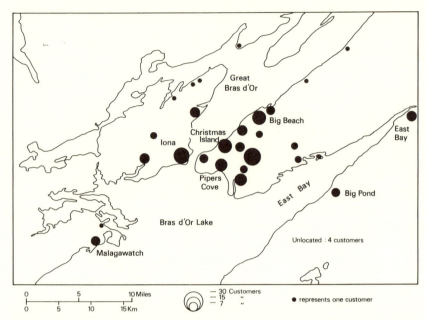

Figure 6.12
The economic hinterland of Malcolm MacDougall, merchant at Christmas Island,
Cape Breton County, 1880
Source: Ledger of Malcolm MacDougall, 1873–1921, MG 14/62, Beaton Institute.

centres, such as West Bay (Figure 6.13), there were general stores,
grist mills, sawmills, blacksmiths, livery stables, schools, and
churches. Apart from Baddeck, which was beginning to attract summer tourists from the United States, there was little prospect of
further development in these settlements unless the agricultural
economy improved.

Although agricultural settlement continued to expand in Cape Breton during the late nineteenth century, the rural population had
clearly overrun its landed resources. Widespread squatting and the
poverty of much of the rural population testified to the difficulties
of backland farming. For many backland farmers, supplementary
employment remained essential. The commercial farmers on the
frontlands still made relatively comfortable livings but faced increasing competition from larger, more efficient producers. The limited
rural trade supported only a small merchant class. Given the widespread poverty, there was little incentive for merchants or affluent
farmers to invest in consumer manufacturing industry on the Island.
The agricultural sector of the Cape Breton economy supplied cheap

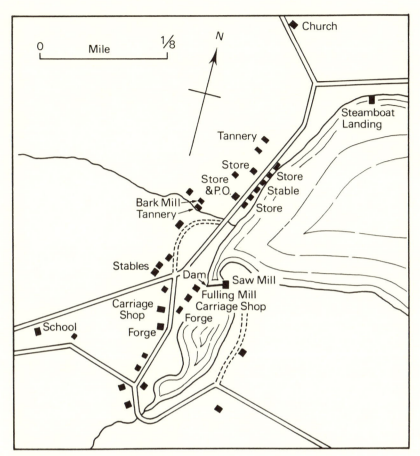

Figure 6.13
West Bay, Inverness County, 1883–87
Source: A.F. Church, *Topographical Township Map of Inverness County Nova Scotia* (Bedford, NS: A.F. Church & Co., 1883–87).

and plentiful labour to the staple industries on the Island and to the shipyards and affluent households in New England, but little capital for investment in the Island's internal economic development. The weakness of the agricultural economy and lack of good land also deflected later waves of immigrants away from Cape Breton shores, allowing Highland culture and the Gaelic language to take hold on the Island. Yet the weakness of the economy threatened their very survival. By the late nineteenth century, the Highland culture re-created in Cape Breton had run out of room. For the younger generations, there was little alternative to emigration, and that almost always meant assimilation into the larger English-speaking world.

7 The Staple Industries in the Late Nineteenth Century

Cape Breton's two staple industries experienced considerable expansion during the late nineteenth century. In both the fishery and coal industry, new capital was invested, production was substantially increased, new markets were developed, more modern technology was introduced, and larger workforces were recruited. Fishing settlements were established in the few remaining unsettled coves, and more mining villages were built on the eastern coalfield. Surplus rural labour continued to find employment in the staples, particularly in the coal industry. As elsewhere in eastern North America, a growing number of farmers on the Island gave up an independent living on the land for industrial wage-labour.

THE FISHERY

The number of men engaged in the Island's fishery more than tripled in the late nineteenth century, increasing from about 2,700 in 1851 to 8,200 in 1891.[1] Most likely, fewer than half of these men were full-time fishermen; most were farmers who did some part-time fishing. Apart from the immigration of Newfoundlanders to the northeast coast in the 1880s and some internal migration from farm to outport,[2] virtually all of the growth in the workforce was accounted for by natural increase. The bulk of the fishermen continued to be concentrated in the traditional centres of the fishery (Figure 7.1). There was also considerable expansion along the northeast coast, particularly at Ingonish and Neil's Harbour and at the

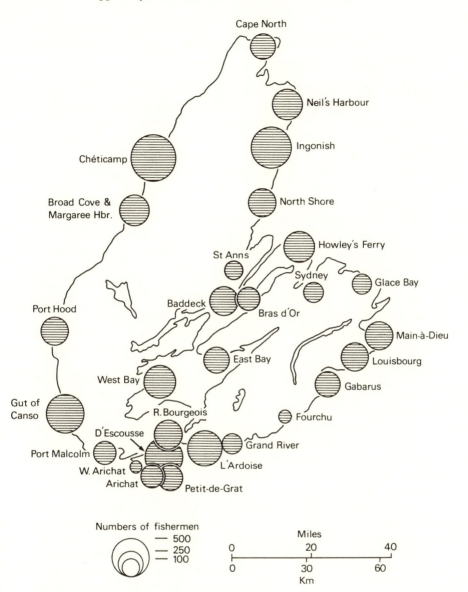

Figure 7.1
Distribution of fishermen on Cape Breton Island, 1891
Source: Sessional Papers, 11A, 1892.

new fishing stations of New Haven and White Point. Many farmers along both the east and west coasts and around Bras d'Or Lake continued to combine farming with fishing.

The cod fishery remained the backbone of the Cape Breton fishery, yielding about half the catch (by value), and was still dominated by the Channel Island companies. Although only two Channel Island companies remained in Cape Breton, they were among the largest businesses on the Island in the late nineteenth century. In the early 1870s, the Robin empire (including its branches in Gaspé) was capitalized at more than $1,000,000, while DeCarteret & LeVesconte, described as "a rich house" by the local R.G. Dun agent in 1857, was worth between $25,000 and $50,000.[3] Even so, the long dominance of the Channel Islands was waning. In the mid-1860s, DeCarteret & LeVesconte, probably as a result of the death of Peter LeVesconte in Jersey, relocated to Cape Breton and became to all intents and purposes an Arichat business.[4] Twenty years later, in 1886, Charles Robin & Co., the huge Gaspé firm and parent company of Philip Robin & Co. in Cape Breton, went bankrupt and had to be rescued by another Jersey company.[5] Although the company continued to trade as Charles Robin, Collas & Co., the days of Channel Island involvement in the New World cod fishery were coming to an end.

Until these changes of fortune, the pattern of sending men, capital, and supplies from Europe to Cape Breton and shipping dried fish to markets in southern Europe, the West Indies, and South America continued. Even in the late 1880s, the Robin Company recruited some 20 shoremen – agents, clerks, beach-masters, and foremen – in the Channel Islands each year to staff its fishing stations at Arichat and Chéticamp.[6] Salt and manufactured goods were also imported from Europe, although by the last quarter of the century an increasing proportion of supplies was coming from North American sources: sugar, rice, oatmeal, pot barley, ground coffee, round peas, raisins, rolled bacon, hams, beef, and pickles from merchants in Halifax; stoves and deck irons from manufacturers in Yarmouth; pork and lard from Charlottetown; cotton warp and kerosene oil from Saint John; hats and tea from Montreal; tar, pitch, pork, and flour from Boston.[7] Although data on dried-fish exports are scarce, it appears that the two Channel Island companies still shipped prime merchantable codfish to markets in southern Europe and fish of lesser quality to Brazil and the West Indies. In 1865, for example, the Cape Breton fishery exported 4,907 quintals of dried fish to Italy, 1,040 to Spain, and 221 to Portugal. A further 3,112 quintals went to Jersey, probably for re-export to the Mediterranean. Another 2,474 quintals were shipped to Brazil.[8] By the 1890s, the Brazil market was dominant. In 1894, the Robin Company's shipments

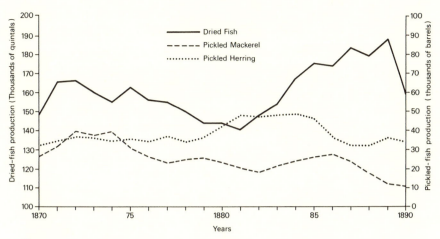

Figure 7.2
Fish production in Cape Breton, showing three-year moving averages for dried
and pickled fish
Source: Sessional Papers.

from Chéticamp comprised 8,646 quintals sent to Santos and Rio de
Janeiro in Brazil, 306 to Jamaica, and 219 to Havana, Cuba.[9] No
fish were exported to southern Europe that year.

As the cod fishery expanded, more resident merchants became
involved in the industry. By the early 1870s, there were approximately 100 fish dealers and merchants in the outports. The greatest
concentration was on Île Madame, where there were 21 merchants;
elsewhere, there were 1 or 2 merchants in each outport. According
to the credit rating agency, Dun, Wiman & Co., most of these merchants were worth less than $2,000.[10] They were the outport equiv-
alents of the country merchants, and many dealt in country produce
as well as fish. They also continued to depend upon Halifax for
supplies and a market connection.

Apart from the depressed years of the late 1870s, production in
the cod fishery rose steadily from 65,500 quintals in 1851 to more
than 180,000 in the late 1880s (Figure 7.2). This growth was largely
due to the increase in labour and the introduction of new technology,
particularly the "bultow" or trawl. Much of the cod came from the
traditional inshore grounds off Île Madame, Chéticamp, Main-à-
Dieu, Louisbourg, and Gabarus (Figure 7.3); in 1891, they accounted
for 54 percent of total dried-fish production. A considerable part of
the remaining fish came from fishing grounds along the northeast
coast, particularly at Ingonish, Neil's Harbour, and Cape North; in
1891, they contributed a further 21 percent to the total. Although

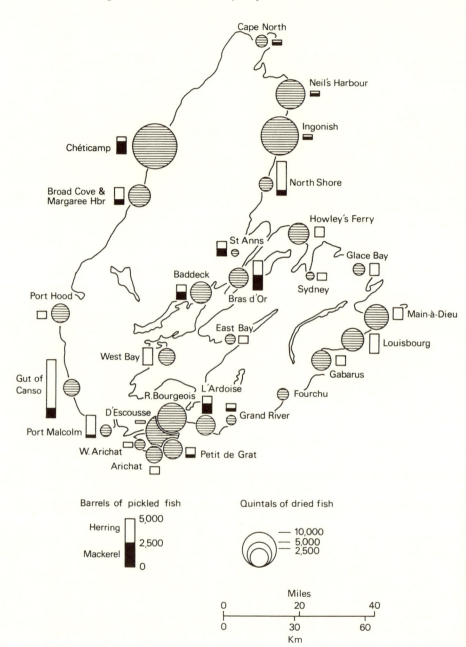

Figure 7.3
Distribution of dried- and pickled-fish production in Cape Breton, 1891
Source: Sessional Papers, 11A, 1892.

Table 7.1
Boats and vessels in Cape Breton, 1891

County		Vessels			Boats	
	No.	Tonnage	Average tonnage	Men	No.	Men
Cape Breton	8	148	18.5	38	811	1,614
Inverness	16	442	27.5	112	879	2,325
Richmond	69	2,122	31	505	1,032	1,645
Victoria	2	71	35.5	7	1,197	1,996
Total	95	2,783	29	662	3,919	7,580

Source: Sessional Papers, 11A, 1892.

no formal property rights to these fishing grounds existed, informal, customary rights certainly did exist and were increasingly exercised as pressure on existing grounds increased. In 1865, for example, fishermen at Cape North were so incensed about the encroachment on their grounds by fishermen from New Haven that they petitioned the Nova Scotia House of Assembly for redress.[11] The same year, fishermen at Caribou Cove, Judique, Port Hood, and Little Mabou complained about the continual "disputes ... among the fishermen which often end in disgraceful rows as to the location of the different bouys, fishing stations on the different fishing grounds" around Port Hood Island, and requested a "competent person" to adjudicate disputes "so that order may be preserved and justice ensured for all."[12] Such complaints suggest that the inshore fishery had expanded as far as it could around the coast of Cape Breton.

Much of the technology of the cod fishery remained unchanged. Most fishermen continued to fish from shallops and other small boats; the rest were employed in the small-vessel fishery (Table 7.1; Figure 7.4). According to the Fish Bounty records of 1891, vessel owners collected $3,915 of the $30,121 paid to Cape Breton fishermen.[13] That year there were 95 fishing vessels (totalling 2,783 tons) engaged in the cod fishery, many of them in inshore waters. Only a few vessels fished the banks, mostly those in the Gulf of St Lawrence; in 1877, a Fishery Protection officer observed 12 Cape Breton vessels, ranging in size from 19 to 62 tons and with crews of six to ten men, fishing around the Magdalen Islands.[14] The smaller vessels caught some 200-300 quintals each trip and generally made three voyages during the season. Each of the larger vessels caught about 1,000 quintals during a voyage of four weeks. Both the Robin

Figure 7.4
Inshore fishing craft at Chéticamp, c. 1915. Schooners are visible in the right background.
Source: Notman Photographic Archives, McCord Museum, McGill University.

Company and DeCarteret & LeVesconte continued to send vessels to Anticosti and North Shore.[15]

Hand-lining remained the standard method of catching cod, although from the 1860s it was gradually supplemented by the French bultow or trawl.[16] Consisting of a long line with numerous shorter hook-lines or "snoods" attached at regular intervals, the trawl was fixed to the seabed by anchors while buoys held the line in position and marked its location on the surface. Usually the baited lines were set in the water for six to eight hours, sometimes longer if bad weather prevented the fishermen from getting out. The increase in productivity was so enormous that fishery officials worried about the effect on fish stocks. The Island's fishery officer, A.C. Bertram, claimed that the trawl was "exceedingly destructive to the codfishery of the coast," but the charge that the trawl led to overfishing was never proved.[17] Trawls were also used in the vessel fishery and were set from dories – small, flat-bottomed boats – crewed by two men.[18] The dories were "nested" on the deck until the vessel got to the fishing grounds and were then launched each day for fishing. Although the combination of trawls and dories greatly increased production on the banks, dory fishing was a risky venture and fishermen were easily lost and drowned in a fog or "blow."

Until the rise of the lobster industry in the early 1870s, the rest of the Island's fishery continued to focus on herring, mackerel, and salmon. The herring fishery was probably the most important part of the pickled fishery in the late nineteenth century; one observer thought that the herring fishery was second only to the cod fishery on Canada's east coast.[19] With a market in the Caribbean and growing demand in Quebec and Ontario, herring production rose from 12,000 barrels in 1851 to nearly 50,000 barrels in the early 1880s, falling back to 30,000–40,000 barrels later in the decade (Figure 7.2). Much of this fish was still caught in inshore waters, particularly along the Strait of Canso (Figure 7.3). The fortunes of the mackerel fishery were more mixed. In the third quarter of the century, production fell from some 30,000 barrels in 1851 to almost half that ten years later, only to rebound in the early 1870s (Figure 7.2). After that brief recovery, production gradually declined until only 11,000 barrels were produced in 1890. Most of the pickled mackerel produced during those years were exported to the American market. Between 1862 and 1865, during reciprocity, 97 percent of the pickled mackerel exported directly from Cape Breton went to the United States.[20] Although reciprocity ended in 1865 and tariffs on Nova Scotian fish were reimposed, free access to the American market was assured by the Treaty of Washington in 1871. Nevertheless, the trade depression of the 1870s and the growing American preference for fresh fish affected sales.[21] By the late 1880s, the mackerel fishery in Cape Breton had lost much of its former importance. Production in the salmon fishery also fluctuated considerably, increasing from 579 barrels in 1851 to 1,171 barrels in 1871, but decreasing to 383 barrels ten years later.[22] By 1891, salmon was being exported in ice and cans, as well as in salt; of the salmon produced that year, some 71,662 pounds were packed in ice, 9,560 pounds were canned, and 228 barrels were put up.[23] Much of the fish was exported to the United States.

In the inshore fishery, herring, mackerel, and salmon continued to be caught in nets, but in the offshore mackerel fishery, technology changed radically. In the early 1850s, hand-lining for mackerel was introduced. First used by the Americans in the Gulf of St Lawrence, the hand-line technique was similar to that in the cod fishery and allowed vessels to follow the shoals of mackerel rather than wait for the fish to be trapped in nets.[24] In 1851, the provincial government encouraged use of the new method by paying bounties, but out of 75 vessels entered for bounties, only 6 were from Cape Breton.[25] The few Cape Breton vessels that participated in this fishery usually combined a summer voyage for cod with a fall trip for mackerel.[26] Large, expensive seine nets were also used in the mackerel and herring fishery. When a shoal of mackerel or herring was spotted close to the shore, a seine boat was launched and the net let out as the boat encircled the fish. The trapped fish were then pulled out with a "spiller" or small bag-net and landed on shore. As many as 800 barrels of fish could be taken in a single sweep.[27]

The most dramatic development in the Island's fishery was the rapid growth of the lobster industry in the early 1870s.[28] Before the advent of canning, lobster was virtually worthless and ignored by the fishermen, but with the introduction of canning, lobster could be preserved for export, principally to the United States, the main centre of demand. In the early years of the industry, much of the investment came from New England entrepreneurs attracted by an undeveloped resource. In later years, local tinsmiths, ex-employees of the larger American companies, and Island storekeepers invested in the industry. The first canneries were opened in Richmond County in 1872 and then in Inverness and Cape Breton counties the following year. By 1874, canneries were open in all four counties. In 1891, there were 32 canneries on the Island, 13 of them in Richmond County.[29] Production increased from 144,000 cans in 1872 to a peak of 2,078,906 cans in 1890 (Figure 7.5). The best lobster grounds – at Port Hood, Judique, Isle Madame, Fourchu, L'Archeveque, Point Michaud, St Peters Island, Gabarus, and Ingonish – were readily accessible to most inshore fishermen, and the traps and pots needed to catch the shellfish were easily made. Fishermen sold lobsters to canners, usually at cash prices. The canneries also gave work during the six-month lobster season to men, women, and children. By 1891, there were some 950 people employed.[30] A single firm could employ as many as 200–250 men and women and about 15 boys. Working from the first of May to the first of October, men could earn $25 to $40 a month with board and lodging, and women and boys about $12 without lodging. The commercial exploitation of lobster was a considerable fillip for the fishing communities, providing much-needed cash for fishermen and their families.

The American fishery also continued to provide employment. In 1878, Roderick MacDonald, a fisherman at Low Point, which over-

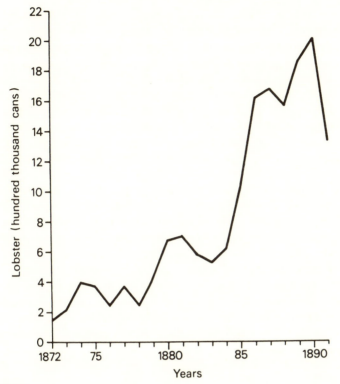

Figure 7.5
Lobster production in Cape Breton, 1872–91
Source: Sessional Papers.

looked the Strait of Canso, estimated "that about half of our fishermen from Cape Breton and on the Nova Scotian side of the Strait
of Canso find employment in American fishing vessels and if they
were not so employed they would have very hard times."[31] D'Escousse merchant William LeVesconte reckoned that 200 men on
average left Îsle Madame each year for the American fishery.[32] They
usually shipped to Boston or Gloucester in April or May and hired
"on shares" on Grand Banks schooners for the season. In a voyage
of three months, a man could earn between $120 and $150.[33] In
the fall, many of these men returned to their homes in Cape Breton;
in late November 1885, an Arichat fisherman noted laconically in
his diary: "Most of crew back from Boston."[34] Yet each year some
stayed in the United States, and a handful never made it back to
either a Canadian or an American port. At the end of each fishing
season, the *North Sydney Herald* reprinted a list from the *Cape Ann
Advertiser* of Gloucester recording the Cape Bretoners lost from

American fishing vessels. During 1889, for example, the Island lost the following: "Simon Sampson, of Arichat, one of the crew of the schr. J.J. Clark, fell overboard off Cape Sable. Peter Landry, a native of Arichat, C.B., about 38 years of age, a widower with one child, was washed overboard from schooner J.H. Carey on the Banks, March 9. William Babineau, 38 years old, married, and Samuel Vineau, 25, single, both of Arichat, C.B., fishing from schooner Senator Frye, were capsized from a dory and drowned at Cape North, May 9th."[35] Bank fishing was at least as dangerous as coal mining.

Until the decline of the American mackerel fishery in the Gulf of St Lawrence in the late 1860s, American vessels continued to provide a large demand for salt, ice, barrels, bait, provisions, and fresh vegetables from Cape Breton merchants and fishermen. Indeed, several merchants along the Strait of Canso advertised their goods in the *Cape Ann Advertiser*.[36] With American skippers each spending $700 on average to outfit their vessels,[37] it was hardly surprising that "money circulated freely" among the communities along the west coast of Cape Breton,[38] and that to the chagrin of Royal Navy officers on Fishery Protection service, "the sympathies of the inhabitants [were] entirely with the Americans."[39] Even in the early 1880s, many American and Nova Scotian fishing vessels operating in the gulf continued to call at ports along the Strait of Canso (particularly at Port Hood and Big Rory's Cove at Judique) to buy bait. Such trade was highly remunerative to local fishermen.[40]

The domestic economy also remained important, although the growing population was putting great pressure on the limited agricultural land in the outports. In many of the older settlements, all the available agricultural land had been granted, while in the newer settlements, located on steep, rocky parts of the coast, there was simply not much arable land. As a result, the growing population was accommodated on existing landholdings. Subdivision and fragmentation of lots became common. On Isle Madame, where the number of occupiers increased from 667 in 1871 to 876 in 1891, the percentage of holdings smaller than 10 acres rose from 64.5 percent to 73 percent. At the newer settlements of Neil's Harbour and New Haven, 41 of the 47 holdings in 1891 were smaller than 10 acres, and 429 people lived on one and a quarter square miles.[41]

Given the pressure on land, much of the occupied area in the fishing settlements was cleared and cultivated by the late nineteenth century. In 1891, 65 percent of occupied land at Neil's Harbour was improved, and as much as 83 percent at Petit-de-Grat on Isle Madame.[42] A considerable portion of this cleared land continued to be in hay or pasture, the rest in potatoes, oats, barley, and hardy vegetables. The small arable plots were intensively cultivated, often cropped year after year. To maintain soil fertility, the fishermen, like the crofters of western Scotland, collected kelp from the shore to spread on the fields, dragged muck from marshland, and shovelled out barn manure over the soil. In October 1884, Dougald Boyle, a fisherman at West Arichat, reminded himself to "get enough kelp or shells to manure the best part of the island. I must have a big manure pile annually or my hay crop will be slight."[43] Stones and rocks were picked off the land, weeds rooted out, and marshes drained to provide rich soil. In August 1883, Boyle noted in his diary: "In P.M. nearly finished draining pond – the remaining being only through mud. Except in centre there is about a foot of rich vegetable loam on top of stiff clay. It is certainly a mine and will obviate any necessity on my part to gather kelp or muzzle mud for manure. A good many envious of the result."[44] Such work was extremely labour intensive, requiring the participation of the fisherman's family and often hired workers. In some outports, fishermen still trekked inland to hunt, trap, pick berries, and remove timber, but in densely settled villages, such resources were in short supply by the late nineteenth century. On Île Madame, many fishermen no longer had access to woodland, a vital source of fuel, building materials, and cattle fodder. At West Arichat, Dougald Boyle had to burn coal in his grate, order fence poles from a local timber merchant, and confine his cow and heifers to a few acres of pasture.[45]

Although the fishing settlements were still dominated by the premises belonging to the Channel Island and resident merchants (Figure 7.6), the form of the settlements changed considerably in the late nineteenth century. From being loose, straggling collections of buildings, they became more concentrated as the population density increased. As lots were subdivided, houses crowded together, often forming a continuous street village, somewhat like the French settlements along the Lower St Lawrence. Behind the houses were long, thin strips or gardens, usually enclosed by post-and-wire fences (Figure 7.7). Many fishermen also had shingled barns and chicken coops at the back of their houses. In the larger settlements, such as Arichat, a second street parallel to the first one along the waterfront was laid out to accommodate the increase in population (Figure 7.6). With its harbour lined with wharves, the county court-house, churches and schools for the Acadian and English populations, a convent, and numerous stores, Arichat was a substantial port and service centre in the late nineteenth century. More typical of the small outports were Neil's Harbour and New Haven. In these settlements, the houses were clustered together, forming nucleated

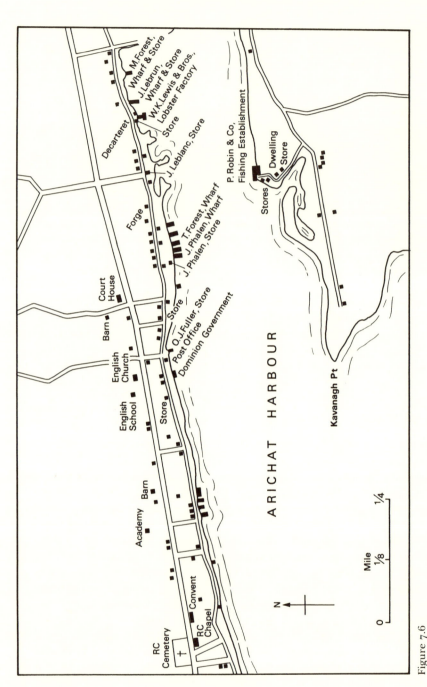

Figure 7.6
Fishing settlement, Arichat, Richmond County, 1883–87

Source: A.F. Church, *Topographical Township Map of Richmond County Nova Scotia* (Bedford, NS: A.F. Church & Co., 1883–87).

Figure 7.7
Fishing settlement, Petit-de-Grat, Richmond County
Source: National Archives of Canada, PA 48066.

villages (figures 7.8 and 7.9). Apart from the local school and church, the substantial merchant premises, and a general store in each place, there were no other services. The economy and life of these two settlements revolved completely around the fishery.

As the decline of agriculture made people even more dependent on the fishery, the economic stratification of outport society may well have increased during the late nineteenth century. The fishermen's dependence on local merchants for outfits and winter supplies probably grew; certainly, chronic indebtedness remained a problem. In March 1880, the *Arichat News Budget* reported that "even with the greatest success it is barely possible for the fishermen to pay their advances and live during the time they are employed."[46] After a bad season, many merchants refused to extend further credit, leaving the fishermen to face a six-month winter without supplies. Destitution soon followed, and several fishing communities were forced to appeal to the government for relief. In the spring of 1880, relief supplies were distributed to more than a hundred poor families on Îsle Madame.[47]

Although poverty, if not destitution, appears to have been common in the Cape Breton outports, fishermen occasionally benefited from competition between merchants or from collective action. When fish were in short supply and prices were high, fishermen were in a relatively strong bargaining position. Dougald Boyle wrote

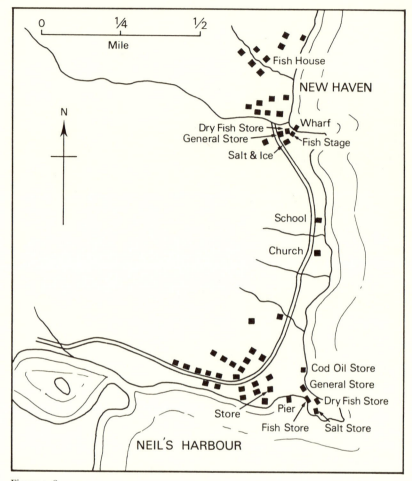

Figure 7.8
Fishing settlements, Neil's Harbour and New Haven, Victoria County, 1883–87
Source: A.F. Church, *Topographical Township Map of Victoria County Nova Scotia* (Bedford, NS: A.F. Church & Co., 1883–87).

in his diary on 5 June 1884 that Bosdet, a West Arichat merchant, was "giving miserable prices and charging scandalously." As a result, Boyle rowed over to Arichat with his catch and "agreed to sell P. Campbell all my herring. He will give me $3.50 at cash prices, by which I will make a dollar per barrel more than by selling to Bosdet."[48] Fishermen also played the Jersey houses off against Halifax merchants. As Peter DeCarteret explained to his partner Isaac LeVesconte in 1858, "It is not surprising to see the Halifax merchants

Figure 7.9
Fishing settlement, Neil's Harbour, Victoria County. Note the dried fish piled up on the flakes in anticipation of rain.
Source: Notman Photographic Archives, McCord Museum, McGill University.

givin those high prices for fish, from the high prices they have been receiving in the West Indies, and trying to get all your good dealers from the River [Bourgeois] and other places, we suppose that you will not be able to do much business in the River for the time to come, you must only give the good dealers all the incouragement in your powor in order to keep them, if the fish keep high you will have to give them high prices in order to prevent them going to Halifax."[49] The Robin Company faced similar problems at Chéti-camp. At the start of the fishing season in May 1889, the local Robin agent made the following report: "We drove in the afternoon to Cheticamp and in the evening the fishermen congregated on the Room to know the price of Green fish. They first asked same price as last year $1.35 per 100 lbs. then came down to $1.20 which we refused to entertain and offered $1.10 which is even too high in proportion to the price of dry in Halifax, this the fishermen would not accept & as a compromise we offered to divide the difference & to pay $1.15 and we now wait to see what they will do as some of them threatened to take their fish elsewhere so we may have to give the $1.20 rather than lose the fish, but will wait to see what the other merchants will do."[50] Once it became clear that "the Cadians had decided to keep the fish if it was not paid 1.20," the company raised its price. To recoup its outlay, the company put a premium of 10 percent on its goods "so as to meet the high price of fresh fish."[51] But in a competitive environment, this tactic was counter-productive. Many of the company's dealers went to local Halifax-supplied merchants who were offering provisions at a cheaper rate. In the following two years, both the planters and hired men who crewed the Robin Company's boats formed combinations and withheld their fish or labour until prices were raised.[52] Such was the tension between the company and its dealers that when the company took out judgments against debtors, the Robin agent observed "a little commotion and serious talk amongst the hard crowd they threaten to fire our Buildings etc have not paid any attention to it on the contrary will add more pressure."[53] Fishermen exercised similar collective action in the lobster industry. In early May 1884, the start of the lobster fishing season, the lobster fishermen of Port Hood refused to work unless local canners increased the price from 50 to 60 cents per 100 pounds of lobster.[54] Fishermen were not passive pawns exploited by the merchants but could, and did, strengthen their position when circumstances permitted.[55]

To some extent, economic relations were cushioned by the growth of community sentiment and the influence of the church. Apart from the handful of single men who looked after the Jersey fishing stations and returned to the Channel Islands for the winter, the population of the fishing villages was stable and deeply rooted. Many families had lived in the same outport for generations, their endogamous marriages preserving ethnic patterns established in the late eighteenth and early nineteenth centuries. The French-speaking Acadians still clung together at Îsle Madame, River Bourgeois, L'Ardoise, and Chéticamp; Irish families lived at Louisbourg, Main-à-Dieu, and Ingonish; and Scots inhabited many of the other outports. The maze of blood relations helped tie people together and provided support for individual fishermen. The church, too, increasingly underpinned community life. Churches had been built in most outports by 1850, and the clergy were firmly entrenched by the late nineteenth century. Such was the importance of the Catholic community at Arichat that the Bishop's See for eastern Nova Scotia was located there from 1844 until 1866, when it was transferred to Antigonish on the Nova Scotian mainland.[56] In addition, the Catholic Church opened a convent at Arichat in 1856 and another at West Arichat in 1863. For many fishermen, life was measured as surely by the religious calendar as by the rhythms of wind, tide, and fish. Religion also offered spiritual support for those in economic distress. Faced with the daily task of providing for his family, Dougald Boyle, a devout Roman Catholic, was probably not alone when he admitted to "suffering terrible anxieties of mind, fearful that I won't be able to make both ends meet, but God will not allow an industrious person to starve, for He has said 'Take no thought of the morrow': therefore I put all trust in His providing for self and family."[57]

THE COAL INDUSTRY

In 1858, after a complex and protracted struggle, the General Mining Association's monopoly of all mineral reserves in Nova Scotia was broken.[58] With the legal impediment to developing the rest of the province's coal reserves removed and the Reciprocity Treaty with the United States signed, the way was open for exploration and development of the coal deposits in Cape Breton. In the late 1850s and early 1860s, the Island's eastern coalfield entered a period of "cyclonic" development.[59] Dozens of prospectors moved in, obtained exploratory leases, dug adits, and when they found a workable seam, obtained a licence to mine. At that point, many prospectors, lacking the capital to develop a mine, sold out. Although this was a golden opportunity for Cape Breton merchants to enter a new and dynamic industry, few had the necessary resources. The agricultural sector, the backbone of the Cape Breton economy, had not produced great fortunes. Charles J. Campbell of Baddeck, the most prosperous country merchant on the Island, invested "the greater part of his capital" in the Campbellton mine at Great Bras d'Or, which the local R.G. Dun agent thought was a "good invest[ment]."[60] But that was not the case. Opened from 1863 to 1881, the mine produced only 66,900 tons of coal, a minute proportion of Cape Breton's total output during those years. Although the Channel Island merchants did not invest in the new mines, some of Cape Breton's leading fish and shipping merchants did make the transition. Archibald & Co., the largest merchant house in North Sydney, was heavily engaged in Cape Breton's traditional sectors of shipping, shipbuilding, and fishing. It owned fishing stations along the northeast coast at Ingonish, Neil's Harbour, Cape North, and Bay St Lawrence, outfitted a vessel for the Newfoundland seal hunt (in 1858 it brought back "the largest catch ever ... to St. John[s]"), shipped coal, built vessels, and was the only house in North Sydney to trade directly with Great Britain. With the breaking of the GMA's monopoly, Archibald & Co. invested in the Gowrie mine (Figure 7.10), spending $120,000 in

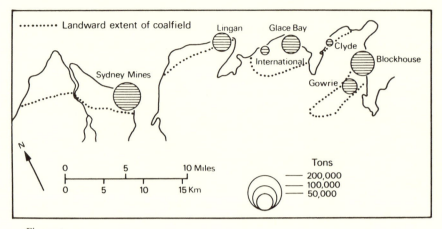

Figure 7.10
Distribution and output of the principal coal mines on Cape Breton Island, 1865–66
Source: Journals of the House of Assembly of Nova Scotia.

1859 alone. Gradually, the company withdrew from shipbuilding and devoted its energies to coal mining; between 1861 and 1893, the Gowrie mine was the largest independent producer in Cape Breton.[61] Another local merchant, E.P. Archbold, who ran a general store, grocery, and dry goods business in Sydney, invested in the Glace Bay mine. But a shortage of capital forced him to seek backing in 1862 from Halifax and New England businessmen.[62] It was a pattern repeated at the Blockhouse mine. Marshall Bourinot, scion of a wealthy Sydney family, opened the mine in 1858 but through lack of capital was forced to sell the lease in 1863 to the Belloni brothers of New York.[63] Americans also invested in the International mine, while British capital supported the Reserve mine.[64] Apart from Archibald's Gowrie mine, British and American interests controlled all the principal mines on the Island by the early 1860s. Cape Breton merchants had failed to make the crucial transition from the old mercantile economy to the new industrial economy. This failure had less to do with their entrepreneurial spirit than with the fundamental weakness of the Cape Breton agricultural and commercial sectors. The traditional economy had not generated sufficient capital among the Island's merchant class to ward off more highly capitalized foreign predators.[65] The Island's nascent industrial class had virtually been strangled at birth.

Although reciprocity allowed free trade between the United States and Nova Scotia, the stimulus for developing the Cape Breton mines came from New England industry working at full capacity during

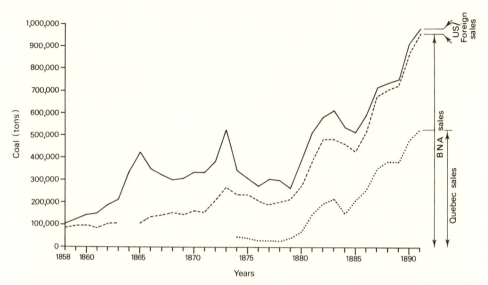

Figure 7.11
Production and export of coal from Cape Breton, 1858–91
Source: *Journals of the House of Assembly of Nova Scotia.*

the Civil War: urban and industrial users desperately needed Cape Breton coal. By 1863, more than half the coal produced in Cape Breton was sold in the United States (Figure 7.11). Two years later, exports to the United States reached three-quarters of total output, 320,610 tons. For the coal companies, this was "harvest time" and many investors saw a quick return on capital.[66] Yet the boom was not to last. In 1866, the Reciprocity Treaty was abrogated and American tariffs on Nova Scotian coal were reimposed. Sales to the United States collapsed. By 1869, only 147,381 tons, half the total output, were shipped to the United States. The few alternative markets were well supplied. The GMA dominated the Maritime market; Ohio coal was sold in Ontario; and British coal, shipped across the Atlantic as ballast, supplied Quebec and Montreal.[67] For the new mines, the outlook was bleak,[68] although temporary respite came in 1873 when strikes curtailed coal exports from Britain at a time when coal stocks were low in the United States.[69] Cape Breton collieries stepped in to meet the shortfall in supply and exported a record 520,777 tons, almost half of it to the United States. But the recovery of the British coal trade and the onset of world depression curtailed further exports. By 1874, output had fallen 35 percent to 341,602 tons, and less than a third of exports went to the United States. Two years later, exports were almost half what they had been in 1873.

Faced with American tariffs, British competition in the St Lawrence market, and small Maritime demand, the Nova Scotia Coal Owners' Association lobbied the Dominion government for protection. The association claimed that a tariff on American coal sold in Ontario would "create within the Dominion a coal trade that will be equivalent for that with the United States."[70] In 1878, the Conservative government of Sir John A. Macdonald was elected, committed to protecting nascent Canadian industry. Under the guidelines of the National Policy, a tariff of 50 cents per ton was placed on American coal in 1879, and this was raised to 60 cents the following year. Even so, pressure from Ontario consumers for cheap coal ensured that the tariff would not cover the cost of transporting Maritime coal beyond Montreal, leaving the valuable Toronto-Hamilton market in the hands of American companies. Nevertheless, Nova Scotian producers now had a new, secure market. Coal was shipped by steamer to Quebec City and Montreal in return for flour and manufactured goods.[71]

Exports of Cape Breton coal increased from 385,066 tons in 1880 to 982,582 tons in 1891 (Figure 7.11). Sales to Quebec accounted for much of this growth, increasing from 164,151 tons in 1880 to 703,897 tons in 1891, 71 percent of total output. At least three-quarters of the coal was shipped to Montreal, the most populous Canadian city and the leading industrial centre in Quebec; the rest was shipped to Sorel, Trois-Rivières, and Quebec City.[72] At the same time, new industries in the Maritimes pushed up local demand from 112,802 tons to 258,483 tons. American trade, meanwhile, slumped from 108,113 tons to an insignificant 20,202 tons. The National Policy had successfully reoriented the coal trade of Cape Breton Island towards central Canada, virtually ending the industry's dependence on intermittent American markets and lessening its dependence on small Maritime markets.

Much of the coal produced during the late nineteenth century came from the independent collieries. In 1865–66, at the height of reciprocity, there were seven major collieries on the Island: the two GMA pits at Sydney Mines and Lingan and five new pits located in the south of the coalfield close to the sea (Figure 7.10). These new mines produced 55 percent of total output that year, with the Blockhouse and Glace Bay mines each producing more than 60,000 tons. After the GMA closed its Lingan mine in 1886, the independents expanded their share of output. By 1890, they produced 83 percent of the coal mined in Cape Breton. Much of it came from the Gowrie, Glace Bay, Reserve, International, and Caledonia mines, which each produced more than 100,000 tons that year (Figure 7.12). Although

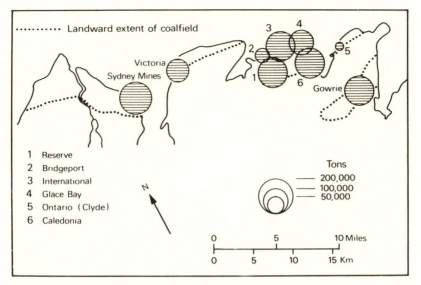

Figure 7.12
Distribution and output of the principal coal mines on Cape Breton Island, 1890
Source: *Journals of the House of Assembly of Nova Scotia.*

Sydney Mines was still the largest single colliery on the Island, the GMA had lost its former dominance.

When the new mines opened in the early 1860s, much of the technology was pre-industrial. Seams were tapped by adits driven through the sea cliffs, and coal was hauled out by men. Water drained out along the adits, and the circulation of air was generally poor.[73] But as production increased and shafts replaced adits, more efficient means of haulage, drainage, and ventilation became necessary. Steam power was introduced, taking over the more arduous haulage from men and improving the drainage. By 1866, seven of the new mines had installed 13 steam engines, totalling 266 horsepower (Figure 7.13).[74] The GMA also improved its engines; Richard Brown considered the 240-horsepower Cornish pumping engine and the 160-horsepower winding engine built at Sydney Mines in the 1860s to be "beyond all doubt the most perfect and most powerful that have been erected for mining purposes in British America."[75] Underground haulage was also mechanized. Although ponies were still used in the 1890s, stationary engines were installed in several pits to haul tubs along the levels. By means of an endless rope moving in one direction and passed around a powered pulley at either end of the level, tubs were pulled along tracks to the shaft bottom or up

Figure 7.13
Mining scenes, Caledonia Mines, Cape Breton County, late nineteenth century
Source: G.M. Grant, *Picturesque Canada*, vol. 2 (Toronto: Belden Bros, 1882).

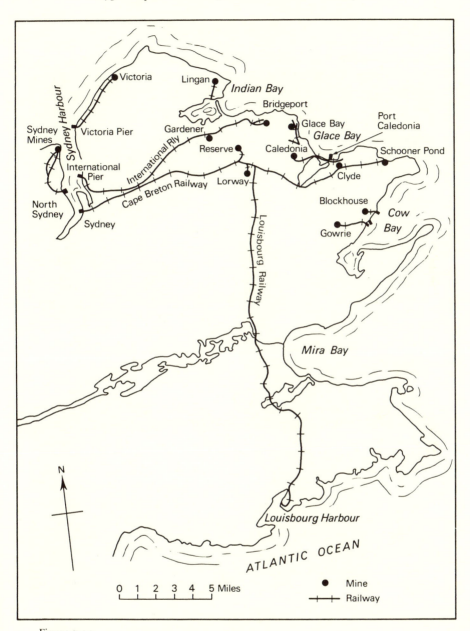

Figure 7.14
Colliery railways in eastern Cape Breton County
Source: A.F. Church, *Topographical Township Map of Cape Breton County Nova Scotia* (Bedford, NS: A.F. Church & Co., 1877).

the slope to the surface.[76] Ventilation, too, was mechanized. Furnaces had never been very efficient, particularly in the larger mines, and in the 1870s, mechanical fans were introduced. A Guibal fan at Sydney Mines was claimed to pass 67,000 cubic feet of air per minute compared to the 20,000–50,000 cubic feet of furnace systems.[77] On the surface, new railways and shipping facilities were constructed. Most railways were short spur lines of one to three miles connecting colliery to coast, but longer lines were built to the best shipping ports (Figure 7.14). The GMA opened a railway to North Sydney to use the better harbour facilities, and similar lines were built to connect the Reserve, International, and Bridgeport mines with two new piers at Sydney. A more ambitious railway was constructed from the coalfield to Louisbourg to take advantage of its ice-free harbour, but the line closed during the depression of the 1870s.[78]

Despite the massive expansion of the mines, there was relatively little spin-off to other sectors of the Cape Breton economy. As in the early nineteenth century, the GMA continued to import much of its equipment and stores from Britain each year. This equipment included parts for pumps as well as such basic items as iron tubs.[79] Given this linkage back to Britain and the small size of the Nova Scotia market, there was no incentive to make mining equipment locally. The railways and port facilities were still used for coal and were not adapted for shipping agricultural produce. They were not the basis of further economic development.

The most important linkage was to the Island's large pool of surplus rural labour. As production expanded, more men were taken on, particularly in boom periods (Figure 7.15). In 1865–66, some 1,800 men and boys were employed at the mines: 442 men and 107 boys at Sydney Mines; 314 men and 62 boys at Blockhouse; 204 men and 17 boys at Gowrie; and 161 men and 27 boys at Glace Bay. Apart from the brief boom of 1872–73, when some 2,600 men and boys were hired, labour was laid off during the depressed years of the late 1860s and 1870s; only 1,156 men and 266 boys worked at the mines in 1879. But as production picked up during the 1880s, more miners were employed, and by 1890, there were some 2,500 men and boys at work. That year, there were 444 men and 160 boys at Sydney Mines; 249 men and 63 boys at Reserve; 224 men and 50 boys at Caledonia; and 259 men and 58 boys at International. These were still the largest individual workforces on the Island.

Since the 1840s, a growing proportion of miners were from Cape Breton, and by 1871, they formed a majority. A sample of 330 miners drawn from Sydney Mines and the Gowrie, Blockhouse, and Schooner Pond mines near Glace Bay shows that 201 men, 60 percent

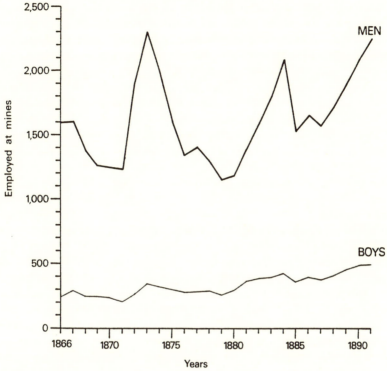

Figure 7.15
Men and boys employed at the coal mines in Cape Breton County, 1866–91
Source: Journals of the House of Assembly of Nova Scotia.

of the total, were from Nova Scotia. Another 86 men, 26 percent of the total, were from Scotland, and the remainder from England and Ireland.[80] In 1889, R.H. Brown, the GMA manager, in testimony to the Royal Commission on Labour, reckoned that the "great majority of our men" were born in Cape Breton.[81]

As most of the workforce was drawn from the pre-industrial worlds of farming and fishing, colliery management continued to inculcate "time-thrift" and "regularity." For example, superstitious belief – which often led to stoppages – was curbed. In 1881, the men laid off work at Sydney Mines after a disaster had been prophesied. The GMA management visited the Presbyterian and Roman Catholic clergy and urged them to speak to their respective congregations. After sermons "about absurdity of laying idle on strength of predictions," the men returned to work.[82] Drunkenness was also attacked. The monthly pay-day was usually "celebrated" by the miners for several days, leading to widespread absenteeism.[83] In 1889, R.H.

Brown, before the royal commission, paternalistically argued against fortnightly pay because "there are men who get drunk regularly every pay night ... these men would get drunk once a fortnight if they were paid in that way."[84] In 1881 an act was passed prohibiting the sale of liquor around the mines.[85]

Management also attempted to regulate the workplace. Traditionally, the hewer had considerable "independence" at work. He was paid by the piece and set his own hours and output; for example, John McNeil, a hewer at Sydney Mines in the 1880s, "quit [work] as I think proper," while another hewer, Alexander McLellan, left "at three or four o'clock and sometimes later" depending on "when I am tired."[86] According to union leader Robert Drummond, "The miner [was] his own master."[87] But although hewers had considerable leeway over their hours and output, overseers carefully monitored the driving of bords and imposed fines on men who exceeded the permitted dimensions.[88] Fines also discouraged hewers from sending up too much stone or slack coal in their tubs: at Sydney Mines, a hewer could forfeit 1,000 pounds of coal from his tally if his tub contained 8–10 pounds of stone, or lose half a ton if it had more than 200 pounds of slack. Unskilled men also found their routine organized. Paid by the day, their shifts were measured by whistles and their tasks assigned by overseers: "Such imposition," complained one labourer at Sydney Mines, "was hardly carried on among the slaves in olden times."[89]

As the new mines developed, company villages were established to accommodate the permanent mining workforce. By the 1880s, there was a string of mining settlements around the east coast of Cape Breton County – Sydney Mines, Victoria, Bridgeport, Reserve, Glace Bay, Caledonia, Blockhouse, and Gowrie – each entirely dependent upon its local colliery. Most had about 700–1,000 inhabitants, but the largest – Sydney Mines and Glace Bay – had some 2,400 people each in 1891. Colliery villages were laid out much like the earlier GMA settlements: parallel rows of one-storey duplex houses built on company land close to the pit-head (Figure 7.16). Living conditions were often cramped and at some of the new mines, unsanitary. At Little Glace Bay mine, the only privy, located on the pit premises, served 30–40 families.[90] Communal wells were frequently contaminated, and there were some outbreaks of diptheria.[91] Like those in GMA rows, most houses had a garden where miners kept a pig, some chickens, perhaps a cow, and grew potatoes and vegetables. The rest of a typical mining village comprised pit buildings, manager's house, company store, school, several churches, and, off company land, bars and independent stores.

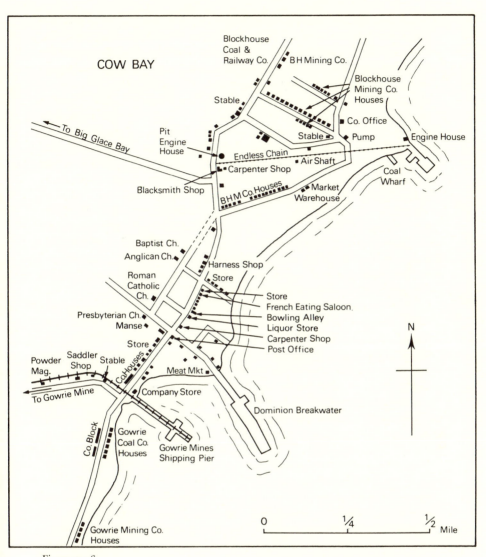

Figure 7.16
The Blockhouse and Gowrie mining villages at Cow Bay, Cape Breton County,
1877
Source: A.F. Church, *Topographical Township Map of Cape Breton County Nova Scotia* (Bedford,
NS: A.F. Church & Co., 1877).

Compared to any part of rural Cape Breton, the mining population was markedly diverse. Most of the miners were from different
parts of the Island and brought different ethnic and religious back-
grounds to the mines. About half the population was of Scottish

descent, a quarter Irish, and the rest divided among Acadians and English.[92] Most of the miners were either Roman Catholic or Presbyterian, the remainder Anglicans, Methodists, and Baptists. Although English was the dominant language, Gaelic and French were spoken underground and in many homes. Yet conditions of work cut across ethnic, religious, and linguistic differences. Men lived in similar company housing, worked in the same mine, were paid standard rates, and joined the same union. Over time, a common mining culture developed. Despite considerable transiency among the miners, some men spent all their working lives mining coal in Cape Breton and their sons followed them into the industry. Stability helped encourage the development of a shared culture. Ethnicity became less a way of life than a symbolic attachment. Scottish miners had pipe bands; the Irish celebrated St Patrick's Day. Yet even some religious holidays succumbed to the demands of work. In 1883, the Roman Catholic clergy, under pressure from the companies, agreed to exempt men from mass on saint's days in return for the collection of church dues at the pay office.[93]

The miners' standard of living scarcely improved during the late nineteenth century. The availability of cheap rural labour ensured that the mines were frequently "overstocked" with men during the summer, reducing the amount of work available for full-time miners and depressing their wages.[94] In 1875, for instance, the GMA proposed a 25 percent "reduction in wages all round now that labour is so superabundant in C. Breton."[95] In a working year of about 200 days, a hewer earned approximately $300 in the 1880s.[96] Deductions for rent, coal, powder, oil, school, doctor, and tally claimed between $50 and $60, leaving about $250 for food, clothing, furniture, taxes, and dues. If work was steady from one year to the next, most miners earned enough to live, though few had money set aside. In evidence to the Royal Commission on Labour, a Sydney miner reckoned that "not many of them [have any money ahead]. There may be an odd one who has not a family to keep who has a little money."[97] Yet working sons were an asset, contributing, at least for a few years, to the family income. In 1891, a Bridgeport miner explained his situation: "A few years ago myself an' son could only make three hundred dollars a year, an' that I thought was not so bad. Last year meself an' two boys made over nine hundred. I have a nest egg in the Co-operative Store. My family is well rigged fer the winter. I have plenty of grub laid by fer the next three months."[98] Yet long winters could easily erase summer savings. Like fishermen, miners depended upon credit from the company store to carry them through the winter and they used their summer earnings to pay off their arrears.[99] A poor season could leave men in debt, facing the need for further advances for the coming winter; many miners were continually in debt to the company. At Sydney Mines, for example, 162 men owed $9,422 in July 1862 and 66 of them still owed $2,833 in March 1868.[100] Indebtedness cost men their freedom to move and increased company control over them.[101] In particularly bad years, men were laid off, often with few savings to carry them through idle months. Some attempted to eke out a living from their vegetable patches and fishing,[102] but many fell dependent upon public support. During the winter of 1876, the provincial government provided relief for destitute miners.[103]

Collective action to improve pay and working conditions had little success during the depressed years of the 1860s and 1870s. In 1876, a long, bitter strike at Sydney Mines ended when "scab" labour was hired and the strikers were evicted from company housing.[104] But as trade improved in the early 1880s, the miners regrouped. During a strike at Springhill Mines on the Nova Scotian mainland in 1879, the local miners formed the Provincial Workmen's Association (PWA) – the first province-wide labour organization in Canada – and soon organized the Cape Breton men.[105] Despite considerable management hostility, the first PWA lodge in Cape Breton was opened in July 1881, and a further eight lodges with nearly a thousand members were opened by September (Figure 7.17). In its first year, the PWA attracted some 67 percent of the mining workforce, although in later years it struggled to hold a majority.[106] Probably most of the permanent miners were union members.

Even though visions of a new social order often inspired editorials and letters in the union newspaper, the aims of the PWA were practical and pragmatic. Union leader Robert Drummond wanted "mutual concession between employers and employed to seek to have the work carried on to the advantage of both" and managed to have a series of reform measures implemented.[107] Amendments to the Mines Regulation Act during the 1880s and early 1890s introduced fortnightly pay, improved colliery safety, and raised the level of competency of mine officials, shot-firers, and miners.[108] By insisting that men have one year's experience in the mine before being allowed to cut coal, the union attempted to restrict the inflow of cheap rural labour and preserve work for full-time miners. The union also provided a measure of social support for its members, organizing dances, picnics, regular lodge meetings, and celebratory marches with pipe bands, regalia, and banners bearing the motto "Unity, Equity, and Progress."[109] The union arranged collections for the injured and fought compensation cases. Funds were made available

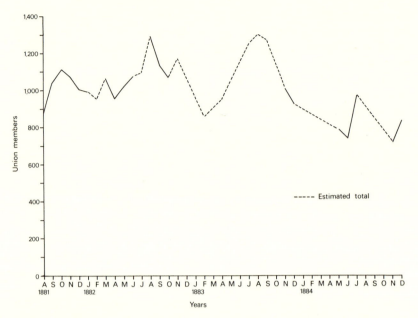

Figure 7.17
Union membership among Cape Breton miners, August 1881–December 1884
Source: Lodge membership rolls, Provincial Workmen's Association, Department of Labour, Ottawa.

for funerals of miners killed in accidents and for their dependents.[110] Cooperative stores were encouraged.[111] The *Trades Journal*, the union newspaper edited by Drummond, was a voice for the working man that tried to instil a sense of self-respect and brotherhood among the men. Miners were "brothers" and union members were "true men." But after the initial enthusiasm, the PWA faced a constant struggle to recruit men as they signed on for work each spring. "An effort is being made to rouse the members of 'Equity' to a sense of duty," reported one lodge secretary in March 1885. "A pretty hard thing to accomplish. Some from whom better things might be expected are only half hearted, good Union men only when any personal end is to be served."[112] Union levies were often ignored; eight months into a strike at Lingan mine in 1882 – the longest strike to that date in Canada – less than half the Cape Breton lodges had contributed to the strike fund.[113]

Although the union had improved the conditions of work and partially slowed the influx of cheap labour, it had probably not managed to raise the miners' standard of living. Many miners lived a hand-to-mouth existence. During the 1870s and 1880s, hardship in the Cape Breton mines and the lure of higher wages in the Pennsylvania coalfields and hardrock mines of the Western Cordillera led many men to leave the Island. Their places were taken by farmers from the backlands of Cape Breton. The coal companies, too, were struggling to survive. Although coal exports increased rapidly during the 1880s, the duplication of management, workshops, railways, and harbours kept production costs high, while intense competition among Maritime producers depressed prices.[114] Sales usually covered the high costs of production, provided an occasional small dividend, but allowed for little capital improvement.[115] Undercapitalized and relatively small producers, the mines were ripe for take-over and consolidation. In 1893, all the important mines with the exception of Sydney Mines were purchased by the Dominion Coal Company, a Boston-based syndicate of American and central Canadian businessmen.[116] Cape Breton interest in the principal mines was extinguished; control over the Island's most important industrial resource now lay completely outside the province.

SHIPPING AND SHIPBUILDING

Continuity and change marked the Cape Breton shipping industry in the late nineteenth century. Dried and pickled fish were still sent along the coast by schooner to Halifax or shipped by schooner or square-rigger to markets in the Caribbean, South America, and Southern Europe. Agricultural produce was also shipped to St John's and Halifax. In the important coal trade, however, an increasing proportion of exports was carried by steamers, many of them owned by the coal companies. The Glace Bay Mining Company, for example, introduced coal barges towed by steam tug in 1891 for its trade to Halifax.[117] Given such developments, local coasters, who had once depended upon the coal trade for much of their business, were squeezed out. Between 1871 and 1881, the number of mariners declined from 1,567 (6.7 percent of the total workforce) to 1,357 (5.1 percent of the total), a trend that probably continued in the 1880s and 1890s.[118] As elsewhere in the North Atlantic, sailing vessels were giving way to faster and more economical steamships.

The coming of the steamship, as well as the decline of ocean freight rates and the lure of landward investment, heralded the end of the wooden shipbuilding industry on the Island. In 1854, 30 vessels totalling 3,992 tons were built on the Island; by 1891, only 7 totalling 165 tons were constructed (Figure 7.18). The industry was all but finished. Merchants who had invested in the old economy of "wood,

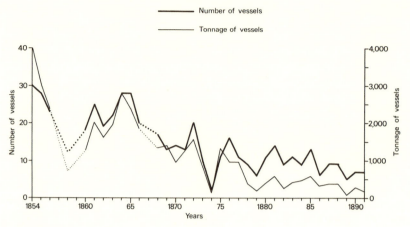

Figure 7.18
Shipbuilding on Cape Breton Island, 1854–91
Source: Journals of the House of Assembly of Nova Scotia.

wind, and sail," such as Archibald & Co. of North Sydney, switched their capital to the new economy of "iron, coal, and rail." The few ships built on the Island during the last years of the century were sold locally for the fishery and coasting trade.

During the late nineteenth century, the age-old transatlantic connections of Cape Breton's staple trades were gradually replaced by new continental ties. As the hold of the Channel Island companies and the GMA on the Island's resources slackened, so the tentacles of American and central Canadian capital tightened. Too weak to compete successfully, Cape Breton merchants were squeezed out, particularly in the all-important coal industry. New Canadian markets for Cape Breton coal and new North American suppliers for the fishery were also part of this continental integration. Within Cape Breton, there were significant changes as well. The workforces of both staples increased substantially. New settlements were established and old settlements were enlarged to accommodate the increased population. Kinship ties became stronger. There was also a growing sense of collective identity among the individual staple workforces, particularly among the coal miners. Yet at a fundamental level, the structure of the Island's staple economy had not changed much. The staples were still dominated by external capital (North American capital had merely replaced British capital), they still exported much of their production to overseas markets, and they continued to rely on imported foreign technology. Ties between the staples were virtually non-existent, and apart from shipping and shipbuilding, there had been little other economic spin-off. Many of the settlements remained totally dependent upon their local staple industry. The social divisions between capital and labour were still acute, and cultural patterns had barely changed. Although the population of the mining villages was mixed (as it had been since 1800), the fishing settlements were culturally homogeneous and distinct. The ethnic enclaves endured. From being a hinterland of Great Britain, Cape Breton had become a hinterland of the eastern United States and central Canada.

8 The Exodus

Even as thousands of Highland Scots were pouring into Cape Breton in the late 1820s and early 1830s, a new cycle of emigration, this time from Cape Breton, began. Discouraged by the lack of good land and shortage of jobs, Cape Bretoners started to drift away. In the 1820s, Acadians from the Chéticamp-Margaree coast moved across the Cabot Strait to settle the west coast of Newfoundland, particularly around St. George's Bay and on the Port-au-Port Peninsula.[1] They were followed in the early 1840s by Scots and a few Irish from the Broad Cove–Margaree area, drawn to the unsettled Codroy Valley.[2] Settlers from other parts of the Island were also leaving. In 1838, the price of land and the cost of clearance were claimed to "have deterred hundreds of young men from attempting to [take] up Land under the present system, some of whom have abandoned their native Province."[3] Yet these first tentative emigrations were to be dwarfed by the great exodus in the second half of the century.

The potato blight marked its beginning. The widespread destitution caused by the blight forced many backland settlers to leave the Island, at least temporarily, in search of work. The Crown surveyor in Victoria County reckoned that the blight was "the chief cause of the young men leaving home to seek employment elsewhere."[4] Many established settlers also wanted to leave, but like Captain Donald McNeil of Mira River, few had sufficient funds to emigrate. "I have a grant of five hundred acres," McNeil explained to his brother back in Scotland, "& would I get for it as *much money* as would bring us up to Canada and purchase a small farm then I would not hesitate to try the chance but under the present circumstances that is entirely out of the question."[5] Some settlers put their trust in the government. In 1849, 16 families at St Anns petitioned Lieutenant-Governor Harvey for help in moving to Canada:

That your petitioners are British subjects natives of Sutherland and Rosshire in the North of Scotland that some of your petitioners are younger branches of families that emigrated to this Island about twenty years ago and who could not get land fit for supporting them after becoming of years, and others ... have only emigrated from the Highlands in later years when all the good lots were also occupied, this keeping your petitioners in a constant state of dependence. That the chief part of your petitioners have large families, and owing to the failure of the crops for years past found it difficult to get means of subsistence, and from the experience of the past, dread the future.[6]

Within a few years, several hundred families would leave the St Anns district. After receiving favourable accounts from his son in Australia, the Reverend Norman McLeod, preacher and community leader at St Anns, organized a mass emigration of families from the area. Between 1851 and 1859, six ships left Cape Breton for Australia and New Zealand carrying 876 people, mostly from the St Anns, Boularderie, Baddeck, and Middle River districts.[7] Some of these migrants were religious followers of McLeod, others were fortune-seekers lured by tales of the gold discoveries in South Australia, but many were dissatisfied by the poor economic conditions caused by the blight and hoped for better circumstances in Australia.[8] Settlers from other parts of the Island were also emigrating. A "great number of persons" were reported to have left for the United States and the Canadas in 1853, and "a still greater exodus of our population" was expected to leave the following year.[9] In the late 1850s, tradesmen, labourers, "as well as others" were still "leaving ... as fast as their means will enable them ... Hundreds are said to have gone away during the past year."[10]

Although the economy of Cape Breton was more buoyant during the reciprocity years of the late 1850s and early 1860s, the upsurge in economic activity did not stem the outflow. In 1865, the *Acadian Recorder* claimed that in spite of free trade, "the bone and sinew of the land" had annually left the province for the past ten or fifteen years.[11] Certainly, the abrogation of the Reciprocity Treaty and the onset of depression in the 1870s caused massive emigration. In the coal industry, for example, some 400 men lost their jobs between

Table 8.1
Total net migration from Cape Breton, 1871–91

County	Total migrants	Migrants per 1,000 head of population
1871–81		
Cape Breton	1178.6	38
Inverness	1768.0	69
Richmond	1233.8	81
Victoria	800.4	64
Cape Breton Island	4980.8	59
1881–91		
Cape Breton	1880.9	55
Inverness	3027.1	117
Richmond	2643.6	212
Victoria	1445.3	116
Cape Breton Island	8996.9	103

Source: P.A. Thornton, "The Problem of Out-Migration from Atlantic Canada, 1871–1921: A New Look," Acadiensis 15, no. 1 (1985): 3–34.

1867 and 1871, and without alternative employment, many must have left.[12] In 1869, it was reported that "the inhabitants of Cape Breton ... are flocking across the [American] border by scores."[13] Between 1871 and 1881, some 5,000 people left the Island, 59 emigrants per 1,000 inhabitants (Table 8.1). The decadal growth rate slowed to 11.9 percent, a rate too low to sustain the natural increase of population (Table 8.2). In the mines, as many as 1,200 men lost their jobs between 1873 and 1880, while elsewhere, more and more families trying to eke out a living from farming and fishing were finding that ends could not be met.[14] Many left. In April 1872, the *Acadian Recorder* observed: "Now that spring is opening, we already see the commencement of that annual exodus of people from this Province which we have been accustomed to see for several years past."[15] In 1879, the same newspaper noted that "week after week, the tide of emigration set from our shores with greater impetus," while the *Port Hood Eastern Beacon* reported "the weekly leave-taking of so many Cape Bretoners for the United States by every Boston-bound steamer, as well as by Gloucester and Boston sailing vessels, from this port."[16]

In the 1880s, almost 9,000 people emigrated, 103 of every 1,000 inhabitants (Table 8.1). The decadal growth rate slowed to only 2.8 percent, and in Richmond and Victoria counties, the population

Table 8.2
Percentage change of population, 1851–91

County	1851–61	1861–71	1871–81	1881–91
Cape Breton	10.7	26.8	18.1	9.4
Inverness	18.0	17.3	9.5	0.5
Richmond	21.4	13.2	6.0	−4.8
Victoria	10.9	17.6	9.8	−0.2
Cape Breton Island	15.1	19.6	11.9	2.8

Source: Census of 1851, RG 1/453, Public Archives of Nova Scotia; Census of 1861, RG 12/21, Public Archives of Nova Scotia; and *Census of Canada, 1870–1871, Census of Canada, 1881*, and *Census of Canada, 1891*, Canada, Department of Agriculture.

decreased (Table 8.2). Contempories appear to have been aware of the greater outflow. The New Glasgow *Eastern Chronicle* reported in April 1882 that "the exodus goes on increasing week after week ... Every train from the east for some four weeks past may be said to be an emigrant train."[17] Many aboard were from Cape Breton, for in the same month the *Chignecto Post* recorded that "one hundred and fifty persons passed through last night [on the train] ... One hundred were Cape Bretoners."[18] Later that year, in October, when seasonal migrants usually returned, the *Port Hood Referee* reported a continued outflow: "The emigration from this part of Cape Breton is becoming greater and more alarming every succeeding week ... From this electoral district alone the emigrants within the past three weeks can be counted by hundreds. Among these no fewer than seven whole families have left this small town for the United States."[19] The National Policy and expansion of the coal industry failed to stop the haemorrhage of population from Cape Breton during these years.

Most of the emigrants were young, usually in their twenties and thirties, and often single. In 1881, it was calculated that of the passengers on board the steamers leaving Halifax for Boston, "three fourths at least were individuals, mostly the young."[20] Newspapers searched for remedies to "cure our young people of the 'foreign fever.'"[21] Roughly the same numbers of men and women emigrated,[22] although during the 1880s most emigrants from the mining communities were women, probably leaving home because of the lack of suitable local employment. The *Trades Journal* observed in October 1885 that the "young men grumble a good deal at this."[23]

Between 1871 and 1891, the largest proportion of migrants were from Richmond County, suggesting a considerable outflow of fishermen and backland farmers (Table 8.1). Victoria and Inverness, both predominantly farming and fishing counties, also had high proportions of migrants. Cape Breton County had the lowest proportion, mainly because its large number of emigrants were replaced by people from the other counties moving to the mines.[24] Contemporary comment further suggests that emigrants were drawn from all major occupations on the Island. The *Acadian Recorder* noted in 1872 that "young farmers – ay, and old ones too [are] selling off their lands, their cattle, the means of a life-long independence for themselves and a comfortable inheritance for their children after them" and leaving the province.[25] A Louisbourg fisherman, questioned by an American traveller, replied that his two sons, aged 11 and 13, who helped him fish from a dory, "won't be with me many years ... all our boys go to the States just as they get old enough."[26]

At the mines, men were leaving, especially during the depressed years of the late 1860s, 1870s, and early 1880s. In October 1881, a Sydney miner reported to the *Trades Journal* that "the exodus at present threatens to be the largest that has been known for years, in this locality. Among the working class, especially the colliers, the question is heard passing from lip to lip. 'Are you going to the States this fall?' and the answer 'Well, I don't know, but believe me, if I could raise money enough I would not stay long here.' This is the 'cry' among young and old, married and single."[27] The reason for the exodus, according to this correspondent, was the "same reason in a manner, that the Scotchman and Irishman have left their native shores, viz: to try and procure a better living for themselves and families."[28] In April the following year, the *Trades Journal* reported that another Sydney miner claimed "the miners ... have been miserably paid and are greatly dissatisfied ... There will likely be a big exodus from here during the course of the summer."[29] Later in the decade, "B.C. fever" gripped the mining population. In May 1884, a miner at Little Glace Bay expected "quite an exodus" at the end of the month because all the "young men" intended to go "out west."[30] In November 1887, more "able bodied young men" were reported to have left for British Columbia, many to work in the coal mines at Nanaimo, Vancouver Island.[31] The GMA manager at Sydney Mines was so concerned about the loss of skilled men to the Nanaimo mines that he requested the GMA secretary in London to contact the British owners of the Nanaimo mines to tell them "that they are paying a big price for colliers and advise them to send more men out there from England."[32] Yet the appeal was in vain, for in May 1888 "a crowd" left Sydney Mines, again for British Columbia, and it was reported that a "great many more would follow if their means would allow them."[33] After working that summer, many had

Table 8.3
Distribution of Nova Scotians in Canada, 1881–91

Year	PEI	%	NB	%	Que.	%	Ont.	%	Man.	%	BC	%
1881	2,507	17	6,160	43	813	6	3,799	26	727	5	379	3
1891	1,950	11	5,527	31	1,402	8	4,659	27	1,402	8	2,656	15

Source: Canada, Dominion Bureau of Statistics, Seventh Census, 1931, vol. 1, 1182–3.

earned enough to emigrate, and in October a Sydney miner reported that "the place is being fast depopulated of its best workmen. Of late a large number of men, with their families, in some instances, have left for British Columbia, and there are more to follow."[34] The emigration continued. In March 1889, a Bridgeport miner remarked sardonically that "a few winters like this as regards work, and we will all be forced to go West."[35] Again many left at the end of that summer; in October, a miner reported that "Cow Bay is fast becoming a 'one-horse' place, and a broken-winded horse at that." According to this miner, with colliers earning less than two-thirds of the wages of the previous year, "an emigration fever has consequently seized our young men and several are making preperations to go West."[36]

Yet the most common Canadian destination for Cape Breton emigrants was another part of the Maritimes. Of the Nova Scotians who moved to other parts of Canada, some 60 percent lived in New Brunswick and Prince Edward Island in 1881, and 42 percent in 1891 (Table 8.3). A survey of 208 emigrant obituaries published in the North Sydney Herald between 1880 and 1893 shows that 51 people, 24 percent of the total, remained in Nova Scotia and neighbouring New Brunswick (Figure 8.1). At least three-quarters of these emigrants moved to Halifax, and most of the rest to the new industrial towns of Pictou County. For many, this change of residence was associated with industrial employment. The traditional Maritime economy based on "wood, wind and sail" was giving way in the 1880s and 1890s to one based on "iron, coal and rail."[37] Protected by National Policy tariffs and connected to central Canadian markets by the Intercolonial Railway, new industries developed in the Maritimes, drawing rural labour to the expanding towns and cities. With a population of about 40,000 during these years, Halifax added new manufacturing to its old commercial economy and became Canada's largest producer of rope and second-largest refiner of sugar, as well as a considerable manufacturer of cotton, confectionary, paint, and lamps. Meanwhile, in Pictou County, New Glasgow emerged as one

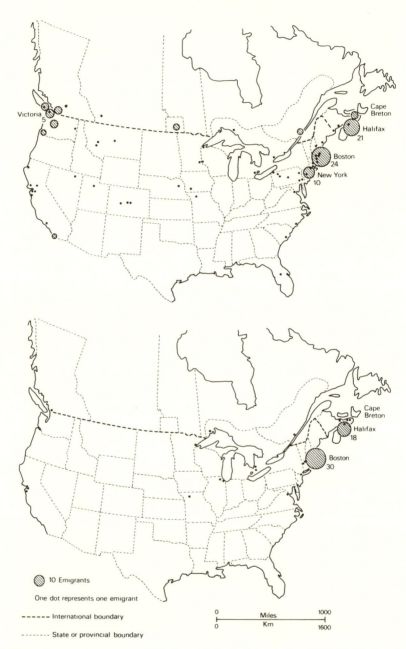

Figure 8.1
Distribution of male emigrants (top) and female emigrants (bottom) from
Cape Breton by place or state/province of death, 1880–93
Source: North Sydney Herald, 1880–93, obituaries.

of the foremost industrial towns in the province. Located on the Pictou coalfield, the town was a suitable site for heavy manufacturing, and with the formation of the Nova Scotia Forge Company in 1889, it became home to the largest producer of primary steel in the country. With the increased demand for coal, the local mines took on more men, many of them from Cape Breton. Across the border in New Brunswick, Moncton was growing as a railway centre, with workshops and factories; while at Saint John, also a town of about 40,000 people, the new industries of smelting, rope and cotton manufacture, and brass and rail production joined the old sawmilling and shipping trades. The transformation of a rural labour force into an urban industrial one was not new to Cape Bretoners: many had either worked or known friends and relatives employed in the Island's coal mines.

Few Cape Bretoners appear to have moved to Quebec or Ontario, and most of those who did apparently settled in Montreal, Toronto, or the townships along Lake Huron (Figure 8.1). On the other hand, the completion of the Canadian Pacific Railway (CPR) to Winnipeg in 1882 offered Cape Bretoners a new agricultural frontier, some 40 years after the meagre Codroy Valley had been settled. With its "fertile fields" and "bountiful harvests" that "almost surpass belief," the province was held up by one Cape Breton newspaper as "a remedy for the annual exodus."[38] Manitoba offered, the newspaper went on, "a new prospect ... an opportunity, which, if seized, will lead to comparative wealth, a happy home, and, in a short time, to comparative independence of others."[39] In 1881, the *North Sydney Herald* announced that 26 Cape Bretoners had given a celebratory party in Winnipeg: 22 people were from Whycocomagh, 2 from West Bay, and 2 from Little Narrows.[40] The following year, the same newspaper observed that "some of our farmers are making preparations to leave their old homes for the Prairie Province."[41] Perhaps some of these emigrants were among the 50 farmers and mechanics from Port Hood, Mabou, and Whycocomagh who were reported, "on good authority," to be planning to take advantage of a special rate on an emigrant train from New Glasgow to Winnipeg that spring.[42] By the early 1890s, emigration agents such as J.C. McLean, a farmer at Manitou, Manitoba, but formerly of Middle River, were recruiting on the Island.[43] In the summer of 1892, the CPR inaugurated its first "Harvest Specials," running three trains from Halifax to prairie destinations.[44] For $28, passengers could buy a return ticket to Moosomin; another $12 took them as far as Edmonton. For many Cape Bretoners, seasonal work on the prairies became permanent.

Table 8.4
Distribution of Nova Scotians in selected states and
territories of the United States, 1870–80

Year	Mass.	Maine	NY	Calif.	RI	Minn.
1870	58%	6	5	4	3	–
1880	57	7	4	5	3	3

Source: U.S. Census Office, Ninth Census, 1870, vol. 1, 336–7;
Tenth Census, 1880, vol. 1, 492–5.

Cape Bretoners had probably begun arriving in British Columbia in the late 1850s, drawn north from the California diggings by the gold rushes along the lower Fraser River and then later in the Cariboo. As the placer mines were exhausted, they probably drifted back south, for it was not until the 1880s that much employment was again available in the province. The coal mines at Nanaimo drew experienced men from Cape Breton, and the logging industry offered some employment. A few Islanders crewed schooners that were sailed from Cape Breton around Cape Horn to Victoria; there, the vessels formed a small Cape Breton fleet that hunted for seals off Alaska in the Bering Sea.[45]

Yet far more Cape Bretoners emigrated to the United States. In 1880–81, the only year for which statistics are available, there were 65,561 Nova Scotians outside their native province, 22 percent elsewhere in Canada, the remaining 78 percent in the United States.[46] The survey of Cape Breton obituaries shows that 61 percent of emigrants had crossed the international border. Between 1870 and 1880, 70 percent of Nova Scotians in America were in the New England states, and 52 percent of the Cape Breton sample. Most Nova Scotians and Cape Bretoners were in Massachusetts, with lesser numbers in Maine, New Hampshire, Rhode Island, and Connecticut (Table 8.4 and Figure 8.1). In 1880, 29,307 Nova Scotians lived in Massachusetts, most of them in Boston and few west of Worcester.

The connection between Cape Breton and Boston had been close for much of the century. Since the early 1830s, Cape Breton coal companies had tried to penetrate the New England market, and during the reciprocity years they sold much of their output to buyers in New England. Cape Breton fishermen had hired on Massachusetts fishing vessels, and others had sold their catch to Yankee traders. Commercial contacts were well established, and during the exodus many Islanders no doubt secured a berth to Boston on American or Maritime fishing schooners and coasters. By 1865, regular steamer services connected Halifax to Boston, offering a one-way fare for less than $10.[47] Cape Bretoners reached Halifax easily enough, either by taking a steamer from Port Hawkesbury or by travelling overland on the stage via Antigonish, New Glasgow, and Truro. From the 1880s, the stage was replaced by the railway that left Port Mulgrave on the mainland side of the Gut of Canso. There were also many vessels coasting between the Island and the provincial capital.

Boston was a rapidly expanding city where suitable jobs for Maritimers were available: fishing and shipping; retail and domestic service; and woodworking crafts such as shipbuilding, carpentry, coopering, and cabinet-making.[48] Nova Scotian "hatchet and saw men," for example, turned from building wooden ships to building wooden houses and in 1880 comprised over 20 percent of all carpenters in Boston and Worcester. Within Boston, the two major clusters of Nova Scotians were in East Boston, a centre of wooden shipbuilding, and in Dorchester, an expanding suburb of wooden houses. Not surprisingly, several Cape Bretoners ended their days in these two places. The 1880 census shows that outside the city, 2,383 Nova Scotians, including several Cape Bretoners, lived in the principal fishing port of Gloucester,[49] more than double the number of Nova Scotians living in Manitoba and BC. There were also 193 Nova Scotians in the seafaring town of Newburyport, a few miles north of Gloucester. Significantly, relatively few of the Nova Scotians and none of the Cape Breton sample lived in the industrial mill towns along the Merrimack River. Boston and the neighbouring port towns allowed Cape Bretoners and other Nova Scotians an opportunity to continue using traditional skills, albeit in an urban setting, rather than make the wholesale transition to factory "hand."

Although based on a small sample, some 80 percent of the women who emigrated from Cape Breton to the United States stayed in Massachusetts compared to 36 percent of the men (Figure 8.1). A similar finding comes from a sample of 190 emigrants from Canning, King's County, Nova Scotia: 88 percent of women compared to 62 percent of men remained in Massachusetts. While many men emigrated to start new households, women often remained in close contact with their families in Cape Breton, sending back money to help the household economy. Boston, the closest centre offering significant employment to women, was easily accessible from Cape Breton. There was little need for women to move farther away in search of work.[50]

Beyond Massachusetts, some 6–7 percent of Nova Scotians were found in Maine, 3 percent in Rhode Island, and a few others in New

Hampshire and Connecticut. Several of the Cape Breton sample lived in these states, no doubt using their traditional skills in the ports and shipyards. Outside New England, some 4–5 percent of Nova Scotians were in New York State and probably almost all of the Cape Bretoners were in New York or Brooklyn. Although relatively few Nova Scotians appear to have emigrated to Pennsylvania, the Cape Breton obituary data suggests that the state drew a disproportionate number of Islanders. Since the 1830s, Cape Breton miners had been attracted by jobs in the anthracite mines between Scranton and Pottstown and in the bituminous coal mines in the Alleghenies.[51] Farther west, 3 percent of the Nova Scotians in the United States were in Minnesota in 1880 and Cape Bretoners were also found in Michigan, Missouri, Nebraska, and Iowa. They were probably employed in farming, lumbering, or small trades. Stillwater, Minnesota, had some 30 Islanders in 1882, many living on contiguous lots.[52] The migrants had arrived with "some means" and hoped to profit from judicious investment in the expanding town. The prairie states offered Cape Bretoners opportunities in agriculture or small business much like those farther north in Manitoba.

As early as the California gold rush of 1849, Cape Bretoners had been moving to the Far West, working either at the placer deposits or in hardrock mines. Later, lumbering offered alternative employment. Between 1870 and 1880, 4–5 percent of Nova Scotians were in California and Cape Bretoners were to be found in southern California from San Diego to San Francisco Bay. Farther north, they worked in the logging camps, sawmills, and ports situated along most of the inlets from Eureka, northern California, through Oregon, and into western Washington, particularly around Puget Sound. Some spilled over the international border to take similar jobs in British Columbia. Inland, Cape Bretoners, especially those from the coal mines, worked in the Cordilleran hardrock camps stretching from Colorado, through Utah and Nevada, into Idaho, Montana, and eastern Washington.[53] Like the loggers, some men moved farther north, working in Nanaimo during the 1880s and in the Kootenays in the next decade.[54] In isolated mountain mines, displaced Cape Breton miners continued to practise their skills, while former farmhands were initiated into a particularly raw form of industrial employment.

Of the several hundred Cape Bretoners who sailed for Australia in the 1850s, many ended up in New Zealand, where most settled in Waipu, North Island, creating a distinctive Scottish colony.[55] A few mariners and gold seekers also fetched up in Australia. Little information about these extensive individual wanderings survives, but the careers of two Campbell brothers from Whycocomagh may be indicative.[56] Hugh Oig Campbell and Hugh Ban Campbell left Cape Breton in 1845 and, like many others, moved to Boston, where they gained traditional employment at a boat-building yard in Back Bay. With the California gold rush, the two young men joined another Cape Bretoner, Malcolm Blue from River Denys, and a MacDonald from Pictou Island and travelled overland to the diggings. In California, Hugh Ban and the Pictou Islander died from disease; soon after, the remaining two men joined thousands of others leaving San Francisco for the other side of the Pacific. At the Victoria diggings in 1852, the two men excavated gold worth $10,000 and decided to return home. A ship took them to Britain, where Hugh Oig visited relatives in Oban, Argyllshire, and then they returned to Nova Scotia. No doubt few emigrants to the South Pacific ever managed to return to the Maritimes.

Hugh Oig Campbell was probably born in Cape Breton, but at least some of those who emigrated from the western Highlands to Cape Breton eventually ended their days in Australia or New Zealand. In 1892, the *North Sydney Herald* reprinted from an Auckland newspaper the obituary of one John Finlayson, who had died at his home "Braemar" in Waipu.[57] Born at Loch Alsh, Wester Ross, Finlayson had emigrated to Cape Breton in "early life" and settled at Baddeck. After he and his wife raised several children, the family left on the *Highland Lass* in 1852, first for Australia and then for New Zealand. Finlayson's life encapsulated the complete cycle of emigration from western Scotland, settlement and population growth in Cape Breton, followed by renewed emigration.[58]

Like the original Scottish emigration to Cape Breton, chain migration facilitated these transcontinental and intercontinental movements. Frequently, a younger son emigrated first and sent back information and perhaps money to other members of his family or for friends so that they could join him. In the migration to the Codroy Valley, for example, related Clan McIsaac families from the Margaree–Broad Cove district settled together, often on contiguous lots.[59] Similarly, families from Canning, Nova Scotia, settled close to relatives in Boston;[60] no doubt it was the same for Cape Breton emigrants.

Although the best surviving evidence of individual migration to Boston does not include family members, it does demonstrate the close contact maintained with friends. Fisherman Dougald Boyle, originally from Glenora Falls near Mabou, spent the summer of 1872 in Boston before moving to West Arichat. After several months teaching at Mabou and making "no money, but what I barely required," Boyle, then 25, "determined to go either to Canada or the States." With no savings, he gave up his post at the end of the spring term and worked for a month to earn the passage money. On 11 July, he left Mabou "in company with big Rory McLeod, for Boston." Nevertheless, friend McLeod went only as far as Creignish, still in Inverness County. At Port Hawkesbury, where the ferry left for the mainland, Boyle saw "Ben Hawley and others" and on board the boat fell in with "Wm. McNeil, Gillis, Campbell and others, bound for Pictou to work." He left them at New Glasgow, and when he arrived at Halifax, he spent most of the day with "Paddy Wallis's son from Margaree." So far, Boyle was in almost constant contact with Cape Bretoners.

After an eventful voyage during which he nearly lost his life after becoming entangled in the ship's winch, Boyle arrived in Boston and was stood lunch, "the bounty of a Lunenburger." Then he went to "Mckillop's [probably McKillop, Cazmay & Co. – a commercial agency] where the Campbells and lots of Mabou fellows soon congregated." In the following two weeks, Boyle went from job to job with evidently little satisfaction: at Glendon & Pitchers (an iron company), he "found the work too heavy and its nature too hot"; at Campbell's, "the work did not suit"; and at Quincy, he "got disappointed." At the end of July, he moved to East Cambridge with McIsaac, another Inverness man, and hired with one William Nixon (possibly a grocery and provisions business). Boyle stayed with Nixon until 3 November, when he joined McCuigan's. Moving from one job to another in different parts of the city, Boyle continued to meet Cape Bretoners: "Lauch. McNeil, John McDonald, Allen, Angus McDonald, Saddler, etc." No doubt he saw more at that "grand affair" in August, the Scotch Picnic. But despite the conviviality of friends, Boyle had had his "fill of Boston" by October and with the outbreak of a smallpox epidemic (which took away Lauchlin McNeil "without the consolation of a priest"), he decided to leave for Cape Breton. Boyle "bade all friends goodbye" on 23 November and left on the Halifax steamer "with crowds from River Inhabitants."[61] Throughout his trip, he had been in touch with friends from Inverness County who were probably also Roman Catholics. Information about jobs, accommodation, and acquaintances undoubtedly passed among them, facilitating Boyle's migration to Boston.

Whether in the form of letters or oral communication, information was relayed back to family and friends in Cape Breton to help them decide when and where to emigrate. Letters were avidly read, passed from hand to hand around the family and community, and occasionally published in the local newspaper. The letters from Norman

McLeod's son in Australia, for example, were read by many in St Anns and would have been sent to friends in Pictou County had they been available. "I have thought to inclose my son's letter," McLeod wrote in June 1849, "but I cannot now lay my hands on it, as it is seldom in the house; for its information is so interesting to all intending emigrants for that New Colony, that it is already in half tatters, by frequent perusal, from place to place."[62] Letters published in the Conservative *North Sydney Herald* during the great exodus of the 1880s usually stressed the negative features of emigration "out West" and recommended that Cape Bretoners stay home,[63] but occasionally a more balanced view slipped through:

Quite a number of Cape Breton boys who have made British Columbia their home have done well and are doing well ... Men coming to this country should be good mechanics *able* and *willing* to work, men who are willing to rough it at first for a year or two ... in western parlance they are known as "rustlers." The man who is comfortably situated in Cape Breton who makes a fair living and has a family had better stay there so far as *British Columbia* is concerned, UNLESS thinking there is no prospect in store for his family he is willing to undergo *hardships* and *privations* for to get his boys and girls a chance in this country. A young man free from family cares coming here can generally make a comfortable living if steady and a tradesman. Clerks, book-keepers and people looking for "soft snaps" had better stay home or go to "Boston," this is no country for such.[64]

Apart from news about employment, information about friends and accommodation was sent back. From Victoria, Vancouver Island, J.H. McDougall, formerly of North Sydney, reported meeting "several Cape Breton boys from the 'old sod' from Low Point to Lochlomond, from Gabarus to Judique," and he recommended that those looking for lodgings in Victoria should contact "Mrs Langley formerly of Sydney [who] is conducting a nice private boarding house on Pandora St., where all Cape Breton folks will receive a genuine welcome."[65] Cape Bretoners living on islands at either side of the continent kept in touch.

Some emigrants also returned home, visiting friends and family and keeping them informed of places hundreds and perhaps thousands of miles away. In 1889, the *North Sydney Herald* reported that "a number of our Boularderie 'Boys' who have been for the past few years in the Western States, where they have been successful in accumulating the 'hard flint' are daily expected home."[66] Such men were respected. "A SUCCESSFUL CAPE BRETONIAN VISITS HIS FRIENDS," proclaimed the *Herald* in May 1887: "Mr Angus Campbell, of Silver City, New Mexico, U.S. is on a visit to his friends at Mabou."[67] After leaving Cape Breton in 1867, Campbell had been a miner in California and Colorado before settling in New Mexico, where he purchased "a large tract of land comprising 1,500,000 acres," which he stocked with 30,000 head of cattle and 500 horses. Whether or not Campbell exaggerated the size of his new operation to impress the Islanders, the newspaper was impressed: "It always gives us pleasure to note the success of Cape Bretonians abroad." The *Herald* proudly concluded that "Mr Campbell may be classed among the most successful."

More often obituaries were sent home, poignant reminders of a young son's emigration and death in a far-off mine or logging camp. The *Trades Journal*, for example, reported in May 1884 that "intelligence reached Sydney Mines ... of the death of Mr Neil McLean, a native of the former place. Mr McLean, who had worked in B.C. for a few years came home on a visit a year ago, and took back with him his brother and the other members of his family. His death was occasioned by a fall of 'till.'"[68] The exodus of Cape Breton miners during the 1880s was so great that whole communities on the Island could be touched by a mining disaster thousands of miles away. The explosion at Nanaimo mines in 1887 killed six from Cape Breton: "William B. Campbell, a native of Sydney Mines ... age 28 years, single. James Hoggan, native of Cape Breton, aged 21 years, single. William Hoyt, native of Sydney Mines ... aged 21 years, leaves wife and child ... Michael Corcoron, a native of County Kerry, Ireland, recently of Sydney Mines ... aged 36 years; wife and six children. Malcolm McLean, native of Sydney Mines ... aged 31 years, single. Roderick McDonald, native of Cape Breton, aged 37 years; wife and child."[69] Occasionally, bodies were returned, at least from Boston, for burial in Cape Breton, while family gravestones in Island cemeteries recorded those buried elsewhere.[70]

9 Cape Breton Island at the End of the Nineteenth Century

By the early 1890s, Cape Breton was thickly settled, relatively well cultivated, and an important part of the growing industrial economy of Maritime Canada. Although comprising only 19 percent of the population of Nova Scotia, the nearly 87,000 people on the Island compared well to the 98,000 in British Columbia at the farthest reach of the Dominion or the 109,000 in neighbouring Prince Edward Island (Figure 9.1).[1] For the inhabitants of Cape Breton, the 1890s was a period of intense change. The expansion of the traditional economy based on farming and fishing had all but ceased, and many people looked to the railway being built across the Island and the ambitious plans of Boston businessmen for the coal mines as promise of a prosperous industrial future. Contempories were aware that the Island was at a turning-point in its history, and in retrospect, the early 1890s provide a useful point to take stock of the Island's nineteenth-century development.

In 1890, as at the beginning of the century, the pattern of settlement around the coast of Cape Breton was largely the result of the cod fishery. Channel Island and resident merchants still organized the fishery, importing supplies, outfitting fishermen, and exporting fish to markets around the Atlantic. Apart from the development of the lobster industry, the technology of the fishery remained much as it was in 1800. Fishermen hand-lined or set nets from small boats in inshore waters, and dried or pickled their catches on land. Virtually all the labour for the fishery was from Cape Breton, but a handful of men from the Channel Islands still came out to Cape

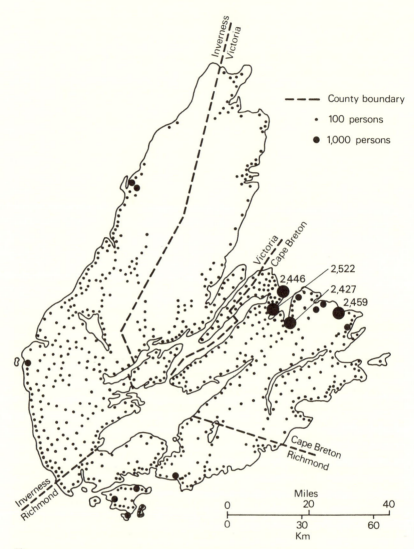

Figure 9.1
Distribution of population on Cape Breton Island, 1891
Source: Census of Canada, 1891, Canada, Department of Agriculture.

Breton each year to staff the fishing stations – late vestiges of a
seasonal movement that was four centuries old. On the coast of Cape
Breton County, coal mining, rather than the fishery, had dictated
the pattern of settlement. Like the fishery, the mines were largely
controlled by outside capital. In 1890, the mines were operated by
British, American, and Nova Scotian interests, but within three years

the coalfield was divided between the London-based General Mining Association and the Boston-backed Dominion Coal Company.[2] Almost all coal production was exported to markets outside Cape Breton, although that pattern changed in the mid-1890s when the development of an iron and steel industry provided a major local market. The workforce in the mines was mostly from Cape Breton, but immigrant miners from Scotland occasionally arrived looking for work – a link that began in the late 1820s. Inland, much of the population depended upon farming. Along the intervales, second- and third-generation settlers operated substantial farms, raising livestock for the Newfoundland market and supplying dairy products to the towns of eastern Cape Breton. On the backlands, settlers struggled to make a living, cobbling together livelihoods from subsistence farming and off-the-farm employment. Just as crofters in Scotland looked for seasonal work in the Lowlands or smallholders in the Channel Islands once crossed the Atlantic to work in the fishery, so backlanders left their farms in spring to find work in the mines, fishery, and cities of Halifax and Boston.

Overall, the Cape Breton economy was still relatively fragmented. The staples had created enclaves of specialized work around the coast that were more connected to external economies than to the rest of the Island. The staples relied heavily on imported capital and, to a lesser extent, imported technology and skilled labour. They were tied to distant, often fluctuating markets but had little to trade with each other. Economic multipliers were limited. The export of fish and coal, as well as agricultural produce, had generated some shipping and shipbuilding, but shipbuilding was in decline by the 1890s, a victim of changing technology and shipping practices. The fishery and mines also supported some commercial farming on the Island. Given the nature of the export staples, there was little need for processing industries. The few processing industries on the Island consisted of lobster- and meat-canning factories and some sawmills and tanneries. The widespread poverty of the staple workforces also ensured that few consumer or service industries had been established. Agricultural settlement, driven initially by economic pressures in western Scotland and later by demographic imperatives in Cape Breton, had created an extensive landscape of family farms. Land, climate, and market competition had limited the development of commercial agriculture. A handful of farmers sold produce to the staple industries; a few country merchants profited from agricultural trade. There was not much spare capital to reinvest in the Island. Cape Breton merchants had largely failed to make the transition to industrial entrepreneurs. Some of the surplus rural labour found work locally in the staple trades; the rest had to look farther afield in Halifax, Boston, or Gloucester. These three ingredients of the nineteenth-century Cape Breton economy were only loosely connected; they were more integrated into external economies than with each other. The Island's economy had not become much more than a sum of its constituent parts.[3]

Such an economic structure supported different societies. Both staple trades societies were stratified according to occupational ranking. Life within the outports and mining villages was dominated by merchants or coal companies and the rhythms of the staple trade. While wealth accumulated outside Cape Breton among the Channel Island merchants and shareholders of the mining companies, the staple workforces were frequently characterized by poverty and debt. Many miners and fishermen turned to collective action to improve their lot. Although rural society was also stratified, the divisions were less marked than in the staple trades. The comparative weakness of the agricultural economy and the availability of land had compressed the social range. Such different circumstances of work gave rise to diverse ideologies, ranging, at their extremes, from the socialist rhetoric of the Provincial Workmen's Association, with its millennial vision of the cooperative commonwealth, to the liberal individualism of the frontland farmer.

The Island's fractured economy also underlay a relatively complex cultural mosaic. Although the mines drew different peoples together, the fishing and farming sectors largely separated them: Scots, Acadians, and Irish in the fishery, descendants of Loyalists and Scots in farming. Many settlements were almost completely populated by a single ethnic group. Religious affiliation and endogamous marriage preserved each group's ethnic identity; few marriages crossed the Protestant/Catholic divide. Moreover, the relative isolation of rural Cape Breton ensured that the dialects and languages of the different ethnic groups were under less pressure to conform to Standard English than in other parts of Canada. Much vernacular culture survived. The different social and ethnic groups on the Island still maintained their own distinct "limited identity."[4]

For a time in the nineteenth century, Cape Breton provided a meagre rural niche in a rapidly industrializing world. Changing industrial demand for kelp and wool lay behind the Clearances from western Scotland that had largely settled the Island. Cape Breton gave some of these emigrants an opportunity – denied them in Scotland – to make an independent living on the land. Gaelic language and culture were given an extended lease on life. Yet the niche was filled very quickly, and later settlers could make a living only by combining subsistence farming with another occupation. An independent living on the land depended upon part-time work elsewhere. Within a generation, settlers were faced with renewed migration. Although a few found another rural niche in Manitoba or New Zealand – perhaps meeting later migrants from western Scotland – most moved into the urban-industrial world. There, Gaelic-speaking Scots from Cape Breton encountered English speakers. Despite the Scotch picnics held for a few years in Boston and the recounting of Gaelic tales in far-off mining camps,[5] there was no critical mass beyond Cape Breton to support Gaelic culture and language. Assimilation was rapid.

Patterns similar to those in Cape Breton were found elsewhere in the Maritimes. The penetration of British and Maritime mercantile capital into the region during the late eighteenth and nineteenth centuries created a series of staple enclaves supplying fish, timber, and minerals to markets around the North Atlantic rim. Dried fish was shipped from Nova Scotia's Atlantic shore to the West Indies and southern Europe; timber was exported from the interiors of Nova Scotia, Prince Edward Island, and New Brunswick to Great Britain; coal was exported from eastern and central Nova Scotia to regional and eastern seaboard markets. These staples created functional, single-industry resource settlements and workforces dominated by the economic and social divisions between capital and labour and the demands of the staple trade. Life within the "company towns" created by the timber barons along the Miramichi in New Brunswick was much the same as in the mining villages of eastern Cape Breton.[6] Although the staples generated some linkages – commercial farming, sawmilling, shipbuilding, a huge merchant marine – there was little economic integration among them. Even in particular staple economies, there was fragmentation. Control over Nova Scotia's cod fishery was divided between merchants in Halifax and the Channel Islands, while the New Brunswick timber industry, split between the Saint John and Miramichi watersheds, was controlled by Chatham, Saint John, and Glasgow merchants.[7] The scattered location of the staple enclaves and the lack of economic interconnections made it virtually impossible for any one Maritime port to capture and control the region's staple trades. The staples had not generated much internal economic momentum in the region.

Interspersed among these staple enclaves were pockets of agricultural land – the Saint John Valley, the Bay of Fundy marshlands, the Annapolis Valley, the larger intervales, and Prince Edward Island – that supported much of the nineteenth-century Maritime population. At first, this land was available far more cheaply than land in Europe. Attractive to immigrant labour, it provided support for farm families but not for large capital investment or for Old World landed wealth. Rural society was less differentiated than in Europe or in the staple trade settlements. Yet as population increased or markets improved, the pressure on land intensified. As land prices rose, so the opportunity declined for settlers with little capital to acquire land. Rural society became much more stratified.[8] As in Cape Breton, poorer settlers moved onto the uplands to scratch a living from scrub farms; occupational pluralism became common. Men worked in the timber trade, mines, and fishery; women in domestic service.[9] Staples developed on the backs of cheap rural labour. The pockets of commercial agriculture supported some basic manufacturing – grist mills, tanneries, forges, cooperages – and rural services, but much of this development was small scale and dispersed. Moreover, agricultural exports were shipped out from different parts of the region. Eastern Nova Scotia (including Cape Breton) exported livestock to St John's; Prince Edward Island sent livestock, roots, and grains to St John's, Cape Breton, and northern New Brunswick; the Annapolis Valley and Bay of Fundy marshes shipped livestock to Saint John or overland to Halifax.[10] Given the dispersal of agricultural trade, port hinterlands tended to be small, and profits from trade limited.[11] Unlike Toronto, which captured much of the wheat export trade from southern Ontario during the mid-nineteenth century,[12] there was no port in the Maritimes which organized the region's back-country trade. A fragmented, diverse economy supporting many relatively small urban centres characterized the nineteenth-century Maritimes. Like Cape Breton, the region was oriented to an Atlantic economy supplying a variety of products to many different markets.

The dispersed and fragmented staple and agricultural economies meant that during the Maritimes' transition to industrial manufacturing in the late nineteenth century, no dominant centre of industry, finance, trade, and transport emerged.[13] Instead, manufacturing was dispersed among many communites engaged in staples, agriculture, or shipping. Old mercantile towns such as Saint John, Halifax, Yarmouth, St Stephen, and New Glasgow, as well as new centres such as Amherst and Truro along the Intercolonial Railway, developed new industries: textiles, steel making, rope-yards, sugar refining. Although many merchants made the transition to industrial manufacturing, their factories were usually small and weakly capitalized. Many of the new industries proved too frail to resist external take-over. In the 1890s and early twentieth century, Maritime industry was bought up by Montreal and Toronto businesses and rationalized.[14] Such a process had taken place in Cape Breton some

30 years earlier when the coal industry expanded with a surge of local investment only to give way to foreign capital. The roots of the loss of Cape Breton and Maritime control over their industry lay in the late eighteenth- and nineteenth-century development of the region's staple and agricultural economies.

The cultural fragmentation that characterized Cape Breton was also found elsewhere in the Maritimes. After the collapse of the French regime in 1758, the region was settled by a variety of ethnic groups: Acadians, returning from exile, scattered around the coasts; Methodist Yorkshiremen at the head of the Bay of Fundy; Congregational and Baptist New Englanders in the Annapolis Valley and along Nova Scotia's south shore; Protestant Highland Scots in Pictou County; Catholic Highlanders in Antigonish County and much of Cape Breton and Prince Edward Island; Catholic Irish in Saint John and the Miramichi. A religious, linguistic, and cultural mosaic was created.[15] Nevertheless, these patches, like those in Cape Breton that supported the Acadians and Highland Scots, were limited. The shortage of good agricultural land, the weakness of manufacturing and services, the rise and fall of the staple trades, and the increase of population all combined to threaten these communities. Out-migration became inevitable. A trail of Maritimers led from the region's farms and fishing villages to its towns and cities or to the "Boston States."[16] Rural communities became depleted; their culture increasingly fossilized.[17]

Farther afield, the details of the Cape Breton experience become less relevant, but the underlying pattern of the Island's settlement and economy was repeated. The staples of fish, fur, timber, and minerals were all important motors of Canadian economic development in the nineteenth century. Staple trade settlements were scattered across the country from the outports of Newfoundland to the lumber camps in the Ottawa Valley, the fur posts farther west, and the salmon canneries and sawmills along the Pacific coast. Like the staple settlements in Cape Breton, they were tied to distant sources of capital and foreign markets, employed specialized work-forces, and created societies marked by clear divisions between capital and labour. Economic multipliers varied according to the nature of the staple, but at least in Ontario the wheat staple led to considerable economic development.[18] Toronto, and to a lesser extent Montreal, captured much of the wheat trade, providing profits that were reinvested in economic development. The provincial economies of Ontario and Quebec had considerable internal momentum.

Furthermore, the pockets of fertile land were very much larger in these provinces than in Cape Breton, and farming, at least in much of southern Ontario and across the Montreal plain, was more commercial. The growth of Ontario's wheat staple allowed for much more economic development than the corresponding livestock staple in the Maritimes. Even so, fertile land along the St Lawrence Valley and in peninsular Ontario was eventually taken. Social and economic stratification became more common, and settlement spread onto the marginal lands of the Canadian Shield and northern front of the Appalachian Mountains.[19] There, the close juxtaposition of staple trades and subsistence agriculture that characterized Cape Breton became widespread. In Quebec and Ontario, the timber industry created work camps that depended upon external capital and markets but drew labour from surrounding, largely subsistence farms. In the Clay Belt of northern Ontario, farming was frequently combined with pulpwood harvesting and hardrock mining. In Sorel parish, Quebec, subsistence farmers found work as voyageurs in the fur trade. Cheap farm labour manned mines, mills, and camps; staple earnings helped maintain marginal farms. Seasonal migration from farm to camp was part of the rhythm of life.[20]

A patchwork cultural pattern, too, developed in other parts of the country. From the Irish and English shores of Newfoundland to the French settlements along the St Lawrence, the New Englanders in the Eastern Townships, and the Loyalists, English, and Protestant and Catholic Irish and Scots in Ontario, an intricate cultural mosaic had taken shape in Canada by the late nineteenth century.[21] In Quebec and Ontario, the patches of fertile land supported these cultural groups for a while, but eventually people faced a shortage of good land. Where staple trades could not employ all the surplus rural labour, migration paths frequently led south of the border. As early as the 1830s, Quebecers were leaving to work in the woods of Maine or on the farms of Vermont; by the 1860s, they were moving to the textile factories of Maine, Massachusetts, New Hampshire, and Rhode Island.[22] At the same time, people were leaving Ontario for the Dakotas.[23] Cheap farm labour from Quebec was incorporated into American industrialization and eventually formed part of an emerging American working class, while Ontarians were assimilated on the American frontier.[24]

Although the patterns that emerged in nineteenth-century Cape Breton – the export enclaves, the patches of agriculture amid a generally niggardly land, the cycle of immigration, population growth, and emigration, the cultural communities – were also found in the United States, particularly in northern New England, Appalachia, and parts of northern Michigan and Washington State, they were much less common than in Canada.[25] In the late eighteenth and nineteenth centuries, the "virgin land" of the American

West supported many more farmers than Appalachia or northern New England and gave rise to a national mythology of abundance and plenitude.[26] In Canada, the land was much more meagre, staple trades were much more to the fore, and the pattern of settlement in places like Cape Breton was much more central to the national experience.

Notes

All abbreviated references in the notes are given in full in the Manuscript Sources section of the Bibliography.

INTRODUCTION

1 These two patterns were identified long ago by Canadian economist Harold Adams Innis and American historian Frederick Jackson Turner. In *The Fur Trade in Canada* and *The Cod Fisheries*, Innis focused attention on the vital role that staples played in shaping the early Canadian economy. In "The Significance of the Frontier in American History," Turner argued that agricultural opportunity in the New World had been crucial to the development of American society and democracy. Although the staple and frontier theses can be questioned, they do identify important elements of colonial development in North America.

  Some of the best contemporary discussions of the relevance of these two patterns to our understanding of early North America are in Harris, ed., *Historical Atlas of Canada* (hereafter cited as *HAC*), and McCusker and Menard, *The Economy of British America 1607–1789*, chap. 1. Many of the ideas in the following discussion are drawn from these two works, as well as from Harris, "European Beginnings in the Northwest Atlantic" and "The Pattern of Early Canada," and Wynn, "Settler Societies in Geographic Focus." Meinig's *The Shaping of America* is also useful in providing a larger context for this study. He identifies a "northern circuit" of European involvement in the New World, a circuit that encompassed early Cape Breton.

Of course, staples and agriculture do not include all the economic activity in colonial North America. A third pattern, centred on urban areas, has been identified, but it is well to remember that only a small proportion of the colonial population lived in towns and cities. The urban population of nineteenth-century Cape Breton was also relatively small and is considered only incidentally in this study.

2 For example, the immigration of indentured servants to seventeenth-century Virginia ensured that the early European population of the colony was predominantly male.

3 The rise and fall of the Chesapeake tobacco economy is charted in McCusker and Menard, *British America*, chap. 6, and in Earle, *The Evolution of a Tidewater Settlement System*, 14–17.

4 Wynn, *Timber Colony*, 53. Wynn details the evolution of New Brunswick's dependent economy in chap. 2.

5 Hirschman, "A Generalized Linkage Approach to Development, with Special Reference to Staples"; McCusker and Menard, *British America*, chap. 1; and Watkins, "A Staple Theory of Economic Growth."

6 For example, the late nineteenth-century British Columbian mining town of Sandon, discussed in Harris, "Industry and the Good Life around Idaho Peak."

7 Lemon, "Colonial America in the Eighteenth Century," 128–31.

8 For elaboration, see Harris, "The Simplification of Europe Overseas."

9 For the Malthusian argument that growth of population led to the subdivision of holdings and increasing social and economic differentiation, see Lockridge, "Land, Population, and the Evolution of New England Society, 1630–1790." For the argument that westward migration acted as a safety-valve, see Rutman, "People in Process." Bumsted and Lemon in "New Approaches in Early American Studies" have suggestively argued that rural communities in colonial New England went through three stages – "fluidity, stabilization, and stagnation" – or a cycle of immigration, population growth, and emigration.

10 Lemon, *The Best Poor Man's Country.*

11 Lockridge, *A New England Town*, and Innes, *Labor in a New Land.*

12 Daniels, "Economic Development in Colonial and Revolutionary Connecticut."

13 Quotations in Smith, *Virgin Land*, 127–8.

14 Harris, ed., *HAC.*

15 Frye, *The Bush Garden*, 226.

16 Harris, "Regionalism and the Canadian Archipelago."

17 Cell, *English Enterprise in Newfoundland 1577–1660*; Harris, ed., *HAC*, 47–51, pls 21–28; Head, *Eighteenth Century Newfoundland*; and Innis, *Cod Fisheries.*

18 Balcom, *The Cod Fishery of Isle Royale 1713–58*; Harris, ed., *HAC*, pl. 24; and Moore, "The Other Louisbourg."

CHAPTER ONE

1 The population return is enclosed in General Despard to Lord Hobart, 24 December 1801, CO/CB/A/22 NAC, and reprinted in Brown, *A History of the Island of Cape Breton*, 421.

2 The larger context is treated in Wynn, "A Province Too Much Dependent on New England" and "A Region of Scattered Settlements and Bounded Possibilities," and Harris, ed., *HAC*, pl. 68.

3 The following is based on Brown, *History*, 367–9. Lawrence Kavanagh Sr, the Newfoundland merchant, was reported to be living at Louisbourg in 1768 and probably had been there for several years. Lawrence Kavanagh is discussed in Wagg, "Lawrence Kavanagh I."

4 Shipping Returns for Arichat and Sydney, 1796, CO 221/34, 132, 135, 141–2 NAC.

5 The populations were calculated by comparing the distribution of people in the militia muster of 1793, quoted in Brown, *History*, 406–7, with the population return of 1801.

6 Shipping Returns.

7 For the Channel Island involvement in the cod fishery, see *Dictionary of Canadian Biography* (hereafter cited as *DCB*), vol. 6, *1821 to 1835*, for Janvrin; Lee, *The Robins in Gaspé, 1766 to 1825*; and, especially, Ommer, *From Outpost to Outport*. Also useful is Samson, *Fishermen and Merchants in 19th Century Gaspé*. The Nova Scotia fishery is meticulously dealt with in Balcom, "Production and Marketing in Nova Scotia's Dried Fish Trade 1850–1914."

8 The Shipping Returns reveal Janvrin's connections with the Magdalen Islands and Gaspé; see also Harris, ed., *HAC*, pl. 54. Remon is more elusive. His trade through the port of Sydney suggests that he had a fishing station somewhere in eastern Cape Breton, while the shipment of fishing supplies to Chaleur Bay suggests a further station in Gaspé. Remon disappears from the Shipping Returns after 1797. The Robin connection is treated in Lee, *Robins*.

9 Shipping Returns.

10 For the trade of these three merchants, see Shipping Returns; see also *DCB*, vol. 5, *1801 to 1820*, for Stout, and *DCB*, vol. 6, *1821 to 1835*, for Kavanagh.

11 W. Macarmick to H. Dundas, 6 October 1792, CO/CB/A/10, 125–33 NAC.

12 The planter also appeared in the Newfoundland fishery and the earlier French fishery; see Harris, ed., *HAC*, pls 23, 25, and 26, and Balcom, *Cod*. The extent of trade with the Channel Island merchants is suggested by Fish Bounty Returns. For example, Moses Martell of L'Ardoise, master of the shallop *Three Brothers*, caught and cured 146 quintals of dry merchantable codfish during the season of 1830 "and

placed that the same was sold to John Janvrin Esquire and placed to the credit of Moses Martell & Co. Act. in his books" (RG 31/111/3 PANS).

13 I. Brookes, "Physical Geography of the Atlantic Provinces," 24–6, and Knight, *Shore and Deep Sea Fisheries of Nova Scotia.*

14 Knight, *Shore,* 39.

15 Shipping Returns; Parker, *Cape Breton Ships and Men.*

16 For the following description of cod fishing and curing, see Chiasson, *Chéticamp,* 297; Joncas, *The Fisheries of Canada;* and Knight, *Shore,* 87–9.

17 E. Orange to F. Briard, 15 June 1861, CRC Letterbooks, MG 23/G 111/18 vol. 250 NAC.

18 For the following, see Knight, *Shore,* 27–35, 45–57, and Shipping Returns.

19 Harris, ed., *HAC,* pls 21–6.

20 J. Miller to the Duke of Portland, 31 October 1794, CO/CB/A/12, 250 NAC.

21 *Guernsey and Jersey Magazine,* 309.

22 *Guernsey and Jersey Magazine,* 311, and Knight, *Shore,* 87–9.

23 This is an important qualification of Harris's argument that the work-forces were "bound to a rigid, specialized work discipline in what were virtual unmechanized seasonal factories" (Harris, ed., *HAC,* 48).

24 The classic discussion of pre-industrial work patterns is E.P. Thompson, "Time, Work Discipline and Industrial Capitalism."

25 For the landholdings of the Channel Island firms, see Nova Scotia Department of Lands and Forests, Crown Land Index Sheets, 111–12, 118–20.

26 A good description of a large fishing station is in Knight, *Shore,* 87.

27 The fishermen's cabins and gardens are noted in T. Crawley to W. Bruce, 13 January 1817, CO/CB/A/38, 215 NAC, and described in Bishop Plessis's diary, quoted in A.A. Johnston, *A History of the Catholic Church in Eastern Nova Scotia,* vol. 1, 286.

28 Father Gaulin, missionary to Arichat in 1819, quoted in A.A. Johnston, *History,* vol. 1, 422.

29 Chiasson, *Chéticamp,* 29.

30 For the early history of the coal mines, see Brown, *The Coal Fields and Coal Trade of the Island of Cape Breton,* and Martell, "Early Coal Mining in Nova Scotia." The geographical development of the coalfield is dealt with in Millward, "A Model of Coalfield Development."

31 Brown, *Coal,* 55.

32 Miller to Portland, 249.

33 Miller to Portland, 257.

34 Brown, *Coal,* 51–2.

35 "Memorial of William Campbell, leasee of H.M. Coal Mines, to General Despard," 17 January 1803, CO/CB/A/24, pt 2, 277–87 NAC; and "Pay List of persons employed at His Majesty's Coal Mines, Cape Breton, for One Month from 25th September to 24th October 1807, both days inclusive," RG 21/A/1/141 PANS.

36 Miller to Portland, 277.

37 "Pay List."

38 "Pay List."

39 Miller to Portland, 252.

40 Brown, *History*, 53–4.

41 W. Campbell to Brig.-Gen. N. Nepean, 24 January 1808, CO/CB/A/29 NAC.

42 Miller to Portland, 250.

43 Miller to Portland, 250–1, 253.

44 "Pay List."

45 Miller to Portland, 253.

46 Miller to Portland, 254.

47 For a good summary of staple theory and spread effects, see McCusker and Menard, *British America*, 17–32, and Watkins, "Staple Theory." For an application of staple theory to the cod fishery, see Ommer, *From Outpost to Outport*.

48 Shipping Returns. This figure does not include multiple clearances by the same vessel.

49 Shipping Returns.

50 Nominal census of Arichat, Little Arichat, Upper Arichat, Barrachois, Petit-de-Grat, D'Escousse, Grand Digue, River Bourgeois, St Peters, and L'Ardoise, 1811, RG 1/333/84–98 PANS.

51 The importance of the carrying trade to colonial economies is stressed in McCusker and Menard, *British America*, 71–88. For shipbuilding in Cape Breton, see Parker, *Ships and Men*, a work that could have been more useful if it had included reference notes. On the importance of shipping and shipbuilding for the Maritime economy, see Sager and Panting, *Maritime Capital*.

52 Shipping Returns.

53 "A Sketch of Memorandums taken from Observations made in Exploring the Island of Cape Breton," Anon., 1804, CO/CB/A/37, 132, 136, 145, 147 NAC.

54 Morgan, "The Loyalists of Cape Breton" and "Orphan Outpost"; see also Wynn, "Region."

55 Brown, *History*, 424.

56 Estimated from census return of 1801.

57 For the following physical description, see Cann et al., *Soil Survey of Cape Breton Island Nova Scotia*, and I. Brookes, "Physical Geography."

58 Loucks, "A Forest Classification for the Maritime Provinces," and Bentley and Smith, "The Forests of Cape Breton in the Seventeenth and Eighteenth Centuries."

59 "Sketch," 145–6.

60 Cann et al., *Soil Survey*, 11–13.

61 Shipping Returns.

62 Wynn, "Region," 320.

63 General Nepean to Lord Liverpool, 8 February 1811, CO/CB/A/32, 9 NAC.

64 General Swayne to Lord Bathurst, 1 March 1814, CO/CB/A/35, 5 NAC.

65 "Sketch," 133.

66 General Swayne to Lord Bathurst, 26 July 1814, CO/CB/A/35, 20–1 NAC.

67 Estimated from the nominal census of Cape Breton, 1811, RG 1/333/ 84–98 PANS.

68 "Plan of Sydney River, 5 September 1788," H3/240/Sydney and Sydney River/1788 NAC.

69 McNabb, *Old Sydney Town*, and Nova Scotia Museum, *Cossit House*.

70 J. Miller to the Duke of Portland, 4 December 1794, CO/CB/A/12, 304 NAC.

71 Morgan, "Loyalists," and Jackson, "Some of North Sydney's Loyalists."

72 Morgan, "Loyalists" and "Orphan Outpost."

73 J. Miller to J. King, 17 July 1795, CO/CB/A/13, 131 NAC.

74 "Map of the Town of Sydney, 10 July 1795," H3/240/Sydney/1795 NAC.

75 Miller to King, 133, and W. Smith, "State of the Island of Cape Breton, from the year 1784 to the present time," MG 1/1848/8, 12 PANS.

76 The governor's residence is depicted by John Hames in his "View of Sydney in the Island of Cape Breton," 1799, C-24939 NAC. It is likely that the building is exaggerated in size.

77 Duffus et al., *Thy Dwellings Fair*, 71–4.

78 "A Diary of someone from Sydney, Cape Breton in 1802," RG 21/A/ 40/7 PANS.

79 "Diary."

80 Morgan, "Loyalists."

81 "Letter written by a soldier newly arrived from England, 5 August 1789," MG 23/J11 NAC.

CHAPTER TWO

1 The standard accounts of British emigration to Canada are Cowan, *British Emigration to British North America*, and N. MacDonald, *Canada,*

1763–1841 Immigration and Settlement. Also useful is H.J.M. Johnston, *British Emigration Policy 1815–1830.* For discussion of the conservative nature of emigration and the desire for an "independence" in the New World, see Erickson, *Invisible Immigrants,* and Harris et al., "The Settlement of Mono Township."

2 Gray, *The Highland Economy 1750–1850*; Hunter, *The Making of the Crofting Community*; Richards, *A History of the Highland Clearances: Agrarian Transformation and the Evictions 1746–1886* and *A History of the Highland Clearances: Emigration, Protest, Reasons*; and Youngson, *After the Forty-Five.*

3 Bumsted, *The People's Clearance*; Cameron, "The Role of Shipping from Scottish Ports in Emigration to the Canadas, 1815–1855"; Campbell and MacLean, *Beyond the Atlantic Roar*; Gentilcore, "The Agricultural Background of Settlement in Eastern Nova Scotia"; Goldring, "Lewis and the Hudson's Bay Company in the Nineteenth Century"; Harvey, "Scottish Immigration to Cape Breton"; Kincaid, "Scottish Immigration to Cape Breton, 1758–1838"; D. MacKay, *Scotland Farewell*; M. Mackay, "Poets and Pioneers" and "Nineteenth Century Tiree Emigrant Communities in Ontario"; McLean, "'In the new land a new Glengarry,'" "Peopling Glengarry County," and "Achd an Rhigh"; Ommer, "Highland Scots Migration to Southwestern Newfoundland"; and Wynn, "A Share of the Necessaries of Life."

4 It is impossible to know exactly how many Highlanders arrived in Cape Breton, but given the rapid rise in population, the estimate of 20,000 in Harvey, "Scottish Immigration," must be close.

5 It is impossible to be completely certain on this point, but a reading of the evidence published in *Report of the Select Committee on Emigration from the United Kingdom,* 1826, and *Report of the Select Committee on the Condition of the Population of the Highlands and Islands of Scotland,* 1841, suggests that Prince Edward Island and Cape Breton were the most popular destinations in the early nineteenth century. Given the earlier Scottish settlement on Prince Edward Island and the problems of land tenure in that colony, it is likely that most Highland emigrants in the 1820s and 1830s were heading for Cape Breton.

6 *Census of Canada 1870–1871.* The ethnic composition was Scots 66 percent, Acadians 14 percent, Irish 9 percent, and English (Loyalists) 8 percent.

7 For example, see General Ainslie to Lord Bathurst, 25 November 1816, CO 217/134 NAC, and Sir James Kempt to Wilmot Horton, 14 September 1826, CO 217/146 NAC.

8 The survey of gravestones was conducted by Sandra Ferguson and her manuscript is deposited in the Beaton Institute. The genealogies are collected in MacDougall, *History of Inverness County.*

9 Gailey, "The Evolution of Highland Rural Settlement with Particular Reference to Argyllshire"; Gray, *Highland Economy*, 3–54; and Skene, *Celtic Scotland: A History of Ancient Alban*, 368–94.

10 Gray, *Highland Economy*, 66–75; and Youngson, *Forty-Five*.

11 Hunter, *Crofting Community*. The actual laying out of the crofting townships is best described in Caird, "Land Use in the Uists Since 1800."

12 Crawford, "Feannagan Taomaidh (Lazy Beds)."

13 Grant, *Highland Folk Ways*, 96.

14 Gray, *Highland Economy*, 207–8, and Salaman, *The History and Social Influence of the Potato*, 346–85.

15 D. Macdonald, *Lewis*, 74.

16 J. MacDonald, *General View of the Agriculture of the Hebrides*, 152.

17 *Evidence Taken by Her Majesty's Commissioners of Inquiry into the Condition of the Crofters and Cottars in the Highlands and Islands of Scotland*, vol. 1, 651.

18 *Crofters and Cottars*, vol. 1, 660; vol. 2, 2079.

19 D. Shaw to A. Hunter, 25 February 1827, GD 201/4/97 SRO.

20 Marshall, *General View of the Agriculture of the Central Highlands of Scotland*, 37–8, and Sinclair, *General View of the Agriculture of the Northern Counties and Islands of Scotland*, 114. In the islands of Tiree and Coll, it was reported that "crofters have no winter pasture, and the utmost they can often do is keep their cows from starving, during, the winter and the spring" (*New Statistical Account of Scotland*, vol. 7, 213).

21 Crawford, "Kelp Burning."

22 Gittens, "Soapmaking in Britain, 1824–1851."

23 J. MacDonald, *General View*, 120.

24 Gray, *Highland Economy*, 197–8.

25 Shaw to Hunter.

26 Shaw to Hunter.

27 South Uist in the *New Statistical Account of Scotland*, vol. 14, 189, and Fenton, *Scottish Country Life*, 159–80.

28 Grant, *Folk Ways*, 295.

29 Fenton, *The Island Blackhouse*; and D. Macdonald, *Lewis*, 57–62.

30 Shaw to Hunter.

31 J. MacDonald, *General View*, 119; see also Devine, "Temporary Migration and the Scottish Highlands in the Nineteenth Century" and "Highland Migration to Lowland Scotland, 1760–1860," and Howatson, "The Scottish Hairst and Seasonal Labour 1600–1870."

32 J. MacDonald reported that "many hundreds of families or individuals ... are tenants at will, without leases, without definite boundaries of landed possessions, without anything, excepting debts, which they call their own; and, alas! without any prospect before them but beggary and the grave" (*General View*, 111).

33 Personal communication to author from Dr Margaret Mackay, School of Scottish Studies, University of Edinburgh. Mackay deduces this from her recent important research on the demography of the island of Tiree in the late nineteenth and twentieth centuries.

34 *New Statistical Account of Scotland*, vol. 14, 173.

35 Buchanan, *Travels in the Western Hebrides: From 1782 to 1790*, 52–3.

36 Bumsted, "Highland Emigration to the Island of St. John and the Scottish Catholic Church, 1769–1774."

37 Hunter, "The Emergence of the Crofting Community," 99.

38 Quotations from Hunter, *Crofting Community*, 20, 23.

39 Bumsted, *People's Clearance*, Appendix A, Table 2.

40 Evidence of R.J. Uniacke published in *Report of the Select Committee on Emigration*, 38.

41 General Despard to J. Sullivan, 10 September 1802, CO/Cape Breton A Papers/23/127 NAC.

42 Hunter, *Crofting Community*, 24–5.

43 Bumsted, *People's Clearance*, Appendix A, Table 2.

44 Gittins, "Soapmaking," 33, and Hunter, *Crofting Community*, 34–5.

45 Gray, *Highland Economy*, 182.

46 Factor's Report, 21 April 1823, GD 201/1/352 SRO.

47 "Particulars of the Estate of Clan Ranald, 1836 and 1837," GD 201/5/1235/16–17 SRO.

48 Quotation from Hunter, *Crofting Community*, 37.

49 Although Bumsted, in *The People's Clearance*, dates the voluntary clearances from 1770 to 1815, the evidence suggests that the "people's clearance" extended into the mid-1820s, when the collapse of the kelp industry led to the landlord-initiated clearances.

50 "A Statement relative to the treatment received by the Passengers in the Ship William Tell and Brig Hope from Greenock to this Island," enclosed in General Ainslie to Lord Bathurst, 1 October 1817, CO 217/135 NAC.

51 Evidence of Alexander Hunter published in *Report of the Select Committee on Emigration*, 288; J. Adam to Lord Seaforth, 31 March 1827, GD 46/17/72 SRO; and Shaw to Hunter.

52 Hunter, *Crofting Community*, 35.

53 Factor's Report, 19 November 1827, GD 201/1/338 SRO.

54 Gray, *Highland Economy*, 158.

55 R. Brown to R. Swinton, 16 February 1827, GD 201/5/1228/3 SRO.

56 Factor's Report, 19 November 1827, GD 201/1/338 SRO.

57 "Note of Leases on Clan Ranald's Estate," 29 January 1833, GD 201/5/1217/70 SRO; "Particulars of the Estate of Clan Ranald"; and Caird, "Land Use," 515.

58 Hunter, *Crofting Community*, 45–7, and Caird, "The Isle of Harris."

59 Quotation from Hunter, *Crofting Community*, 47.

60 Caird, "Land Use," 515.
61 Factor's Report, 19 November 1827, GD 201/1/338 SRO, and Factor's Report, 8 May 1827, GD 201/1/354 SRO.
62 *Acadian Recorder*, 23 July 1831.
63 Evidence of A. Hunter published in *Report of the Select Committee on Emigration*, 287–9.
64 Hunter, *Crofting Community*, 46.
65 Hunter, *Crofting Community*, 47.
66 "A Return of Emigrants arrived in the Island of Cape Breton for the years 1821 to the present time," enclosed in Sir Peregrine Maitland to Viscount Goderich, 24 June 1831, CO 217/152 NAC.
67 This passenger list, the only one that appears to have survived for Cape Breton, is reprinted in MacDougall, *History of Inverness*, 126–31.
68 MacGregor, *Observations on Emigration to British America*, 41.
69 Knoydart is in the parish of Glenelg. The quotation is in Fraser-Mackintosh, ed., *Letters of Two Centuries chiefly connected with Inverness and the Highlands, from 1616 to 1815*, 311–12.
70 D. Campbell to H. McKay, 7 October 1830, reprinted in the *Stornoway Gazette*, 30 September 1972; also filed in MG 100/115/33 PANS. For a description of the severely congested township of Tong in the 1820s, see Hunter, *Crofting Community*, 45.
71 Shaw to Hunter.
72 See petition of Mary McIsaac, 9 February 1858, RG 5/P/87/102 PANS.
73 *Novascotian*, 11 October 1832.
74 Sir Colin Campbell to Lord Glenelg, 18 July 1836, CO 217/161 NAC, and "Report of Commissioners of H.M. Council," enclosed in Sir James Kempt to W. Huskisson, 25 November 1827, CO 217/147 NAC.
75 Sir Peregrine Maitland to Viscount Goderich, 16 February 1832, CO 217/147 NAC.
76 Quoted in Martell, *Immigration to and Emigration from Nova Scotia 1815–1838*, 27.
77 *Journals of the House of Assembly of Nova Scotia*, 1843, 395.
78 Petition, 27 February 1844, RG 5/P/82 PANS.
79 H.J.M. Johnston's *British Emigration Policy* is subtitled 'Shovelling out Paupers.'
80 Haliburton, *An Historical and Statistical Account of Nova Scotia*, 260.

CHAPTER THREE

1 Census return for 1828 enclosed in Sir James Kempt to W. Huskisson, 12 May 1828, CO 217/148 NAC. For the 1830 return, see PANS Report 1966, Appendix B, 27–9; for the 1838 return, RG 1/449 PANS; and for the 1851 return, RG 1/453 PANS.

2 The following discussion of settlement is based on the land-grant maps. These maps were created using the records of the Crown Lands Office, 1738–1962, RG 20/A/3 PANS, and Crown Land Index Sheets 108–12, 114–33, and 135–40 (Nova Scotia Department of Lands and Forests). Every grant recorded between 1786 and 1850 was located on the index sheets and mapped. Of course, not every grant was taken up and many grants were made out years after settlement. Nevertheless, the long period covered by each map probably catches many of the settlers who delayed taking out a grant.

3 "Extracts from H.M. General Instructions to the Governors of Nova Scotia, 1789," CO/CB/A/35, 5 NAC.

4 General Swayne to Lord Bathurst, 26 July 1814, CO/CB/A/35, 20–1 NAC.

5 General Nepean to Lord Liverpool, 8 February 1811, CO/CB/A/32, 9 NAC.

6 H.J.M. Johnston, *British Emigration Policy.*

7 Acknowledgment of the new instructions is contained in General Ainslie to Lord Bathurst, 13 October 1818, CO/CB/A/39, 121–3 NAC.

8 Instructions for Captain Crawley, surveyor general of Cape Breton, 1820, CO 217/138 NAC. See also "Memoranda relative to the Grants of Crown Lands in the Province of Nova Scotia during the last twenty years," 14 November 1825, CO 217/145 NAC.

9 Although purchasers of Crown land were expected to pay an annual quit-rent, the cost of collection was too expensive and these rents were never collected. They were eventually abolished in 1834 after the Nova Scotia House of Assembly agreed to commute them for an annual sum of £2,000 sterling to support the Civil List. See the communication from Sir Colin Campbell, 29 December 1834, CO 217/156 NAC. For a table of fees for the Surveyor General's Office, see CO/CB/A/39, 309 NAC.

10 Return of the titles of land registered in Cape Breton, 1821, printed in Haliburton, *Historical and Statistical,* 304.

11 Bittermann, "Middle River," 100–10, and "The Hierarchy of the Soil."

12 Sir James Kempt to Lord Bathurst, 27 April 1827, CO 217/147 NAC. For the background of this change in policy, see Riddell, "A Study in the Land Policy of the Colonial Office, 1763–1855."

13 Evidence of Sir Rupert George, secretary of the Province of Nova Scotia, to Lord Durham's Commission, *Parliamentary Papers,* 1839, vol. 17, 132–3.

14 Sir Peregrine Maitland to Viscount Goderich, 12 August 1831, CO 217/152 NAC.

15 The number of sales are recorded in the annual reports of the Crown Lands Office printed in the *Journals of the House of Assembly of Nova*

Scotia. See also John Morris, commissioner of Crown lands, to Sir Rupert George, 1 April 1837, CO 217/163 NAC.

16 "For the information of emigrants with capital intending to settle on land," 1841, RG 1/384 PANS.

17 Average values of improved dyke land are contained in the census of 1851 (RG 1/453 PANS).

18 Bittermann, "Middle River," 114.

19 H.W. Crawley to Sir Rupert George, 5 April 1837, RG 20/C/54 PANS.

20 H.W. Crawley to Sir Rupert George, 8 May 1844, RG 20/C/56 PANS.

21 H.W. Crawley to Crown Lands Office, 17 February 1844, RG 20/C/56 PANS.

22 H.W. Crawley to Sir Rupert George, 22 January 1844, RG 20/C/56 PANS. Of course, the problem of controlling access to Crown land was not unique to Cape Breton; for similar problems in a neighbouring colony, see Wynn, "Administration in Adversity."

23 D.B. McNab to H.W. Crawley, 28 September 1840, RG 20/C/55 PANS.

24 D.B. McNab to W.A. Hendry, 30 January 1854, RG 20/C/58 PANS.

25 H.W. Crawley, 27 October 1841, CO 217/178 NAC.

26 "Petition of Samuel Campbell residing at the Kempt Road County of Richmond Cape Breton to Sir Colin Campbell," 4 June 1837, RG 5/ GP/1/85 PANS.

27 "James Hawley JP and other inhabitants on behalf of John McPherson to H.W. Crawley," 13 July 1836, RG 20/C/54 PANS. The "moral economy" of the poor is discussed in E.P. Thompson, "The Moral Economy of the English Crowd in the Eighteenth Century."

28 *Journals of the House of Assembly of Nova Scotia,* 1843, Appendix 12.

29 For the struggle between the legislature and the Colonial Office, see the various despatches in *Journals of the House of Assembly of Nova Scotia,* 1841, Appendix 13.

30 *Journals of the House of Assembly of Nova Scotia,* 1842, Appendix 16.

31 *Journals of the House of Assembly of Nova Scotia,* 1843, Appendix 12.

32 Harvey, "The Civil List and Responsible Government in Nova Scotia," and MacNutt, *The Atlantic Provinces,* 228–9.

33 "Memoranda relative to the Grants of Crown Lands."

34 H.W. Crawley to Sir Rupert George, 28 February 1840, RG 20/C/55 PANS.

35 These figures are drawn from the list of prices "For the information of emigrants with capital intending to settle on land," 1841, RG 1/384 PANS. For comparison, see Ankli and Duncan, "Farm Making Costs in Early Ontario," and Wynn, *Timber Colony,* 80.

36 MacGregor, *British America,* 57.

37 D. Campbell to H. Mckay, 7 October 1830, reprinted in the *Stornoway Gazette,* 30 September 1972; also filed in MG 100/115/33 PANS.

38 "For the information of emigrants."

39 MacGregor, *British America*, 57.

40 In evidence to the Durham Commission, James McKenzie reckoned that a settler in Cape Breton needed "about £50, exclusive of the land," to start a farm (*Parliamentary Papers*, 1839, vol. 17, 144). Excluding the cost of land and labour, Ankli and Duncan estimated that £50 was needed to establish a farm in Ontario, while Wynn reckoned that £30 to £40 was required in New Brunswick. See Ankli and Duncan, "Farm Making," 48, and Wynn, *Timber Colony*, 80.

41 General Ainslie to Lord Bathurst, 29 September 1818, co 217/136, 120 nac, and Bouchette, *The British Dominions in North America*, vol. 2, 86. See also Haliburton, *Historical and Statistical*, 236–7, and R. Elmsley, "History of Baddeck," mg 1/1840/7 pans.

42 Shipping Intelligence column, *Newfoundlander*, 1828–39.

43 H.W. Crawley to Sir Rupert George, 28 February 1837, rg 20/c/54 pans.

44 M. McNeil to J. Morris, 16 October 1851, rg 20/c/58 pans.

45 D.B McNab to W.A. Hendry, March 1854, rg 20/c/58 pans.

46 Moorsom, *Letters from Nova Scotia*, 51–2. For an insightful discussion of the close relationship between agriculture and lumbering in a neighbouring colony, see Wynn, "'Deplorably Dark and Demoralized Lumberers'?"

47 *Parliamentary Papers*, 1843, vol. 34, 100, 102. See also "The information for emigrants of the labouring class," 1841, rg 1/384 pans, and Bittermann, "Hierarchy of the Soil."

48 The American mackerel fishery in the gulf expanded rapidly from the early 1830s and often employed labour from Nova Scotia; see Innis, *Cod Fisheries*, 323–8.

49 Evidence of Richard Brown, manager of Sydney Mines, to Lord Durham's Commission, *Parliamentary Papers*, 1839, vol. 17, 141.

50 Petition of Michael Doyle to General Swayne, 4 September 1815, rg 20/b/5/1128 pans, and petition of James Fitzgerald to General Ainslie, 1819, rg 20/b/2124 pans.

51 Mannion, "The Waterford Merchants and the Irish-Newfoundland Provisions Trade, 1770–1820."

52 Shipping Returns for Arichat and Sydney, 1814, co 221/35, 83–4, 88–90 nac.

53 The accuracy of the Blue Book returns of agricultural exports may be questioned. For example, the agricultural societies' returns of exports to Newfoundland provide a check on the Blue Book figures and reveal some discrepancies. In 1844, the Blue Books recorded the export of 2,111 cattle and 1,781 sheep; that year, the Port Hood, Margaree, and Broad Cove agricultural societies recorded the export of 1,650

cattle. The Port Hood society also estimated that cattle equivalent to a third of its exports were exported via the Gut of Canso and Bras d'Or Lake. In total, the agricultural societies estimated that 1,940 cattle were exported to Newfoundland. But this total excludes exports from Sydney (no data), an export outlet for several hundred cattle. Overall, the Blue Book figure of 2,111 cattle was probably reasonably accurate. The figure for sheep exports, however, was an underestimate. The extant returns from the agricultural societies show that 2,200 sheep were exported. When the estimate for the Canso and Bras d'Or trade is included, the total becomes 2,566 – considerably more than the Blue Book total of 1,781. In this light, the Blue Book figures must be considered rough approximations (but not completely inaccurate) of the Island's agricultural exports. See annual report of the Broad Cove Agricultural Society, 17 February 1845; annual report of the Margaree Agricultural Society, 24 January 1845; and annual report of the Port Hood Agricultural Society, 15 January 1845, RG 8/13/22 PANS.

54 The Antigonish cattle trade is discussed in A.R. MacNeil, "A Reconsideration of the State of Agriculture in Eastern Nova Scotia, 1791–1861," 124–9. The Prince Edward Island cattle trade is mentioned in Clark, *Three Centuries and the Island*, 69, but a more detailed view is available in the Shipping Intelligence column of the *Newfoundlander*, 1828–39. Imports from Prince Edward Island appear to have been as important as those from Antigonish and Cape Breton.

55 Stewart & Co., St John's, to James Wilson, merchant at Port Hawkesbury, 17 August 1847, Documents, 1814–29, MG 1/964–76 PANS.

56 Stewart & Co. to Wilson.

57 The dominance of butter imports from northern Europe in the Newfoundland market is clearly revealed in the Shipping Intelligence column of the *Newfoundlander*. In 1839, for example, the *Lord Ravensworth* carried 1,800 barrels of flour, 90 barrels of beef, 600 bags of bread, 125 barrels of oatmeal, 50 barrels of peas, and 750 firkins of butter from Hamburg to St John's. The cargo of butter was equivalent to 53 percent of all recorded butter imports from Cape Breton in 1839. The *Lord Ravensworth* was just one of several vessels bringing butter, flour, and beef from northern Europe to Newfoundland that year. Although prices for butter were infrequently recorded in the *Newfoundlander*, the few price tables in the newspaper during the late 1830s all show that Copenhagen and Hamburg butter was cheaper than Nova Scotian butter. On 19 December 1839, for example, the *Newfoundlander* recorded the price of Copenhagen and Hamburg butter as 9d. to 10d. per pound, and Nova Scotian butter as 10d. to 11d. per pound. The quality of Cape Breton butter was adversely commented upon in the *Journals of the House of Assembly of Nova Scotia*,

1888, Appendix 8. It is unlikely that the quality of the butter was better earlier in the century.

58 Clark, *Three Centuries*, 69. In 1832, the total value of commodity exports from Prince Edward Island was £31,739. Oats and potatoes comprised more than a quarter of this total. Much of this produce was shipped to Newfoundland. According to the Shipping Intelligence column in the *Newfoundlander*, the thousands of bushels of oats and potatoes from Prince Edward Island completely dwarfed the few hundred bushels from Cape Breton, suggesting that Cape Breton farmers found it difficult to compete.

59 Shipping Returns.

60 *Journals of the House of Assembly of Nova Scotia*, 1848, Appendix 39; 1849, Appendix 100.

61 Annual Nova Scotia Blue Books, 1846–48, RG 2/47 PANS.

62 Annual Nova Scotia Blue Books, 1846–48.

63 Annual report of the Richmond Agricultural Society, 31 December 1842, RG 8/13/22 PANS.

64 Bittermann considers "mixed" farming to be an inappropriate description of agriculture in Middle River because of the concentration on livestock raising (Bittermann, "Middle River," 50; Bittermann, "Hierarchy of the Soil," 36). Yet the combination of arable and pastoral farming in Cape Breton was consistent with the traditional mixed farm and was much different from the specialized sheep farms of Highland Scotland or the cattle ranches of the American West. For good overviews of mid-century Nova Scotian agriculture, see MacKinnon and Wynn, "Nova Scotian Agriculture in the 'Golden Age'"; and J.L. Martin, *The Ross Farm Story*. For the development of agriculture in a comparable region, see Danhof, *Change in Agriculture*.

65 The only available data on agricultural improvements at mid-century are average figures for census subdistricts that include both front- and backland.

66 Nominal census of Cape Breton Island, 1811, RG 1/333/84–98 PANS.

67 Martell, "From Central Board to Secretary of Agriculture, 1826–1885"; and Wynn, "Exciting a Spirit of Emulation among the 'Plodholes.'"

68 E. Sutherland, secretary of the Cape Breton Agricultural Society, to T. Smith, 17 May 1841, RG 8/13/22 PANS.

69 Annual report of the Broad Cove Agricultural Society, 17 January 1845.

70 *Journals of the House of Assembly of Nova Scotia*, 1888, Appendix 8.

71 For the importance of the hay crop in a comparable region, see Barron and Bridges, "Making Hay in Northern New England." Also useful is Danhof, "Gathering the Grass."

72 DesBarres, "A Description of the Island of Cape Breton in North America," 74, 80. A typical ox of 600–700 pounds consumed about one ton of hay and a substantial amount of straw during the winter. MacGregor, *British America*, vol. 1, 524.

73 *Journals of the House of Assembly of Nova Scotia*, 1850, Appendix 45.

74 Census of 1851, RG 1/453 PANS; annual report of the Baddeck United Agricultural Society, 2 April 1855, RG 8/13/22 PANS.

75 Martell, "The Achievements of Agricola and the Agricultural Societies, 1818–1825."

76 J. Doyle, secretary of the Mabou Agricultural Society, to J. Young, 27 December 1823, RG 8/7/143 PANS.

77 R. Smith to R.I. Cochran, 5 October 1833, MG 14/19/D8 (a) BI, and D.B. McNab to T. Smith, 16 April 1844, RG 8/13/22 PANS.

78 R. MacDonald, secretary of the Mabou Agricultural Society, wrote to John Young on 21 December 1821, requesting seed for clover, timothy, and ray grass, parsnips, carrots, beets, cabbage, and onions (RG 8/7/132 PANS). A. Taylor, president of the Baddeck United Agricultural Society, made a similar request, 14 April 1848 (RG 8/13/22 PANS).

79 *Journals of the House of Assembly of Nova Scotia*, 1844, Appendix 72.

80 "Scheme of Agricultural Prizes for the year 1822 selected by the Agricultural Society of Sydney, Cape Breton," RG 8/7/136 PANS, and H.W. Crawley to J. Young, 24 April 1824, RG 8/7/158 PANS.

81 H. Blanchard to T. Smith, 15 January 1845, RG 8/13/22 PANS.

82 Annual report of the Broad Cove Agricultural Society, 2 March 1846, 17 February 1845, RG 8/13/22 PANS.

83 "An account of Implements, Stock, Seeds, etc. Imported and Sold by the Inverness Agricultural Society in the Year 1842," RG 8/13/22 PANS; annual report of the Margaree Agricultural Society, 1846, RG 8/13/22 PANS; and Martell, "From Central Board."

84 Annual report of the Margaree Agricultural Society, 1846, RG 8/13/22 PANS.

85 Danhof, *Change in Agriculture*, 189, and "The Tools and Implements of Agriculture," 89.

86 Annual report of the Port Hood Agricultural Society, 5 February 1845, RG 8/13/22 PANS, and Danhof, "Gathering the Grass" and *Change in Agriculture*, 218–21.

87 Without the use of a horse-drawn reaper, a farmer could probably harvest about 12 acres of grain or grass. See Henretta, *The Evolution of American Society, 1700–1815*, 15–18.

88 Haliburton, *Historical and Statistical*, vol. 1, 259.

89 Ennals and Holdsworth, "Vernacular Architecture and the Cultural Landscape of the Maritime Provinces – A Reconnaisance"; Ennals, "The Yankee Origins of Bluenose Vernacular Architecture"; and my own observations in Cape Breton.

90 Ennals, "Nineteenth-Century Barns in Southern Ontario," and my own observations.

91 Annual Nova Scotia Blue Books, 1843.

92 MacDonell, *The Emigrant Experience*, 57–103; D. Campbell to H. Mckay, 7 October 1830, MG 100/115/33 PANS; and D. McNeil to W. McNeil, 25 June 1849, GD 403/27/2 SRO.

93 Census of 1851, RG 1/453 PANS. Although the 1851 census subdistricts are not especially helpful for elucidating frontland agricultural production because the aggregate figures include backland, they are better for backland production. There were several census subdistricts that were coincident with backland, and thus we can be reasonably confident that the production figures accurately reflect the backland economy.

94 Petition, 12 February 1847, RG 5/P/83/109 PANS. A similar petition from settlers on the front and rear of St Patricks Channel, Little Narrows, also spoke of the "well known fact that the inland settlements about the Bras d'or Lakes are no grain country; the potatoes are almost all they have to live upon throughout the year" (25 January 1847, RG 5/P/83/67 PANS).

95 D.B. McNab to T. Smith.

96 Farm accounts of John B. Moore, Documents, 1848–99, MG 1/Biography PANS. See also Bittermann, "Hierarchy of the Soil." For a general discussion of occupational pluralism in the Maritimes, see McCann, "'Living a double life.'"

97 Ledger of John McKay & Co., MG 3/8 PANS.

98 D.B. McNab to J.B. Uniacke, 3 January 1857; reprinted in the *Journals of the House of Assembly of Nova Scotia*, 1857, Appendix 71.

99 Sir Peregrine Maitland to Viscount Goderich, 14 November 1831, CO 217/152 NAC.

100 Gesner, *The Industrial Resources of Nova Scotia*, 310, and MacGregor, *Historical and Descriptive Sketches of the Maritime Colonies of British North America*, 117.

101 Morison, "The Early Scotch Settlers," MG 1/706/40 PANS.

102 Extract of a letter written by Rev. John Stewart quoted in a "Memorial Regarding the Religious State of the Island of Cape Breton, respectfully addressed by the Glasgow North American Colonial Society, to the Right Honorable the Secretary of State for the British Colonies," 1835, CO 217/159 NAC, and Stanley, *The Well-Watered Garden*, 82.

103 Petition, 26 January 1833, RG 5/P/80/67 PANS.

104 *Journals of the House of Assembly of Nova Scotia*, 1834–35, 715.

105 Petition, 5 December 1836, RG 5/P/18/23 PANS.

106 C.R. Ward et al. to Sir Rupert George, 4 April 1837, MG 6/2/1 PANS, and Stanley, *Well-Watered Garden*, 100.

107 Campbell to Mckay, and Sir James Kempt to W. Huskisson, 2 May 1828, CO 217/148 NAC.

108 Bittermann, "Middle River," 114, 117, and "Hierarchy of the Soil," 44–5.

109 Petition of John Mathewson, William Corbet, David Corbet, Robert McCoy, and Farquhar Mathewson, RG 20/B/1774 PANS. For family settlement in Cape Breton, see Ommer, "Highland Scots Migration to Southwestern Newfoundland" and "Primitive Accumulation and the Scottish Clann in the Old World and the New," and Molloy, "'No Inclination to Mix with Strangers.'" For the larger context, see Wynn, "Ethnic Migrations and Atlantic Canada."

110 Campbell to Mckay.

111 Nominal census of Cape Breton Island, 1818, RG 1/333/84–98 PANS.

112 Campbell and MacLean, *Atlantic Roar*, 169–92; Dunn, *Highland Settler*, 34–73, 136–49; J.N. MacNeil, *Tales until Dawn*; Chapman, ed., *Johnson's Journey to the Western Islands of Scotland and Boswell's Journal of a Tour to the Hebrides with Samuel Johnson, L.L.D.*, 86–7.

113 Quoted in Toward, "The Influence of Scottish Clergy on early Education in Cape Breton," 158.

114 Quoted in Stanley, *Well-Watered Garden*, 35.

115 Stanley, *Well-Watered Garden*, 59.

116 Stanley, *Well-Watered Garden*.

117 Stanley, *Well-Watered Garden*, 122.

118 Martell, "Achievements of Agricola" and "From Central Board."

119 Annual report of the Richmond Agricultural Society, 31 December 1841, RG 8/13/22 PANS.

120 Census of 1851, RG 1/453 PANS.

121 Petition, 29 February 1824, RG 5/P/120/55 PANS.

122 Doyle to Young.

123 J. Bull to J. Young, 8 January 1824, RG 8/7/156 PANS.

124 Martell, "Achievements of Agricola."

125 *Journals of the House of Assembly of Nova Scotia*, 1848, Appendix 86; 1852, Appendix 18; 1853, Appendices 11, 12, 62.

126 Census of 1851, RG 1/453 PANS.

127 Bittermann, "Middle River," 137.

128 Petition of Angus McDonald to House of Assembly, 1854, RG 5/P/54/21 PANS.

129 Elmsley, "Baddeck," and MacDougall, *History of Inverness*, 31–2.

130 Bittermann, "Middle River," 137–8.

131 Haliburton, *Historical and Statistical*, 249.

132 The census subdistricts in the 1851 census are too large to allow the accurate identification of the populations of the small urban centres in Cape Breton. Nevertheless, some estimate can be made. In 1840,

the *Cape Breton Advocate* estimated that the population of Sydney was about 500 people; in the 1860s, John Uniacke reckoned that the town's population was about 700 (Fergusson, ed., *Uniacke's Sketches of Cape Breton, and Other Papers Relating to Cape Breton Island*, 80, 153). If the difference is split, the population of Sydney in 1850 was about 600. The other towns must have had only a few hundred people each.

133 McCallum, *Unequal Beginnings*.

CHAPTER FOUR

1 For the end of the migratory fishery to Newfoundland, see Head, *Newfoundland*, 196–242, and Ryan, *Fish out of Water*, 33–7.

2 Remon & Co. does not appear in the Shipping Returns for Sydney, 1797, CO 221/34 NAC.

3 For a brief history of the firm, see the entry for Isaac LeVesconte in DCB, vol. 10, *1871–1880*, and Dennis, *Cape Breton Over*, 12–14.

4 Petition of Joseph Le Blanc, 2 March 1830, RG 5/P/121/89 PANS, and J. Bailleul, agent for Thoume Moullin & Co., to Creighton & Grassie, 9 March 1836, Joseph Wilson Papers, MG 1/964–76 PANS.

5 Shipping Returns for Arichat, 1814, CO 221/35, 83–9 NAC.

6 Shipping Returns.

7 For the development of the Brazil trade, see Ryan, *Fish out of Water*, 205–25.

8 Bill of lading of the *Shamrock*, DeCarteret & LeVesconte Business Papers, MG 3/1/156 PANS.

9 DeCarteret & LeVesconte to Creighton & Grassie, 22 April 1842, DeCarteret & LeVesconte Business Papers, MG 3/5–9 PANS. Grassie later married Mary DeLisle, and in 1853 he left Halifax to join DeLisle, Janvrin & Co. of London. This firm acted as the London agent for the Janvrin and Robin companies. See R.G. Dun Collection, Canada, vol. 11, 229 BLHU, and Ommer, *From Outpost to Outport*, 50–51, 102–3.

10 DeCarteret & LeVesconte to D. Frazer, 1 April 1842, DeCarteret & LeVesconte Business Papers, MG 3/5–9 PANS.

11 P. & H.N. Paint to DeCarteret & LeVesconte, 16 June 1858, DeCarteret & LeVesconte Papers, MG 1/257/289 PANS, and P. De-Carteret to J. Wilson, 29 April 1840, DeCarteret & LeVesconte Business Papers, MG 3/5–9 PANS.

12 For the agents, see the Letter Book, 1839–1843, DeCarteret & LeVesconte Business Papers, MG 3/5–9 PANS.

13 For ship movements, see the Letter Book, 1839–1843, DeCarteret & LeVesconte Business Papers, and Ommer, *Outpost to Outport*, 68–94.

14 P. DeCarteret to P. LeVesconte, 3 August 1842, DeCarteret & LeVesconte Business Papers, MG 3/5–9 PANS.

15 Thoume Moullin & Co. had two fishing stations in Cape Breton, one at River Bourgeois and the other at Port Hawkesbury. It appears that Joseph Wilson first bought the River Bourgeois establishment and then a year later moved to Port Hawkesbury, where he might have purchased the second station. Both properties were advertised by Creighton & Grassie in the *Novascotian*, 5 November 1835. Information on Wilson's property dealings can be gleaned from J. Bailleul to Creighton & Grassie, 9 March 1836, Joseph Wilson Documents, 1814–1929, MG 1/964–976 PANS.

16 "Invoice Sundries shipped by Wm. Pryor & Sons ...," 6 May 1843, and W. Pryor & Sons to J. Wilson, 5 July 1842, Joseph Wilson Documents, 1814–1929.

17 J. Wilson to W. Pryor & Sons, 9 December 1842, Joseph Wilson Documents, 1814–1929.

18 W. Pryor & Sons to J. Wilson, 20 December 1842, Joseph Wilson Documents, 1814–1929.

19 W. Pryor & Sons to J. Wilson, 5 July 1842.

20 Stewart & Co. to J. Wilson, 17 August 1847, Joseph Wilson Documents, 1814–1929.

21 J. Wilson to W. Pryor & Sons, 26 August 1847.

22 The census of 1851 is confusing and contradictory on the number of fishermen in Cape Breton. Under "Nos. engaged in various Occupations," it lists 2,669 people engaged in the fisheries, but in the census of the fisheries, the numbers of men on boats and vessels are much higher. Obviously, there was a considerable problem in defining a fisherman who was also a farmer or a mariner. I have used the occupational data for Figure 4.1 and the fisheries data for Table 4.1.

23 DeCarteret stopped sending ships to Labrador in 1840 "as it is expensive and the fish is bad [i.e. heavily salted] that we receive from that quarter" (P. DeCarteret to P. LeVesconte, 9 June 1840, DeCarteret & LeVesconte Business Papers).

24 J.W. Robin to Charles Robin & Co., 12 April 1853, CRC Letterbooks, MG 23/G 111/18/245 NAC.

25 Knight, *Shore*, 29, and DeCarteret to LeVesconte, 9 June 1840.

26 Census of 1851.

27 P. DeCarteret to P. LeVesconte, 20 November 1840, and P. DeCarteret to D. Frazer, 1 April 1842, DeCarteret & LeVesconte Business Papers.

28 The following is based on Knight, *Shore*, 35, and Seal Bounty Returns, RG 31/111/4 PANS.

29 Innis, *Cod Fisheries*, 321–31.

30 *Journals of the House of Assembly of Nova Scotia*, 1843, Appendix 74.

31 *Journals of the House of Assembly of Nova Scotia*, 1837, Appendix 75.

32 *Journals of the House of Assembly of Nova Scotia*, 1852, Appendix 13.

33 T. Crawley to W. Bruce, 13 January 1817, CO 217/135 NAC.

34 DesBarres, "Island of Cape Breton," 77–8. A similar movement has been documented for Logy Bay, Newfoundland; see Mannion, "Old World Antecedents, New World Adaptations," 156. Mannion's *Point Lance in Transition* contains much that is relevant to understanding the fishing settlements in Cape Breton.

35 Evidence of J. Fairbanks to Lord Durham's Commission, *Parliamentary Papers*, 1839, vol. 17, 145.

36 Of course, many of these people also drew a living from part-time farming.

37 *Guernsey and Jersey Magazine*, 309.

38 Thoume Moullin & Co. property advertised in the *Novascotian*, 5 November 1835.

39 For further discussion of this point, see Ommer, *From Outpost to Outport*, 136.

40 P. DeCarteret to P. LeVesconte, 3 August 1842, and DeCarteret & LeVesconte to Creighton & Grassie, 25 June 1842, DeCarteret & LeVesconte Business Papers.

41 Letter from "A SON OF GRANNAGH," *Novascotian*, 11 July 1839.

42 Sabine, *Report on the Principal Fisheries of the American Seas*, 69.

43 Based on the census of 1851, which gives the religious affiliation of the population, and the *Census of Canada, 1871*, Canada, Department of Agriculture.

44 A.A. Johnston, *History*, vol. 2, 54.

45 Brown, *Coal*, 47–55.

46 Brown, *Coal*, 56–73, and Martell, "Coal Mining."

47 For a biography of Smith, see DCB, vol. 9, *1861–1870*.

48 Brown, *Coal*, 77.

49 Brown, *Coal*, 68–73.

50 Brown, *Coal*, 72.

51 S. Cunard to Viscount Falkland, 22 December 1842, RG 1/459/104 PANS; see also S. Cunard to Earl Gray, 16 May 1848, MG 100/190/21C PANS, and S. Cunard to Sir Rupert George, 5 December 1849, RG 1/465/3 PANS.

52 W.R. Johnson, *The Coal Trade of British America with researches on the characters and practical values of American and Foreign Coals*, 44.

53 *Journals of the House of Assembly of Nova Scotia*, 1854, Appendix 74.

54 Brown, *Coal*, 68.

55 *Canadian Mining Review*, 1894, 142.

56 Gilpin, *Coal Mining in Nova Scotia*, 12–15. See also the "Report of the

Inspector of Mines," 31 December 1858, RG 21/A/7, PANS; reprinted in the *Journals of the House of Assembly of Nova Scotia*, 1859, Appendix 22.

57 "An account of the Numbers, Names and Situations of the Pits of His Majesty's Coal Mines in Bridgeport C. Breton," 1 January 1837, RG 1/464/6, PANS, and "Report of the Inspector of Mines."

58 Gilpin, *Coal Mining*, 16–17.

59 "A Brief History of the early coal hauling in Cape Breton," RG 21/A/39/57 PANS.

60 *Novascotian*, 17 September 1835.

61 W. Crawley, "Memorandum respecting Gypsum Quarries Cape Breton and Coal Mine with list of Mines and Quarries in the Island of Cape Breton," 2 August 1836, RG 1/463/29 PANS.

62 W.R. Johnson, *Coal Trade*, 25.

63 Petition of R. Brown, 4 June 1827, RG 1/459/11 PANS, and Daily Journal, 24 May 1831, MG 14/19/E.1 (a) BI.

64 Workmen's Time Book, June 1832, RG 21/A/40/10 PANS.

65 "Statement of Men, Horses, and Machinery, employed at Sydney Mines in September 1838" and "Statement of Men, and Horses employed at the Bridgeport Mines in September 1838," RG 1/463/32–3 PANS.

66 *Journals of the House of Assembly of Nova Scotia*, 1859, Appendix 22.

67 "Wise men" was a term used in the GMA workmen's Time and Pay books (MG 14/19/A.1 BI).

68 Although based on later practice by the GMA, check-weighmen were possibly employed in the early nineteenth century. See *Report of the Royal Commission on the Relations of Capital and Labour in Canada, Evidence – Nova Scotia*, vol. 5, 407.

69 Petition of R. Brown. See also the Daily Journal, 4 January 1831, MG 14/19/E.1 (a) BI for a reference to Welshmen, and the diary of a GMA employee (probably R. Brown), 2 November 1829, MG 14/19/D.10 (a) BI, for a reference to Cornish labourers.

70 R.M. Martin, *History of Nova Scotia, Cape Breton, the Sable Islands, New Brunswick, Prince Edward Island, the Bermudas, Newfoundland, etc., etc.*, 112.

71 W.R. Johnson, *Coal Trade*, 21.

72 "There are about 500 men constantly employed, and during the shipping season about 100 men more" (Evidence of Richard Brown to the Durham Commission, *Parliamentary Papers*, 1839, vol. 17, 141).

73 Diary of a GMA employee.

74 E.P. Thompson, "Time, Work Discipline."

75 The threat of eviction was eventually used in a strike at Sydney Mines in 1864. For details, see Fergusson Papers Box, 1847, 6, MG 1 PANS.

76 In a letter from R. Smith to J. Smith, 12 June 1833, two brick-makers from England were reported to have arrived at Sydney Mines; they may have supplied bricks for the company housing (MG 14/19/D.8 [a] BI).

77 The interior arrangements of GMA houses are described in the *Report of the Royal Commission on the Relations of Capital and Labour*, 412.

78 W. Cook to A. Belcher & Co., 10 September 1828, MG 14/19/D.8 (a) BI, and J. Madison to J. Stevenson, 28 December 1835, MG 100/185/7 PANS.

79 Census of 1851.

80 The following is based on W.R. Johnson, *Coal Trade*, 20, although his figures have been converted into sterling.

81 Campbell, *The Lanarkshire Miners*, 19. The high cost of labour at the Cape Breton mines was noted by R.M. Martin, *History of Nova Scotia*, 111.

82 On 23 October 1829, Richard Brown "paid off balance due to several of the men who had been discharged for their bad conduct on the 19 inst. Understanding that Alexr. Smith who was one of the party intended going in the Schr. Arichat Boudrot to Hfx. gave him notice that if he took Smith away he would render himself answerable for the debt due by Smith to the Association. R.B[rown] having previously offered Smith work at Bridgeport until the debt should be paid off" (diary of a GMA employee).

83 Madison to Stevenson.

84 Madison to Stevenson.

85 Diary of a GMA employee.

86 Gesner, *Industrial Resources*, 273–4.

87 Workmen's Time Book, 1832, MG 14/19/E.1 (a) BI.

88 R. Smith to A. Belcher, 6 September 1832, MG 14/19/D.8 (a) BI, and A. Belcher to R. Smith, 26 September 1832, MG 14/19/D.9 (a) BI.

89 Madison to Stevenson.

90 W.R. Johnson, *Coal Trade*, 21.

91 Gesner, *Industrial Resources*, 273–4.

92 Bar Letter Book, 1836–39, MG 14/19/D.8 (a) BI.

93 Shipping Returns for Arichat and Sydney, 1814, CO 221/35 NAC. Of the 301 vessels cleared from Cape Breton, 183 carried coal, 28 carried fish, 13 carried agricultural produce, and 46 carried mixed cargoes (coal/agricultural produce, coal/fish, coal/timber, fish/agricultural produce).

94 *Newfoundlander*, 1837. Of the 152 vessels from Cape Breton listed in the Shipping Intelligence column, 83 carried coal, 35 carried agricultural produce, 20 carried timber, 12 carried mixed cargoes (coal/tim-

ber, coal/agricultural produce, timber/agricultural produce), and 2 carried other cargoes.

95 DesBarres, "Island of Cape Breton," 79. See also Muise and Armour, *Shipping and Shipbuilding in the Maritime Provinces in the Nineteenth Century*; Langhout, "Alternative Opportunities"; Parker, *Ships and Men*; and Sager and Panting, *Maritime Capital*.

96 Bouchette, *British Dominions*, 86.

97 Census of 1851.

98 P. DeCarteret to P. LeVesconte, 27 August 1841, and P. DeCarteret to J. Wilson, 29 April 1840, DeCarteret & LeVesconte Business Papers; and J. Wilson to P. DeCarteret, 20 March 1840, Joseph Wilson Documents, 1814–1929.

99 DeCarteret to LeVesconte, 27 August 1841.

100 Parker, *Ships and Men*, 101.

101 This important point is made most effectively in Sager and Panting, *Maritime Capital*, 188–91.

CHAPTER FIVE

1 For details of the disease, see *Journals of the House of Assembly of Nova Scotia*, 1846, Appendix 77, and Salaman, *History and Social Influence*, 289–92. For another account of the potato famine in Cape Breton, see Morgan, "'Poverty, wretchedness, and misery.'"

2 Annual report of the Margaree Agricultural Society, 1846, RG 8/13/22 PANS.

3 W. Ousley to J.W. Johnston, 2 January 1846, RG 8/13/22 PANS.

4 *Journals of the House of Assembly of Nova Scotia*, 1846, Appendix 77.

5 Ousley to Johnston.

6 Annual report of the Margaree Agricultural Society, 1846.

7 Ousley to Johnston.

8 *Presbyterian Witness*, 15 August 1851.

9 *Journals of the House of Assembly of Nova Scotia*, 1846, Appendix 77.

10 *Journals of the House of Assembly of Nova Scotia*, 1846, Appendix 77.

11 Petition from Îsle Madame, Richmond County, 17 January 1846, RG 5/P/124/102 PANS.

12 Petition from Îsle Madame.

13 Petition from Arichat, 10 December 1845, RG 1/278/114 PANS.

14 *Journals of the House of Assembly of Nova Scotia*, 1847, Appendix 39, and "Petition of the Settlers of South Side of St. Patricks Channel," 14 January 1846, RG 5/P/53/53 PANS.

15 *Journals of the House of Assembly of Nova Scotia*, 1847, Appendix 83.

16 *Journals of the House of Assembly of Nova Scotia*, 1847, Appendix 39.

17 *Journals of the House of Assembly of Nova Scotia*, 1847, Appendix 39.

18 "Petition from Settlers on the front and rear of St. Patricks Channel," 25 January 1847, RG 5/P/83/67 PANS.

19 "Petition of the Settlers on the new Road and vicinity from Little Narrows to Lake Ainslie," 12 February 1847, RG 5/P/83/109 PANS.

20 "Petition of the Inhabitants of Loch Lomond and its vicinity," 26 February 1847, RG 5/P/53/85 PANS.

21 A. Brymer to Sir Rupert George, 8 April 1847, RG 5/P/83/133 PANS.

22 Petition from Whycocomagh, River Denys, and Malagawatch, 4 May 1847, RG 5/P/83/139 PANS.

23 "Petition of JPs [justices of the peace], Merchants, Freeholders, and other Inhabitants of Whycocomagh, River Denys, and Malagawatch," 26 April 1847, MG 6/2/1 PANS, and "Petition from South End of Lake Ainslie," 3 May 1847, RG 5/P/83/138 PANS.

24 "Petition from the JPs for Inverness County," 12 May 1847, RG 5/P/83/141 PANS. In a petition from Lake Ainslie, settlers explained that "having lost almost the whole of their cattle, are without credit as well as means; and on that account are refused *all further supplies of meal* from the local merchants" (23 June 1847, RG 5/P/83/157 PANS).

25 Brymer to George.

26 "Petition of JPs, Merchants, Freeholders."

27 "Petition of Merchants, Magistrates, and other Inhabitants of the Township of Lake Ainslie," 5 May 1847, MG 6/2/2 PANS.

28 J. Janvrin to Sir Rupert George, 27 April 1847, RG 5/P/83/135 PANS.

29 "Petition from the JPs for Inverness County."

30 W. Young to Sir John Harvey, 12 May 1847, MG 6/2/1 PANS.

31 *Journals of the House of Assembly of Nova Scotia*, 1847, Appendix 73.

32 Janvrin to George, and petition from George Brymer et al., 29 April 1847, RG 5/P/83/135 PANS.

33 J. Janvrin to Sir Rupert George, 20 May 1847, RG 5/P/83/144 PANS.

34 "Petition from Settlers on Loch Lomond," 12 June 1847, RG 5/P/83/154 PANS. See also D.B. McNab to Sir Rupert George, 12 June 1847, RG 5/P/83/153 PANS.

35 "Petition of the Inhabitants of Whycocomagh, Malagawatch, River Denys, Indian Rear, Skye Glen, etc.," 19 June 1847, RG 5/P/83/156 PANS.

36 *Journals of the House of Assembly of Nova Scotia*, 1848, Appendix 39.

37 *Journals of the House of Assembly of Nova Scotia*, 1847, Appendix 67.

38 K. McLeod, JP, J. Campbell, JP, and A. Farquharson to J.B. Uniacke, 17 November 1847, MG 6/2/1 PANS.

39 See petitions from Grand Narrows, 12 November 1847; Cape North, 6 October 1847; Ingonish, 30 September 1847; Gabarus and Grand Mira, 1847, MG 6/2/1 PANS.

40 *Journals of the House of Assembly of Nova Scotia*, 1848, Appendix 67. For

the distribution of relief supplies, see J.B. Uniacke to Sir Rupert George, 13 December 1847, MG 6/2/1 PANS.

41 C.F. Harrington to Sir Rupert George, 11 December 1847, RG 5/P/83/174 PANS.

42 C.F. Harrington to Sir Rupert George, 29 December 1847, RG 5/P/83/180 PANS.

43 "Petition from Freeholders and other Inhabitants of the East Section of Lake Ainslie," 27 January 1848, RG 5/P/84/19 PANS, and "Letter from Freeholders and other Inhabitants of the Eastern Section of Township of Lake Ainslie" to W. Young and P. Smyth, 27 January 1848, RG 5/84/19 PANS.

44 W. Jones and D. McRae to J.B. Uniacke, 21 February 1848, MG 6/2/1 PANS.

45 J. Frazer and A. Farquharson to J.B. Uniacke, 11 March 1848, MG 6/2/1 PANS.

46 "Petition from Revd. N. McLeod, and others, inhabitants of St. Anns," 16 March 1848, RG 5/P/84/68 PANS.

47 W. Kidston to A. Scott, 18 April 1848, RG 8/13/22 PANS.

48 Petition from H. Thompson, Margaree, 22 April 1848, RG 5/GP/7/30 PANS.

49 *Journals of the House of Assembly of Nova Scotia*, 1848, 179–80.

50 *Journals of the House of Assembly of Nova Scotia*, 1849, Appendix 100.

51 "Petition of the Clergy, Magistrates, and other Respectable Inhabitants residents of the Township of St. Andrews in the County of Cape Breton," 12 January 1849, RG 5/P/53/129 PANS.

52 *Journals of the House of Assembly of Nova Scotia*, 1850, Appendix 80.

53 *Journals of the House of Assembly of Nova Scotia*, 1850, Appendix 45.

54 *Journals of the House of Assembly of Nova Scotia*, 1856, Appendix 36.

55 McNab to George; and Rev. N. McLeod to J. Gordon, 1 June 1848, in Harvey, ed., *Letters of Rev. Norman McLeod, 1835–1851*, 21–2.

56 "Petition from Settlers on Loch Lomond."

57 Ferguson, ed., *Uniacke's Sketches*, 160.

58 See the deeds in the McKeen Papers, Mabou, 1822–1956, MG 12/109 B1.

59 "Petition of the Commissioners for the distribution of provisions for the helpless and needy, County of Inverness," 8 June 1847, RG 5/P/83/151 PANS.

CHAPTER SIX

1 *Census of Canada 1870–1871* and *Census of Canada 1891*, Canada Department of Agriculture.

2 *Census of Canada 1870–1871*.

3 The census of 1851 does not give the amount of land occupied, so the figure of 1,000,000 acres is only a rough estimate. Both the *Census of Canada 1870–1871* and *Census of Canada 1891* give the area of occupied land.

4 The squatters in these settlements later took out land grants, and these are recorded on the Crown Land Index Sheets 108–12, 114–33, 135–40 (Nova Scotia Department of Lands and Forests).

5 *Census of Canada 1870–1871* and *Census of Canada 1891*.

6 *Census of Canada 1870–1871* and *Census of Canada 1891*.

7 For the Malthusian argument, see, for example, Le Roy Ladurie, *Peasants of Languedoc*, and Lockridge, "Land, Population." For the argument that emigration, at least in North America, acted as a safety-valve and relieved population pressure, see Rutman, "People in Process."

8 H.W. Crawley, 10 December 1861; reprinted in Ferguson, ed., *Uniacke's Sketches*, Appendix L.

9 J. Murphy, deputy surveyor of Inverness County, to J.B. Uniacke, 26 January 1857, *Journals of the House of Assembly of Nova Scotia*, 1857, Appendix 71.

10 *Journals of the House of Assembly of Nova Scotia*, 1888, Appendix 9.

11 *Journals of the House of Assembly of Nova Scotia*, 1892, Appendix 9.

12 *Journals of the House of Assembly of Nova Scotia*, 1857, Appendix 71.

13 *Journals of the House of Assembly of Nova Scotia*, 1860, report of the Committee on Crown Property.

14 *Journals of the House of Assembly of Nova Scotia*, 1859, Appendix 7.

15 An Act for Settling Titles to Land in the Island of Cape Breton, 1850, 13 Vic., *Nova Scotia Statutes*.

16 An Act for Settling Titles to Lands in the Island of Cape Breton, 1854, 17 Vic., *Nova Scotia Statutes*.

17 Instructions relating to Squatters Act, 1859, Orders in Council, 17 June 1865, RG 20/C/63 PANS.

18 D. McDonald to S.P. Fairbanks, 11 March 1867, RG 20/C/63 PANS.

19 *Journals of the House of Assembly of Nova Scotia*, 1868, Appendix 8; 1869, Appendix 4.

20 D.B. McNab to W.A. Hendry, 4 October 1862, RG 20/C/61 PANS.

21 *Journals of the House of Assembly of Nova Scotia*, 1871, Appendix 20, and An Act regulating the Price of Crown Lands in the Island of Cape Breton, 1870, 33 Vic., *Nova Scotia Statutes*.

22 *Journals of the House of Assembly of Nova Scotia*, 1873, Appendix 9.

23 *Journals of the House of Assembly of Nova Scotia*, 1879, Appendix 9.

24 An Act to Amend Chapter 11 of the Revised Statutes, 4th Series of Crown Lands, 1879, 42 Vic. C.3, *Nova Scotia Statutes*.

25 *Journals of the House of Assembly of Nova Scotia*, 1880, Appendix 9.

26 An Act to Amend the Laws relating to Crown Lands, 1880, 43 Vic. C.5, *Nova Scotia Statutes.*

27 An Act to Amend the Laws relating to Crown Lands, 1882, 45 Vic. C.4, *Nova Scotia Statutes.*

28 *Journals of the House of Assembly of Nova Scotia,* 1887, Appendix 9.

29 A report giving a general view of the extent and character of the Crown land in the County of Inverness, 26 January 1857, RG 20/C/59 PANS; and *Journals of the House of Assembly of Nova Scotia,* 1857, Appendix 71; 1858, Appendix 47.

30 *Census of Canada 1891* and *North Sydney Herald,* 5 January 1881.

31 For Broad Cove cattle, see *North Sydney Herald,* 16 January 1881, and for Christmas Island livestock, see Ledger of Malcolm McDougall, 1873–1921, MG 14/62 BI.

32 Innis, *Cod Fisheries,* 323–31.

33 *Port Hood Referee,* 6 June 1883, 14 May 1884.

34 *Island Reporter,* 22 May 1889.

35 *Journals of the House of Assembly of Nova Scotia,* 1890, Appendix 8.

36 Gow, *Cape Breton Illustrated,* 407. For an overview of regional specialization of agriculture in the United States, see Meyer, "The National Integration of Regional Economies, 1860–1920."

37 *Census of Canada 1891.*

38 The total sample comprised 300 households randomly sampled from the nominal *Census of Canada 1870–1871.* Of these, 156 (52 percent) comprised farm households.

39 *Census of Canada 1891.*

40 Census subdistricts of Bridgeport, Cow Bay, North Sydney, Sydney Town, Sydney Forks, and Sydney Mines, *Census of Canada 1891.*

41 *Journals of the House of Assembly of Nova Scotia,* 1888, Appendix 8.

42 *Journals of the House of Assembly of Nova Scotia,* 1892, Appendix 8.

43 *Journals of the House of Assembly of Nova Scotia,* 1888, Appendix 8.

44 The *Census of Canada 1891* records no creameries in Cape Breton.

45 *Journals of the House of Assembly of Nova Scotia,* 1888, Appendix 8.

46 *Census of Canada 1870–1871.* See also *Journals of the House of Assembly of Nova Scotia,* 1856, Appendix 36.

47 Shannon, *The Farmer's Last Frontier,* Table of Hours and Wages by Hand and by Machine, 143.

48 In 1873, the Boularderie Agricultural Society passed the following by-law: "The Threshing Mill is at present at Henry McKinnon's. She is to follow down the north side of Little Bras d'Or and then out to the Back Lands and when the Members of the Society is done with it there it is to come up again to McKinnon's Cove and when all members are done Threshing belonging to the Society, then the said Mill is to go to any man that wants it for 6 bushels per hundred three

bushels is for the man that attends the Mill and three for the Society" (Minutes of annual meetings, together with lists of subscribers, Boularderie Agricultural Society, 1864–85, MG 14/56 BI).

49 *Antigonish Casket*, 30 July 1891.

50 Bittermann, "Middle River," 63.

51 Ennals and Holdsworth, "Vernacular Architecture," 92.

52 The following discussion is based on J.B. Moore, Documents, 1848–99, MG 1/Biography PANS.

53 Cann et al., *Soil Survey*, Southeast sheet.

54 Will of Peter Moore, 1852, Cape Breton County, Will Book B, 205, reel 110 PANS, and "Valuation of the estate of the late Peter Moore," Cape Breton Estate Papers, 1853, N.19, reel 126 PANS. The average probable value of real estate in Cape Breton was £106 according to the 1851 census.

55 *Census of Canada 1870–1871*.

56 Farm accounts, J.B. Moore, Documents. The business of John and William Moore is assessed in R.G. Dun, Canada, vol. 11, 564 BLHU.

57 R.G. Dun, Canada, vol. 11, 620 BLHU; Cape Breton County Deed Book U, 118, 287, 494; Book v, 187, 325; Book w, 342; Book y, 83, 104, 132, 136, 421; Book z, 377; Book A.A., 340; Book B.B., 182, 395; Book C.C., 30, 239, 580; Book I.I., 171, 613; Book M.M., 345; Book T.T., 398, 571, 679, 722; Book Y.Y., 497; Book Z.Z., 284, 575, 593, 595, 642, 678, 789; Book 52, 46; Book 61, 772; and Book 69, 728, PANS.

58 R.G. Dun, Canada, vol. 11, 620 BLHU; Assessment roll for the district no. 1 of North Sydney, November A.D. 1862, RG 34–305/A/1 PANS.

59 "Valuation of the estate of J.B. Moore," Cape Breton Estate Papers, 1897, AZ 8, reel 142 PANS.

60 Galbraith uses the term "men of standing" in *The Scotch*, chap. 5.

61 *Census of Canada 1870–1871*.

62 Bittermann, "Middle River," 63, and "Hierarchy of the Soil."

63 *North Sydney Herald*, 11 September 1895.

64 *Trades Journal*, 16 August 1882.

65 *Trades Journal*, 31 October 1883. See also *Trades Journal*, 13 and 21 September 1882; 6 May and 10 June 1885; and 22 May and 5 June 1889.

66 Wage rates at International, Victoria, and Reserve mines, 1875, RG 21/A/12 PANS.

67 Innis, *Cod Fisheries*, 323–31.

68 D.B. McNab to J.B. Uniacke, 3 January 1857, RG 20/C/59 PANS; reprinted in the *Journals of the House of Assembly of Nova Scotia*, 1857, Appendix 71.

69 Beattie, "Dutiful Daughters."

70 Note enclosed in Ledger of Malcolm McDougall.

71 Ennals and Holdsworth, "Vernacular Architecture," 88–91.

72 D. Murray Jr to S.P. Fairbanks, 20 February 1869, RG 20/C/64 PANS, and *Census of Canada 1870–1871*.

73 J. Ross to W.A. Hendry, 13 September 1864, RG 20/C/61 PANS.

74 *North Sydney Herald*, 3 December 1879.

75 Hunter, *Crofting Community*, chaps. 8, 9, and 10.

76 Devine, "Temporary Migration" and "Highland Migration"; Howatson, "Scottish Hairst"; Mewett, "Occupational Pluralism in Crofting"; and Withers, "Highland-Lowland Migration and the Making of the Crofting Community, 1755–1891."

77 Of the 237 marriages in the 1871 random sample, only 3 were mixed Catholic/Protestant marriages, although an unknown number of spouses may have changed their religious denomination at marriage. The pattern of endogamous marriages among the Scots is discussed in Molloy, "'No Inclination to Mix with Strangers.'"

78 W.A. Hendry to S.P. Fairbanks, 20 August 1863, RG 20/C/61 PANS.

79 Farnham, "Cape Breton Folk," 97–8.

80 Ross to Hendry.

81 Warner, *Baddeck, and That Sort of Thing*, 122–9.

82 *Journals of the House of Assembly of Nova Scotia*, 1891, Appendix 8.

83 Census of 1851, RG 1/453 PANS; *Census of Canada 1870–1871*; and *Census of Canada 1891*.

84 *Port Hood Referee*, 13 November 1883, 2 January 1884.

85 *Port Hood Referee*, 12 December 1883.

86 *Port Hood Referee*, 6 December 1882.

87 R.G. Dun, Canada, vol. 11, 625 BLHU; Dun, Wiman & Co., *The Mercantile Agency Reference Book, (and Key,) for the Dominion of Canada, containing names and ratings of the Principal Merchants, Traders, and Manufacturers in Ontario, Quebec, Nova Scotia, New Brunswick, Prince Edward Island, and Newfoundland*, 520.

88 R.G. Dun, Canada, vol. 11, 550 BLHU.

89 Ledger of Malcolm MacDougall; MacKenzie and MacKenzie, *MacKenzie's History of Christmas Island Parish*, chap. 12; and Dun, Wiman & Co., *Mercantile Agency*, 527.

90 *Census of Canada 1890*.

91 Dun, Wiman & Co., *Mercantile Agency*, 516–81.

CHAPTER SEVEN

1 Census of 1851 and *Sessional Papers*, no. 9, 1885, 93.

2 Vernon, *Cape Breton, Canada, at the Beginning of the Twentieth Century*, 145.

3 R.G. Dun, Canada, vol. 11, 554 BLHU; Dun, Wiman & Co., *Mercantile Agency*, 519.

4 R.G. Dun, Canada, vol. 11, 554 BLHU. In 1895, DeCarteret & LeVesconte was taken over by John Le Brun, another Jersey fish merchant who had settled in Arichat. In the report of the take-over in the *Morning Chronicle* (Halifax), 20 August 1895, the DeCarteret property was described as follows: "with fine dwelling house, fish stores, wharf, a deep water frontage of one hundred yards and a rear of a mile and a half, this forms a typical Jersey property, neat and compact. There is, moreover, a very fine English screw press for packing fish for the Brazilian and Mediterranean trade."

5 Ommer, *From Outpost to Outport*, 176–89.

6 "1889, Clerks etc., Summer Stations," 20 June 1889, CRC Letterbooks, MG 14/55/381 BI.

7 CRC Letterbooks, MG 14/55/386 BI.

8 *Journals of the House of Assembly of Nova Scotia*, 1866, Appendix 2.

9 "Dry Fish Received," 1894–99, CRC Fish Record Books, MG 14/55/152 BI.

10 Dun, Wiman & Co., *Mercantile Agency*, 516–81.

11 "Petition of the fishermen of Cape North in the County of Victoria," 8 February 1865, RG 5/P/55/46 PANS.

12 "Petition of the undersigned residents at the Basin Cariboo Cove the foot of River Inhabitants and elsewhere in the County of Richmond," 23 February 1865, RG 5/P/55/47 PANS.

13 *Sessional Papers*, no. 11A, 1892, 132–43.

14 *Sessional Papers*, no. 1, 1878, 79.

15 *Acadian Recorder*, 16 January 1873; E. Orange to F. Briard, 15 June 1861, CRC Letterbooks, MG 23/G III/18/250 NAC; *Sessional Papers*, no. 11A, 1892, 140–1; and Diary of William LeVesconte, 1879, MG 100/175/21 PANS.

16 *Acadian Recorder*, 25 February 1860, and Knight, *Shore*, 40–1.

17 *Sessional Papers*, no. 8, 1889, 50.

18 For a description of dory fishing, see Goode, *The Fisheries and Fishing Industries of the United States*, section 5, vol. 1, 148–56.

19 Joncas, *Fisheries*, 133.

20 *Journals of the House of Assembly of Nova Scotia*, 1863–66, Trade Returns.

21 Innis, *Cod Fisheries*, 331.

22 Census of 1851, *Census of Canada 1870–1871*, and *Census of Canada 1881*.

23 *Sessional Papers*, no. 11A, 1892, 59.

24 Goode, *Fisheries*, 285–94.

25 *Journals of the House of Assembly of Nova Scotia*, 1851–52, Appendix 13.

26 *Sessional Papers*, no. 1, 1878, 79.

27 Knight, *Shore*, 45.

28 R.H. Williams, *Historical Account of the Lobster Canning Industry*; T. Williams, "The Williams Lobster Factory at Neil's Harbour, 1901–1935"; and the *Report of the Select Committee on the causes of the Present Depression of the Manufacturing, Mining, Commercial, Shipping, Lumber, and Fishing Interests*, 69.

29 *Census of Canada 1891*.

30 *Census of Canada 1891*.

31 *Award of the Fishery Commission: Documents and Proceedings of the Halifax Commission, 1877, under the Treaty of Washington of May 8, 1871*, vol. 3, Appendix M, 3271.

32 *Award*, vol. 3, Appendix M, 3255.

33 *Award*, vol. 3, Appendix M, 3214.

34 Boyle diaries, 1847–1964, MG 12 BI.

35 *North Sydney Herald*, 20 November 1889.

36 *Award*, vol. 1, Appendix F, 607.

37 *Award*, vol. 3, Appendix M, 3217.

38 *Award*, vol. 3, Appendix M, 3218.

39 *Sessional Papers*, no. 5, 1871, 342.

40 *Port Hood Referee*, 23 May 1883.

41 *Census of Canada 1870–1871* and *Census of Canada 1891*.

42 *Census of Canada 1891*.

43 Boyle diaries.

44 Boyle diaries.

45 Boyle diaries.

46 *Arichat News Budget*, quoted in *North Sydney Herald*, 24 March 1880.

47 *Arichat News Budget* and Boyle diaries.

48 Boyle diaries.

49 P. DeCarteret to I. LeVesconte, 3 November 1858, DeCarteret & LeVesconte Business Papers, MG 3/5–9 PANS.

50 Agent, CRC, Eastern Harbour, Chéticamp, to CRC, Pasbébiac, 25 May 1889, CRC Letterbooks, MG 14/55/381 BI.

51 Agent, CRC, Chéticamp, to CRC, Arichat, 27 May 1889, and agent, CRC, Eastern Harbour, Chéticamp, to CRC, Pasbébiac, 8 June 1889, CRC Letterbooks, MG 14/55/381 BI.

52 Agent, CRC, Chéticamp, to CRC, Pasbébiac, 16 June 1890, CRC Letterbooks, MG 14/55/405 BI, and agent, CRC, Chéticamp, to CRC, Pasbébiac, 25 April 1891, CRC Letterbooks, MG 14/55/379 BI.

53 Agent, CRC, Eastern Harbour, Chéticamp, to CRC, Pasbébiac, 13 November 1889, CRC Letterbooks, MG 14/55/405 BI.

54 *Port Hood Referee*, 7 May 1884.

55 There is growing evidence from the Newfoundland fishery that fish-

ermen were not passive pawns exploited by outport merchants; see Cadigan, "Battle Harbour in Transition," and Little, "Collective Action in Outport Newfoundland."

56 A.A. Johnston, *History*, vol. 2.

57 Boyle diaries.

58 Details of this wrangle can be found in Muise, "The General Mining Association and Nova Scotia's Coal."

59 The term "cyclonic" was used by Innis to describe very rapid industrial development in the Canadian North.

60 R.G. Dun, Canada, vol. 11, 625, BLHU.

61 R.G. Dun, Canada, vol. 11, 545, 548, BLHU, and Langhout, "Alternative Opportunities."

62 R.G. Dun, Canada, vol. 12, 622, BLHU, and C.O. MacDonald, *The Coal and Iron Industries of Nova Scotia*, 21.

63 R.G. Dun, Canada, vol. 12, 621, BLHU, and C.O. MacDonald, *Coal and Iron*, 27–8.

64 C.O. MacDonald, *Coal and Iron*, 26, 34–5.

65 This pattern was replicated elsewhere in the Maritimes in the decades after Confederation and the National Policy; see Acheson, "The National Policy and the Industrialization of the Maritimes, 1880–1910."

66 C.O. MacDonald, *Coal and Iron*, 23–4.

67 The lack of markets was discussed by John Rutherford, general manager of the GMA, in his evidence published in the *Report of the Select Committee on the Causes of the Present Depression*, 224; see also the *Report of the Select Committee on the State of the Coal Trade, and for Promoting of Interprovincial Trade*.

68 *Journals of the House of Assembly of Nova Scotia*, 1868, Appendix 4; 1873, Appendix 11; and *Acadian Recorder*, 31 January 1870.

69 See the evidence of Rutherford published in the *Report of the Select Committee on the Causes of the Present Depression*, 224, and C.O. MacDonald, *Coal and Iron*, 30.

70 *Halifax Reporter*, 31 October 1867, reporting a meeting of the Nova Scotia Coal Owners' Association.

71 *North Sydney Herald*, 9 November 1881 and 8 January 1890.

72 C.O. MacDonald, *Coal and Iron*, 66.

73 *Journals of the House of Assembly of Nova Scotia*, 1863, Appendix 15.

74 *Journals of the House of Assembly of Nova Scotia*, 1867, Appendix 12.

75 Brown, *Coal*, 109–10.

76 Gilpin, *Coal Mining*, 16.

77 Gilpin, *Coal Mining*, 16–18.

78 Gilpin, *Coal Mining*, 27–9.

79 Richard Brown to R.H. Brown, 19 January 1866, Brown Papers, MG 1/151/1 PANS.

80 *Census of Canada 1870–1871.*

81 Evidence of R.H. Brown published in the *Report of the Royal Commission on the Relations of Capital and Labour*, 418.

82 R.H. Brown Diary, 1881, RG 21/A/38/12 PANS.

83 "Pay-day [at Bridgeport Mines] which took place on the 15th was celebrated with half a dozen disgraceful fights and quarrels," *Trades Journal*, 3 August 1887.

84 Evidence of R.H. Brown published in the *Report of the Royal Commission on the Relations of Capital and Labour*, 417–18.

85 *North Sydney Herald*, 3 August 1892.

86 *Report of the Royal Commission on the Relations of Capital and Labour*, 411, 423.

87 Drummond, *Recollections and Reflections of a Former Trade Union Leader*, 12.

88 *Report of the Royal Commission on the Relations of Capital and Labour*, 419.

89 *Trades Journal*, 19 June 1889.

90 Evidence of Alexander McGillivray published in *Report of the Royal Commission on the Relations of Capital and Labour*, 448.

91 *Report of the Royal Commission on the Relations of Capital and Labour*, 409.

92 *Census of Canada 1870–1871*; Frank, "Tradition and Culture in the Cape Breton Mining Community in the Early Twentieth Century"; and Muise, "The Making of an Industrial Community."

93 Drummond, *Recollections*, 276–7.

94 *Trades Journal*, 1 July and 16 December 1885.

95 Richard Brown to R.H. Brown, 21 September 1875, Brown Papers, MG 1/152/239 PANS.

96 *Report of the Royal Commission on the Relations of Capital and Labour*, 449.

97 Evidence of John McNeil published in the *Report of the Royal Commission on the Relations of Capital and Labour*, 414.

98 *North Sydney Herald*, 11 February 1891.

99 *North Sydney Herald*, 11 May 1887; see also *Trades Journal*, 13 July 1881.

100 Company Store Debt Book, Sydney Mines, July 1862–August 1868, MG 14/19/C2 (a) BI.

101 *Trades Journal*, 20 July 1887.

102 *Journals of the House of Assembly of Nova Scotia*, 1879, Appendix 6.

103 See the evidence of Robert Belloni published in the *Report of the Select Committee on the State of the Coal Trade*, 21; *Morning Chronicle* (Halifax), 11 April 1876; and *North Sydney Herald*, 29 January 1879.

104 *Journals of the House of Assembly of Nova Scotia*, 1877, Appendix 6; *Sydney Record*, 30 November 1920; and I. McKay, "Crisis of Dependent Development."

105 For the PWA, see I. McKay, "'By Wisdom, Wile or War'" and "Crisis of Dependent Development."

106 Calculated from the membership rolls, Provincial Workmen's Association miscellaneous publications, Department of Labour Library, Ottawa.
107 Drummond, *Recollections*, 31.
108 MacLeod, "Colliers, Colliery Safety and Workplace Control."
109 *Trades Journal*, 11 September 1881.
110 Rules for Island Lodge, *Trades Journal*, 14 November 1883.
111 *Trades Journal*, 21 October 1885.
112 *Trades Journal*, 25 March 1885.
113 *Trades Journal*, 23 August and 4 October 1882.
114 Works and Mines, Nova Scotia, "Re forfeitures in coal lease," RG 21/ A/12 PANS.
115 C.O. MacDonald, *Coal and Iron*, 90, and Accounts of R.H. Brown, GMA, RG 21/A/38/5 PANS.
116 Details of the take-over can be found in the *Canadian Mining Review*, 1894. For an extended treatment of the Dominion Coal Company and the Cape Breton coal industry, see Frank, "The Cape Breton Coal Industry and the Rise and Fall of the British Empire Steel Corporation," and Macgillivray, "Henry Melville Whitney Comes to Cape Breton."
117 C.O. MacDonald, *Coal and Iron*, 24.
118 *Census of Canada 1870–1871* and *Census of Canada 1881*.

CHAPTER EIGHT

1 Mannion, "Settlers and Traders in Western Newfoundland," 234.
2 Ommer, "Highland Scots Migration."
3 *Journals of the House of Assembly of Nova Scotia*, 1839, Appendix 69.
4 *Journals of the House of Assembly of Nova Scotia*, 1857, Appendix 71.
5 D. McNeil to W. McNeil, 25 June 1849, GD 403/27/2 SRO.
6 Petition of Murdoch Kerr, John McLeod, Angus McDonald, Murdoch McLeod, Alexander McLeod, Murdoch Beaton, Angus Campbell, and others of St Anns, Island of Cape Breton, 6 February 1849, RG 5/GP/ 6/24 PANS.
7 N.R. McKenzie, *The Gael Fares Forth*, Appendix 2, and Molloy, "'No Inclination to Mix with Strangers.'"
8 The "depression of the times" and the difficulties of selling property in the St Anns area are mentioned in a letter from Hugh McKenzie, St Anns, to Donald McDonald, Adelaide, South Australia, 10 April 1850, MacKenzie Papers, Ms 248/21 NLNZ.
9 *Cape Breton News*, 27 May 1854.
10 *Journals of the House of Assembly of Nova Scotia*, 1857, Appendix 71.
11 *Acadian Recorder*, 1 May 1865.
12 *Journals of the House of Assembly of Nova Scotia*, Mines reports.

13 *Acadian Recorder*, 13 September 1869.

14 *Journals of the House of Assembly of Nova Scotia*, Mines reports.

15 *Acadian Recorder*, 10 April 1872.

16 *Acadian Recorder*, 12 June 1879, and *Port Hood Eastern Beacon*, quoted in the *Morning Chronicle* (Halifax), 26 September 1879.

17 *Eastern Chronicle*, quoted in the *Acadian Recorder*, 2 May 1882.

18 *Chignecto Post*, quoted in the *Acadian Recorder*, 2 May 1882.

19 *Port Hood Referee*, quoted in the *Acadian Recorder*, 13 October 1882.

20 *Acadian Recorder*, 23 August 1881.

21 *Acadian Recorder*, 12 June 1879.

22 Thornton, "Some Preliminary Comments on the Extent and Consequences of Out-Migration from the Atlantic Region, 1870–1920," Appendix 6; see also Thornton, "The Problem of Out-Migration from Atlantic Canada, 1871–1921."

23 *Trades Journal*, 14 October 1885; see also *Trades Journal*, 21 October 1885.

24 *Trades Journal*, 3 June 1891; see also *Trades Journal*, 13 June 1888.

25 *Acadian Recorder*, 4 November 1872.

26 Cozzens, *Acadia, or A Month with the Blue Noses*, 148.

27 *Trades Journal*, 5 October 1881.

28 *Trades Journal*, 5 October 1881.

29 *Trades Journal*, 19 April 1882.

30 *Trades Journal*, 7 May 1884.

31 *Trades Journal*, 2 November 1887.

32 R.H. Brown to C.G. Swann, 10 January 1888, Brown Papers, MG 1/152/433 PANS.

33 *Trades Journal*, 23 May 1888.

34 *Trades Journal*, 24 October 1888.

35 *Trades Journal*, 27 March 1889.

36 *Trades Journal*, 23 October 1889.

37 Acheson, "National Policy and the Industrialization of the Maritimes."

38 *North Sydney Herald*, 11 May 1892.

39 *North Sydney Herald*, 11 May 1892.

40 *North Sydney Herald*, 28 December 1881.

41 *North Sydney Herald*, 5 April 1882.

42 *Port Hood Referee*, 29 March 1881.

43 *North Sydney Herald*, 30 March 1892.

44 *Morning Chronicle* (Halifax), 4 August 1892; see also A.A. MacKenzie, "Cape Breton and the Western Harvest Excursions 1890–1928," and J.H. Thompson, "Bringing in the Sheaves."

45 *North Sydney Herald*, 23 November 1887; see also *North Sydney Herald*, 7 October and 14 October 1891.

46 The figures are cited in A.A. Brookes, "Out-Migration from the Maritime Provinces, 1860–1900," 38, 43.

47 A.A. Brookes, "Out-Migration," 42.
48 A.A. Brookes, "Out-Migration"; A.A. Brookes, ed., "'The Provincials' by A.J. Kennedy"; and Beattie, "Dutiful Daughters."
49 *North Sydney Herald*, 29 October 1884.
50 A.A. Brookes, "The Golden Age and the Exodus," 78.
51 *Trades Journal*, 22 March 1882.
52 *North Sydney Herald*, 11 October 1882.
53 *North Sydney Herald*, 12 May 1880. During the 1880s and early 1890s, the *North Sydney Herald* published many obituaries of Cape Breton men who had died in western hardrock mines.
54 Harris, "Industry and the Good Life around Idaho Peak."
55 N.R. McKenzie, *Gael Fares Forth*, and Molloy, "'No Inclination to Mix with Strangers.'"
56 M.B. MacKenzie, "The Great Gold Rush."
57 *North Sydney Herald*, 16 November 1892.
58 For a similar geographical migration but stretched over several generations, see Wynn, "Necessaries of Life."
59 Ommer, "Highland Scots Migration."
60 A.A. Brookes, "Golden Age."
61 Boyle diaries, 1847–1964, MG 12 BI. Information on Boyle's places of work was gleaned from the *Boston Directory 1872* and the *Cambridge Directory 1872*.
62 Rev. N. McLeod to J. Gordon, 27 June 1849, in Harvey, ed., *Letters of Rev. Norman McLeod*, 25.
63 See, for example, *North Sydney Herald*, 20 June and 26 December 1888.
64 *North Sydney Herald*, 11 January 1888.
65 *North Sydney Herald*, 21 March 1888; see also *North Sydney Herald*, 9 December 1885.
66 *North Sydney Herald*, 25 December 1889; see also *Trades Journal*, 16 September 1891.
67 *North Sydney Herald*, 25 May 1887.
68 *Trades Journal*, 28 May 1884.
69 *North Sydney Herald*, 25 May 1887.
70 *North Sydney Herald*, 1 June 1892. In the cemetery at Middle River, a MacRae family plot records the deaths of Peter, John K., and Hector in Seattle and of Jessie in Vancouver, BC.

CHAPTER NINE

1 *Census of Canada* 1891.
2 Macgillivray, "Henry Melville Whitney Comes to Cape Breton."
3 I. McKay, "Crisis of Dependent Development," and Sager, "Dependency, Underdevelopment, and the Economic History of the Atlantic Provinces."

4 Careless, "'Limited Identities' in Canada"; Macpherson, "People in Transition"; and Wynn, "The Maritimes."

5 Harris, "Industry and the Good Life."

6 Wynn, *Timber Colony*, 167.

7 Balcom, "Nova Scotia's Dried Fish Trade," 21–2, 28–9, and Wynn, *Timber Colony*, 113–37.

8 Acheson, "A Study in the Historical Demography of a Loyalist County"; Craig, "Immigrants in a Frontier Community"; and Wynn, "Necessaries of Life."

9 Craig, "Agriculture and the Lumberman's Frontier in the Upper St. John Valley, 1800–70"; McCann, "'Living a Double Life'"; and Wynn, "'Deplorably Dark'" and *Timber Colony*, 72–86.

10 MacNeil, "State of Agriculture," 124–31, 206–19, and Clark, *Three Centuries*, 69, 114–19.

11 This is suggested by the map showing "Export Values and Destinations by Ports 1858 for Prince Edward Island" in Clark, *Three Centuries*, 119.

12 McCallum, *Unequal Beginnings*, 54–61.

13 Acheson, "National Policy and the Industrialization of the Maritimes."

14 Acheson, "National Policy and the Industrialization of the Maritimes"; McCann, "Metropolitanism and Branch Businesses in the Maritimes, 1881–1931"; and Kerr and Holdsworth, eds., *Historical Atlas of Canada*, pl. 24.

15 Macpherson, "People in Transition"; Clark, "Old World Origins and Religious Adherence in Nova Scotia"; and Millward, *Regional Patterns of Ethnicity*.

16 A.A. Brookes, "Out-Migration"; Thornton, "Preliminary Comments"; Conrad, "Chronicles of the Exodus"; and Beattie, "Dutiful Daughters."

17 Bennett, *The Last Stronghold*; Dunn, *Highland Settler*; and MacNeil, *Tales until Dawn*.

18 McCallum, *Unequal Beginnings*.

19 Gagan, "Land, Population, and Social Change"; L. Johnson, "Land Policy, Population Growth and Social Structure in the Home District, 1793–1851"; and Wynn, "Notes on Society and Environment in Old Ontario."

20 Gaffield, "Boom and Bust"; Harris, "Of Poverty and Helplessness in Petite-Nation"; McDermott, "Frontiers of Settlement in the Great Clay Belt of Ontario and Quebec"; Roach, "The Pulpwood Trade and the Settlers of the New Ontario, 1919–1938"; and Greer, *Peasant, Lord, and Merchant*, 177–93.

21 Clark, "Old World Origins and Religious Adherence in Nova Scotia"; Doucette, *Cultural Retention and Demographic Change*; Elliott, *Irish Mi-*

grants in the Canadas; Handcock, *Soe longe as there comes noe women*;
Mannion, *Irish Settlements in Eastern Canada*; McLean, "Peopling Glengarry County"; and Remiggi, "Ethnic Diversity and Settler Location
on the Eastern Lower North Shore of Quebec."

22 Linteau, Durocher, and Robert, *Quebec*, 28–31, and Vicero, *Immigration of French Canadians to New England, 1840–1900*.

23 Hudson, "Migration to an American Frontier."

24 Earle and Hoffman, "The Foundation of the Modern Economy," and
Montgomery, *The Fall of the House of Labor*, 70.

25 Eller, *Miners, Millhands, and Mountaineers*; and Judd, "Lumbering and
the Farming Frontier in Aroostook County, Maine, 1840–1880" and
Aroostook.

26 Potter, *People of Plenty*, and Smith, *Virgin Land*.

Bibliography

The bibliography is organized into four sections: manuscript sources, printed primary sources, newspapers, and secondary sources. All abbreviated references cited in the notes are given in full here.

MANUSCRIPT SOURCES

BAKER LIBRARY, HARVARD UNIVERSITY, CAMBRIDGE, MASS. (BLHU)
R.G. Dun Collection

BEATON INSTITUTE, UNIVERSITY COLLEGE OF
CAPE BRETON, CAPE BRETON (BI)
MG 12: Personal Papers
MG 14: Business Papers

DEPARTMENT OF LABOUR LIBRARY, OTTAWA
Lodge Membership Rolls, Provincial Workmen's Association

NATIONAL ARCHIVES OF CANADA (NAC)
CO 217: Colonial Office Records, Nova Scotia and Cape Breton (also listed as CO/Cape Breton A Papers)
CO 221: Cape Breton Shipping Returns
MG 23/G 111: Robin, Jones, and Whitman Papers

NATIONAL LIBRARY OF NEW ZEALAND, WELLINGTON (NLNZ)
Ms 248: MacKenzie Papers

PUBLIC ARCHIVES OF NOVA SCOTIA (PANS)
MG 1: Papers of families and individuals
MG 3: Business Papers
MG 6: Agriculture
MG 100: Miscellaneous
RG 1: Bound volumes of Nova Scotia Records, 1624–1867
RG 5: Records of the Legislative Assembly
RG 8: Records of the Central Board of Agriculture of Nova Scotia
RG 12: Census Records
RG 20: Lands and Forests
RG 21: Mines and Mining in Nova Scotia
RG 31: Treasury Papers
RG 34: Court of General Sessions of the Peace

SCOTTISH RECORD OFFICE, EDINBURGH, SCOTLAND (SRO)
GD 46: Seaforth Papers
GD 201: Clanranald Papers
GD 221: Lord MacDonald Papers
GD 403: Mackenzie Papers

PRINTED PRIMARY SOURCES

Boston Directory 1872. Boston: Sampson, Davenport, & Co., 1872.
Cambridge Directory 1872. Boston: Dean Dudley, 1872.
Canada. Department of Agriculture. *Census of Canada, 1870–1871, Census of Canada, 1881, Census of Canada, 1891.*
– *Report of the Royal Commission on the Relations of Capital and Labour in Canada, Evidence – Nova Scotia.* Vol. 5. Ottawa: Queen's Printer, 1889.
– *Report of the Select Committee on the Causes of the Present Depression of the Manufacturing, Mining, Commercial, Shipping, Lumber and Fishing Interests: Appendix to the Journals of the House of Commons of Canada, 1876.* Vol. 10. Ottawa: MacLean, Roger & Co., 1876.
– *Report of the Select Committee on the State of the Coal Trade, and for Inter-provincial Trade: Appendix to the Journals of the House of Commons of Canada, 1877.* Vol. 2. Ottawa: Queen's Printer, 1889.
– *Sessional Papers.*
Dun, Wiman & Co. *The Mercantile Agency Reference Book, (and Key,) for the Dominion of Canada, containing names and ratings of the Principal Merchants, Traders, and Manufacturers in Ontario, Quebec, Nova Scotia, New Brunswick, Prince Edward Island, and Newfoundland.* Vol. 10. Montreal, Toronto, and Halifax: Dun, Wiman & Co., July 1870.
Great Britain. *Evidence Taken by Her Majesty's Commissioners of Inquiry into the Condition of the Crofters and Cottars in the Highlands and Islands of Scotland.* Vols. 1 and 3. Edinburgh, 1884.

– *Parliamentary Papers.* "Select Committee on Emigration from the United Kingdom, 1826," vol. 4; Appendix B to "Report on the Affairs of British North America from the Earl of Durham, 1839," vol. 17; "Select Committee on the Condition of the Population of the Highlands and Islands of Scotland, 1841," vol. 6; "Correspondence Relative to Emigration, 1843," vol. 34.

Nova Scotia. *Journals and Proceedings of the House of Assembly of Nova Scotia.* 1820–92.

– *Statutes of Nova Scotia.*

United States. *Award of the Fishery Commission: Documents and Proceedings of the Halifax Commission, 1877, under the Treaty of Washington of May 8, 1871.* 3 vols. Washington: Government Printing Office, 1878.

NEWSPAPERS

Acadian Recorder, 1821–23, 1854–91
The Antigonish Casket, 1891
Cape Breton News, 1852–55
The Island Reporter, 1889
Morning Chronicle, Halifax, 1895
The Newfoundlander, 1828–39
North Sydney Herald, 1879–1900
Port Hood Referee, 1882–84
Trades Journal, Stellarton, 1880–91

SECONDARY SOURCES

Acheson, T.W. "The National Policy and the Industrialization of the Maritimes, 1880–1910." *Acadiensis* 1, no. 2 (1977): 3–28.

– "A Study in the Historical Demography of a Loyalist County." *Histoire Sociale–Social History* 1 (1968): 53–64.

Akenson, D.H., ed. *Canadian Papers in Rural History.* Vols. 2–5. Gananoque, Ont.: Langdale Press, 1980–86.

Ankli, R.E., and K.J. Duncan. "Farm Making Costs in Early Ontario." In *Canadian Papers in Rural History*, vol. 4, edited by D.H. Akenson, 33–49. Gananoque, Ont.: Langdale Press, 1984.

Balcom, B.A. *The Cod Fishery of Isle Royale, 1714–58.* Ottawa: Parks Canada, 1984.

– "Production and Marketing in Nova Scotia's Dried Fish Trade 1850–1914." MA thesis, Memorial University of Newfoundland, 1980.

Barron, W.R., and A.E. Bridges. "Making Hay in Northern New England: Maine As a Case Study, 1800–1850." *Agricultural History* 57, no. 2 (1983): 165–80.

Beattie, B. "Dutiful Daughters: Maritime-born Women in New England in the Late Nineteenth Century." Graduate paper, Department of History, University of Maine, 1986.

Bennett, M. *The Last Stronghold: Scottish Gaelic Traditions in Newfoundland.* St John's, Nfld: Breakwater Books, 1989.

Bentley, P.A., and E.C. Smith. "The Forests of Cape Breton in the Seventeenth and Eighteenth Centuries." *Proceedings of the Nova Scotia Institute of Science* 24, pt 1 (1954–55): 1–15.

Bittermann, R. "The Hierarchy of the Soil: Land and Labour in a 19th Century Cape Breton Community." *Acadiensis* 18, no. 1 (1988): 33–55.

– "Middle River: The Social Structure of Agriculture in a Nineteenth-Century Cape Breton Community." MA thesis, University of New Brunswick, 1985.

Bouchette, J. *The British Dominions in North America.* Vol. 2. London: Longman, Rees, Orme, Brown, Green, & Longman, 1832.

Brookes, A.A. "The Golden Age and the Exodus: The Case of Canning, Kings County." *Acadiensis* 11, no. 1 (1981): 57–82.

– "Out-Migration from the Maritime Provinces, 1860–1900: Some Preliminary Considerations." *Acadiensis* 5, no. 2 (1976): 26–55.

– , ed. "'The Provincials' by Albert J. Kennedy." *Acadiensis* 4, no. 2 (1975): 85–101.

Brookes, I. "Physical Geography of the Atlantic Provinces." In *The Atlantic Provinces*, edited by A.G. MacPherson, 1–45. Toronto: University of Toronto Press, 1972.

Brown, R. *The Coal Fields and Coal Trade of the Island of Cape Breton.* London: Sampson, Low, Marston, Low, and Searle, 1871.

– *A History of the Island of Cape Breton.* London: Sampson, Low, Son, and Marston, 1869.

Buchanan, J.L. *Travels in the Western Hebrides: From 1782 to 1790.* London: 1793.

Bumsted, J.M. "Highland Emigration to the Island of St. John and the Scottish Catholic Church, 1769–1774." *Dalhousie Review* 58, no. 3 (1978): 511–27.

– *The People's Clearance: Highland Emigration to North America 1770–1815.* Edinburgh: Edinburgh University Press, 1982.

Bumsted, J.M., and J.T. Lemon. "New Approaches in Early American Studies: The Local Community in New England." *Histoire Sociale–Social History* 2 (1968): 98–112.

Cadigan, S. "Battle Harbour in Transition: Merchants, Fishermen, and the State in the Struggle for Relief in a Labrador Community during the 1930s." *Labour/Le Travail* 26 (Fall 1990): 125–50.

Caird, J.B. "The Isle of Harris." *Scottish Geographical Magazine* 67 (1951): 85–100.

– "Land Use in the Uists Since 1800." *Proceedings of the Royal Society of Edinburgh* 77B (1979): 505–26.

Cameron, J.M. "The Role of Shipping from Scottish Ports in Emigration to the Canadas, 1815–1855." In *Canadian Papers in Rural History*, vol. 2, edited by D.H. Akenson, 135–54. Gananoque, Ont.: Langdale Press, 1980.

Campbell, A.B. *The Lanarkshire Miners: A Social History of Their Trade Unions, 1775–1874.* Edinburgh: John Donald Publishers, 1979.

Campbell, D., and R.A. MacLean. *Beyond the Atlantic Roar: A Study of the Nova Scotia Scots.* Toronto: McClelland and Stewart, 1974.

Canadian Mining Review, 1894.

Cann, D.B., J.I. MacDougall, J.D. Hilchey. *Soil Survey of Cape Breton Island Nova Scotia.* Truro, NS: Nova Scotia Soil Survey, 1963.

Careless, J.M.S. "'Limited Identities' in Canada.' *Canadian Historical Review* 50, no. 1 (1969): 1–10.

Cell, G.T. *English Enterprise in Newfoundland 1577–1660.* Toronto: University of Toronto Press, 1969.

Chapman, R.W., ed. *Johnson's Journey to the Western Islands of Scotland and Boswell's Journal of a Tour to the Hebrides with Samuel Johnson, L.L.D.* Oxford: Oxford University Press, 1970.

Chiasson, Fr. A. *Chéticamp: History and Acadian Traditions.* St John's, Nfld: Breakwater Books, 1986.

Clark, A.H. "Old World Origins and Religious Adherence in Nova Scotia." *Geographical Review* 50, no. 3 (1960): 317–44.

– *Three Centuries and the Island: A Historical Geography of Settlement and Agriculture in Prince Edward Island, Canada.* Toronto: University of Toronto Press, 1959.

Conrad, M. "Chronicles of the Exodus: Myths and Realities of Maritime Canadians in the United States, 1870–1930." In *The Northeastern Borderlands: Four Centuries of Interaction*, edited by S.J. Hornsby, V.A. Konrad, and J.J. Herlan, 97–119. Fredericton: Acadiensis Press, 1989.

Cowan, H.I. *British Emigration to British North America: The First Hundred Years.* 2nd ed., revised and enlarged. Toronto: University of Toronto Press, 1961.

Cozzens, F.S. *Acadia or A Month with the Blue Noses.* New York: Derby and Jackson, 1859.

Craig, B. "Agriculture and the Lumberman's Frontier in the Upper St. John Valley, 1800–70." *Journal of Forest History* 32, no. 3 (1988): 125–37.

– "Immigrants in a Frontier Community: Madawaska 1785–1850." *Histoire Sociale–Social History* 19 (1986): 277–97.

Crawford, I.A. "Feannagan Taomaidh (Lazy Beds)." *Scottish Studies* 6 (1962): 244–5.

– "Kelp Burning." *Scottish Studies* 6 (1962): 105–7.

Danhof, C.H. *Change in Agriculture: The Northern United States, 1820–1870.* Cambridge, Mass.: Harvard University Press, 1969.

– "Gathering the Grass." *Agricultural History* 30, no. 4 (1956): 169–73.

– "The Tools and Implements of Agriculture." *Agricultural History* 46, no. 1 (1972): 81–90.

Daniels, B.C. "Economic Development in Colonial and Revolutionary Connecticut: An Overview." *William and Mary Quarterly* 37, no. 3 (1980): 429–50.

Day, D., ed. *Geographical Perspectives on the Maritime Provinces.* Halifax: St Mary's University, 1988.

Dennis, C. *Cape Breton Over.* Toronto: Ryerson Press, 1942.

DesBarres, A.W. "A Description of the Island of Cape Breton, in North America; Including a Brief and Accurate Account of Its Constitution, Laws & Government." In *Impressions of Cape Breton*, edited by B. Tennyson, 73–86. Sydney, NS: University College of Cape Breton Press, 1986.

Devine, T.M. "Highland Migration to Lowland Scotland, 1760–1860." *Scottish Historical Review* 62, no. 2 (1983): 137–49.

– "Temporary Migration and the Scottish Highlands in the Nineteenth Century." *Economic History Review*, Series 2, 32, no. 3 (1979): 344–59.

Dictionary of Canadian Biography. Vols. 5 and 6. Toronto: University of Toronto Press, 1983–87.

Donovan, K., ed. *Cape Breton at 200: Historical Essays in Honour of the Island's Bicentennial 1785–1985.* Sydney, NS: University College of Cape Breton Press, 1985.

– , ed. *The Island: New Perspectives on Cape Breton History, 1713–1990.* Fredericton, NB: Acadiensis Press, 1990.

Doucette, L., ed. *Cultural Retention and Demographic Change: Studies of the Hebridean Scots in the Eastern Townships of Quebec.* National Museum of Man Mercury Series, Canadian Centre for Folk Culture Studies Paper 34. Ottawa: National Museums of Canada, 1980.

Drummond, R. *Recollections and Reflections of a Former Trade Union Leader.* 1926.

Duffus, A.F., G.E. MacFarlane, E.A. Pacey and G.W. Rogers. *Thy Dwellings Fair: Churches of Nova Scotia 1750–1830.* Hantsport, NS: Lancelot Press, 1982.

Dunn, C.W. *Highland Settler: A Portrait of the Scottish Gael in Nova Scotia.* Toronto: University of Toronto Press, 1953.

Earle, C.V. *The Evolution of a Tidewater Settlement System: All Hallow's Parish, Maryland, 1650–1783.* Chicago: Department of Geography, University of Chicago, 1975.

Earle, C.V., and R. Hoffman. "The Foundation of the Modern Economy: Agriculture and the Cost of Labour in the United States and England, 1800–60." *American Historical Review* 85, no. 5 (1980): 1055–94.

Easterbrook, W.T., and M.H. Watkins. *Approaches to Canadian Economic History*. Toronto: McClelland and Stewart, 1967.

Eller, R.D. *Miners, Millhands, and Mountaineers: Industrialization of the Appalachian South, 1880–1930*. Knoxville, Tenn.: University of Tennessee Press, 1982.

Elliott, B.S. *Irish Migrants in the Canadas: A New Approach*. Kingston and Montreal: McGill-Queen's University Press, 1988.

Ennals, P. "Nineteenth-Century Barns in Southern Ontario." *Canadian Geographer* 16, no. 3 (1972): 257–70.

– "The Yankee Origins of Bluenose Vernacular Architecture." *American Review of Canadian Studies* 12, no. 2 (1982): 5–21.

Ennals, P., and D. Holdsworth. "Vernacular Architecture and the Cultural Landscape of the Maritime Provinces – A Reconnaissance." *Acadiensis* 10, no. 2 (1981): 86–106.

Erickson, C. *Invisible Immigrants: The Adaptation of English and Scottish Immigrants in 19th Century America*. Leicester: Leicester University Press, 1972.

Farnham, C.H. "Cape Breton Folk." Introduction by Stephen F. Spencer. *Acadiensis* 8, no. 2 (1979): 90–106.

Fenton, A. *The Island Blackhouse*. Edinburgh: Her Majesty's Stationery Office, 1978.

– *Scottish Country Life*. Edinburgh: John Donald Publishers, 1976.

Fergusson, C.B., ed. *Uniacke's Sketches of Cape Breton, and Other Papers Relating to Cape Breton Island*. Halifax: Public Archives of Nova Scotia, 1958.

Fischer, L.R., and E.W. Sager, eds. *Merchant Shipping and Economic Development in Atlantic Canada*. St John's, Nfld: Memorial University of Newfoundland, 1982.

Flewwelling, R.G. "Immigration to and Emigration from Nova Scotia, 1839–1851." *Nova Scotia Historical Society Collections* 28 (1949): 75–106.

Frank, D. "The Cape Breton Coal Industry and the Rise and Fall of the British Empire Steel Corporation." *Acadiensis* 7, no. 1 (1977): 3–34.

– "Tradition and Culture in the Cape Breton Mining Community in the Early Twentieth Century." In *Cape Breton at 200: Historical Essays in Honour of the Island's Bicentennial 1785–1985*, edited by K. Donovan, 203–18. Sydney, NS: University College of Cape Breton Press, 1985.

Fraser-Mackintosh, C., ed. *Letters of Two Centuries chiefly connected with Inverness and the Highlands, from 1616 to 1815*. Inverness: A. & W. Mackenzie, 1890.

Frye, N. *The Bush Garden: Essays on the Canadian Imagination*. Toronto: House of Anansi Press, 1971.

Gaffield, C. "Boom and Bust: The Demography and Economy of the Lower Ottawa Valley in the Nineteenth Century." Canadian Historical Association. *Historical Papers*, 1982, 172–95.

Gagan, D. "Land, Population, and Social Change: The 'Critical Years' in Rural Canada West." *Canadian Historical Review* 59, no. 3 (1978): 293–318.

Gailey, R.A. "The Evolution of Highland Rural Settlement with Particular Reference to Argyllshire." *Scottish Studies* 6 (1962): 155–77.

Galbraith, J.K. *The Scotch.* Boston: Houghton Mifflin, 1964.

Gentilcore, R.L. "The Agricultural Background of Settlement in Eastern Nova Scotia." *Annals of the Association of American Geographers* 46, no. 2 (1956): 378–404.

Gesner, A. *The Industrial Resources of Nova Scotia.* Halifax: A & W Mackinlay, 1849.

Gilpin, E. *Coal Mining in Nova Scotia.* Montreal: John Lovell & Son, 1888.

Gittens, L. "Soapmaking in Britain, 1824–1851: A Study in Industrial Location." *Journal of Historical Geography* 8, no. 1 (1982): 29–40.

Goldring, P. "Lewis and the Hudson's Bay Company in the Nineteenth Century." *Scottish Studies* 24 (1980): 23–42.

Goode, J.B. *The Fisheries and Fishing Industries of the United States.* Sections 3 and 5. Washington, DC: US Government Printing Office, 1887.

Gow, J.M. *Cape Breton Illustrated.* Toronto: W. Briggs, 1893.

Grant, I.F. *Highland Folk Ways.* London: Routledge & Kegan Paul, 1961.

Gray, M. *The Highland Economy 1750–1850.* Edinburgh: Oliver and Boyd, 1957.

Greer, A. *Peasant, Lord, and Merchant: Rural Society in Three Quebec Parishes 1740–1840.* Toronto: University of Toronto Press, 1985.

Guernsey and Jersey Magazine. Jersey, 1837.

Haliburton, T.C. *An Historical and Statistical Account of Nova Scotia.* Halifax: Joseph Howe, 1829.

Hall, D.D., and D.G. Allen, eds. *Seventeenth-Century New England.* Boston: Colonial Society of Massachusetts, 1985.

Handcock, G. *Soe longe as there comes noe women: Origins of English Settlement in Newfoundland.* St John's, Nfld: Breakwater Books, 1989.

Harris, R.C. "European Beginnings in the Northwest Atlantic: A Comparative View." In *Seventeenth-Century New England*, edited by D.D. Hall and D.G. Allen, 119–52. Boston: Colonial Society of Massachusetts, 1985.

– "Industry and the Good Life around Idaho Peak." *Canadian Historical Review* 66, no. 3 (1985): 315–43.

– "Of Poverty and Helplessness in Petite-Nation." *Canadian Historical Review* 52, no. 1 (1971): 23–50.

– "The Pattern of Early Canada." *Canadian Geographer* 31, no. 4 (1987): 290–8.

– "Regionalism and the Canadian Archipelago." In *Heartland and Hinterland: A Geography of Canada*, edited by L.D. McCann, 459–84. Scarborough, Ont.: Prentice-Hall Canada, 1982.

– "The Simplification of Europe Overseas." *Annals of the Association of American Geographers* 67, no. 4 (1977): 469–83.
– , ed. *Historical Atlas of Canada*. Vol. 1, *From the Beginning to 1800*. Toronto: University of Toronto Press, 1987.

Harris, R.C., P. Roulston and C. De Freitas. "The Settlement of Mono Township." *Canadian Geographer* 19, no. 1 (1975): 1–17.

Harvey, D.C. "The Civil List and Responsible Government in Nova Scotia." *Canadian Historical Review* 28, no. 4 (1947): 365–82.
– "Scottish Immigration to Cape Breton." *Dalhousie Review* 21, no. 3 (1941): 313–24.
– , ed. *Holland's Description of Cape Breton Island and Other Documents*. Halifax: Public Archives of Nova Scotia, 1935.
– , ed. *Letters of Rev. Norman McLeod, 1835–1851*. Halifax: Public Archives of Nova Scotia, 1939.

Head, C.G. *Eighteenth Century Newfoundland: A Geographer's Perspective*. Toronto: McClelland and Stewart, 1976.

Henretta, J.A. *The Evolution of American Society, 1700–1815: An Interdisciplinary Analysis*. Lexington, Mass.: D.C. Heath & Co., 1973.

Hirschman, A.O. "A Generalized Linkage Approach to Development, with Special Reference to Staples." In *Essays on Economic Development and Cultural Change in Honor of Bert F. Hoselitz*, edited by M. Nash, 67–98. Economic and Cultural Change series 25. Chicago: University of Chicago Press, 1977.

Hornsby, S.J. "An Historical Geography of Cape Breton Island in the Nineteenth Century." PhD thesis, University of British Columbia, 1986.
– "Migration and Settlement: The Scots of Cape Breton." In *Geographical Perspectives on the Maritime Provinces*, edited by D. Day, 15–24. Halifax: St Mary's University, 1988.
– "Scottish Emigration and Settlement in Early Nineteenth Century Cape Breton." In *The Island: New Perspectives on Cape Breton History, 1713–1990*, edited by K. Donovan, 49–69. Fredericton, NB: Acadiensis Press, 1990. Reprinted in *People, Places, Patterns, Processes: Geographical Perspectives on the Canadian Past*, edited by G. Wynn, 110–38. Toronto: Copp Clark Pitman, 1990.
– "Staple Trades, Subsistence Agriculture, and Nineteenth-Century Cape Breton Island." *Annals of the Association of American Geographers* 79, no. 3 (1989): 411–34.

Hornsby, S.J., V.A. Konrad and J.J. Herlan eds. *The Northeastern Borderlands: Four Centuries of Interaction*. Fredericton: Acadiensis Press, 1989.

Howatson, W. "The Scottish Hairst and Seasonal Labour 1600–1870." *Scottish Studies* 26 (1982): 13–36.

Hudson, J.C. "Migration to an American Frontier." *Annals of the Association of American Geographers* 66, no. 2 (1976): 242–65.

Hunter, J. "The Emergence of the Crofting Community: The Religious Contribution 1798–1843." *Scottish Studies* 18 (1974): 95–116.

– *The Making of the Crofting Community*. Edinburgh: John Donald Publishers, 1976.

Innes, S. *Labor in a New Land: Economy and Society in Seventeenth-Century Springfield*. Princeton, NJ: Princeton University Press, 1983.

Innis, H.A. *The Cod Fisheries: The Study of an International Economy*. Rev. ed. Toronto: University of Toronto Press, 1954.

– *The Fur Trade in Canada: An Introduction to Canadian Economic History*. New Haven: Yale University Press, 1930.

Jackson, E.A. "Some of North Sydney's Loyalists." *Nova Scotia Historical Review* 3, no. 2 (1983): 5–22.

Johnson, L. "Land Policy, Population Growth and Social Structure in the Home District, 1793–1851." *Ontario History* 63 (1971): 41–60.

Johnson, W.R. *The Coal Trade of British America with researches on the characters and practical values of American and Foreign Coals*. Washington, 1850.

Johnston, A.A. *A History of the Catholic Church in Eastern Nova Scotia*. Vols. 1–2. Antigonish, NS: St Francis Xavier University Press, 1960–71.

Johnston, H.J.M. *British Emigration Policy 1815–1830: 'Shovelling out Paupers.'* Oxford: Oxford University Press, 1972.

Joncas, I.Z. *The Fisheries of Canada: The Fisheries Exhibition Literature*. Vol. 5, Conferences, 2. London: W. Clowes and Sons, 1883.

Judd, R.W. *Aroostook: A Century of Logging in Northern Maine*. Orono, Me: University of Maine Press, 1988.

– "Lumbering and the Farming Frontier in Aroostook County, Maine, 1840–1880." *Journal of Forest History* 28, no. 2 (1984): 56–67.

Kerr, D., and D.W. Holdsworth, eds. *Historical Atlas of Canada*. Vol. 3, Addressing the Twentieth Century. Toronto: University of Toronto Press, 1990.

Kincaid, B.A. "Scottish Immigration to Cape Breton, 1758–1838." MA thesis, Dalhousie University, 1964.

Knight, T.F. *Shore and Deep Sea Fisheries of Nova Scotia*. Halifax, 1867.

Langhout, R. "Alternative Opportunities: The Development of Shipping at Sydney Harbour 1842–1889." In *Cape Breton at 200: Historical Essays in Honour of the Island's Bicentennial 1785–1985*, edited by K. Donovan, 53–69. Sydney, NS: University College of Cape Breton Press, 1985.

Lee, D. *The Robins in Gaspé 1766 to 1825*. Markham, Ont.: Fitzhenry and Whiteside, 1984.

Lemon, J.T. *The Best Poor Man's Country: A Geographical Study of Early Southeastern Pennsylvania*. Baltimore: Johns Hopkins Press, 1972.

– "Colonial America in the Eighteenth Century." In *North America: Historical Geography of a Changing Continent*, edited by R.D. Mitchell and P.A. Groves, 121–46. Totowa, NJ: Rowman and Littlefield, 1987.

Le Roy Ladurie, E. *The Peasants of Languedoc*. Translated J. Day. Urbana: University of Illinois Press, 1976.

Linteau, P-A., R. Durocher and J-C. Robert. *Quebec: A History 1867–1929*. Translated by R. Chodos. Toronto: James Lorimer & Co., 1983.

Little, L. "Collective Action in Outport Newfoundland: A Case Study from the 1830s." *Labour/Le Travail* 26 (Fall 1990): 7–35.

Lockridge, K.A. "Land, Population, and the Evolution of New England Society, 1630–1790." *Past and Present* 39 (1968): 62–80.

– *A New England Town, The First Hundred Years: Dedham, Massachusetts, 1636–1736*. New York: W.W. Norton & Co., 1970.

Loucks, O.L. "A Forest Classification for the Maritime Provinces." *Proceedings of the Nova Scotia Institute of Science* 25, pt 2 (1962): 85–167.

McCallum, J. *Unequal Beginnings: Agriculture and Economic Development in Quebec and Ontario until 1870*. Toronto: University of Toronto Press, 1980.

McCann, L.D. "'Living a Double life': Town and Country in the Industrialization of the Maritimes." In *Geographical Perspectives on the Maritime Provinces*, edited by D. Day, 93–113. Halifax: St Mary's University, 1988.

– "Metropolitanism and Branch Businesses in the Maritimes, 1881–1931." *Acadiensis* 13, no. 1 (1983): 112–25.

– , ed. *Heartland and Hinterland: A Geography of Canada*. Scarborough, Ont.: Prentice-Hall Canada, 1982.

McCullogh, A.B. "Currency Conversion in British North America, 1760–1900." *Archivaria* 16 (1983): 83–94.

McCusker, J.J., and R.R. Menard. *The Economy of British America, 1607–1789*. Chapel Hill, NC: University of North Carolina Press, 1985.

McDermott, G.L. "Frontiers of Settlement in the Great Clay Belt of Ontario and Quebec." *Annals of the Association of American Geographers* 51, no. 3 (1961): 261–73.

MacDonald, C.O. *The Coal and Iron Industries of Nova Scotia*. Halifax: Chronicle, 1909.

Macdonald, D. *Lewis: A History of the Island*. Edinburgh: Gordon Wright Publishing, 1978.

MacDonald, J. *General View of the Agriculture of the Hebrides*. Edinburgh: Phillips, 1811.

MacDonald, N. *Canada, 1763–1841 Immigration and Settlement: The Administration of the Imperial Land Regulations*. London: Longmans, Green and Co., 1939.

MacDonell, M. *The Emigrant Experience: Songs of Highland Emigrants in North America*. Toronto: University of Toronto Press, 1982.

MacDougall, J.L. *History of Inverness County Nova Scotia*. Truro, NS: 1922.

Macgillivray, D. "Henry Melville Whitney Comes to Cape Breton: The Saga of a Gilded Age Entrepreneur." *Acadiensis* 9, no. 1 (1979): 44–70.

Macgillivray, D., and B. Tennyson, eds. *Cape Breton Historical Essays*. Sydney, NS: College of Cape Breton Press, 1980.

MacGregor, J. *Historical and Descriptive Sketches of the Maritime Colonies of British North America*. London, 1828. Reprint. New York: S.R. Publishers, 1968.

– *Observations on Emigration to British America*. London: Longman, Rees, Orme, Brown, and Green, 1829.

MacKay, D. *Scotland Farewell: The People of the Hector*. Toronto: McGraw-Hill Ryerson, 1980.

McKay, I. "The Crisis of Dependent Development: Class Conflict in the Nova Scotia Coalfields, 1872–1876." *Canadian Journal of Sociology* 13 (1988): 9–48.

– "'By Wisdom, Wile, or War': The Provincial Workmen's Association and the Struggle for Working-Class Independence in Nova Scotia, 1879–97." *Labour/Le Travail* 18 (1986): 13–62.

Mackay, M. "Nineteenth Century Tiree Emigrant Communities in Ontario." *Oral History Journal* 9, no. 1 (1981): 49–60.

– "Poets and Pioneers: Nineteenth-century Tiree emigrants in Canada." In *Odyssey: Voices from Scotland's Recent Past*, edited by B. Kay, 59–69. Edinburgh: Polygon Books, 1980.

MacKenzie, A.A. "Cape Breton and the Western Harvest Excursions 1890–1928." In *Cape Breton at 200: Historical Essays in Honour of the Island's Bicentennial 1785–1985*, edited by K. Donovan, 71–83. Sydney, NS: University College of Cape Breton Press, 1985.

MacKenzie, A.A., and A.J. MacKenzie. *MacKenzie's History of Christmas Island Parish*. Sudbury, Ont.: MacKenzie Rothe Publishing, 1984.

MacKenzie, M.B. "The Great Gold Rush." *Cape Breton Mirror* 1, no. 10 (September 1952): 4, 21.

McKenzie, N.R. *The Gael Fares Forth*. Wellington, New Zealand: Whitecombe and Tombs, 1942.

MacKinnon, R., and G. Wynn. "Nova Scotian Agriculture in the 'Golden Age': A New Look." In *Geographical Perspectives on the Maritime Provinces*, edited by D. Day, 47–60. Halifax: St Mary's University, 1988.

McLean, M. "Acdh an Rhigh: A Highland Response to the Assisted Emigration of 1815." In *Canadian Papers in Rural History*, vol. 5, edited by D.H. Akenson, 181–97. Gananoque, Ont.: Langdale Press, 1986.

– "'In the new land a new Glengarry.' Migration from the Scottish Highlands to Upper Canada." PhD thesis, University of Edinburgh, 1982.

– "Peopling Glengarry County: The Scottish Origins of a Canadian Community." Canadian Historical Association. *Historical Papers*, 1982, 156–71.

MacLeod, D. "Colliers, Colliery Safety and Workplace Control: The Nova Scotian Experience, 1873 to 1910." Canadian Historical Association. *Historical Papers*, 1983, 226–53.

McNabb, D. *Old Sydney Town: Historic Buildings of the North End, 1785 to 1938.* Sydney, NS: Old Sydney Society, 1986.

MacNeil, A.R. "A Reconsideration of the State of Agriculture in Eastern Nova Scotia, 1791–1861." MA thesis, Queen's University, Kingston, 1985.

MacNeil, J.N. *Tales until Dawn: The World of a Cape Breton Gaelic Story-Teller.* Kingston and Montreal: McGill-Queen's University Press, 1987.

MacNutt, W.S. *The Atlantic Provinces: The Emergence of Colonial Society 1712–1857.* Toronto: McClelland and Stewart, 1965.

MacPherson, A.G. "People in Transition: The Broken Mosaic." In *The Atlantic Provinces*, edited by A.G. MacPherson, 46–72. Toronto: University of Toronto Press, 1972.

Mannion, J.J. *Irish Settlements in Eastern Canada: A Study of Cultural Transfer and Adaptation.* Toronto: University of Toronto Press, 1974.

– "Old World Antecedents, New World Adaptations: Inistioge (Co. Kilkenny) Immigrants to Newfoundland." *Newfoundland Studies* 5, no. 2 (1989): 103–75.

– *Point Lance in Transition: The Transformation of a Newfoundland Outport.* Toronto: McClelland and Stewart, 1976.

– "Settlers and Traders in Western Newfoundland." In *The Peopling of Newfoundland: Essays in Historical Geography*, edited by J.J. Mannion, 234–75. St John's, Nfld: Institute of Social and Economic Research, Memorial University of Newfoundland, 1977.

– "The Waterford Merchants and the Irish-Newfoundland Provisions Trade, 1770–1820." In *Canadian Papers in Rural History*, vol. 3, edited by D.H. Akenson, 178–203. Gananoque, Ont.: Langdale Press, 1982.

Marshall, W. *General View of the Agriculture of the Central Highlands of Scotland.* London: Board of Agriculture, 1794.

Martell, J.S. "The Achievements of Agricola and the Agricultural Societies, 1818–1825." *Bulletin of the Public Archives of Nova Scotia* 1, no. 3 (1940): 1–48.

– "Early Coal Mining in Nova Scotia." *Dalhousie Review* 25, no. 2 (1945): 156–72.

– "From Central Board to Secretary of Agriculture, 1826–1885." *Bulletin of the Public Archives of Nova Scotia* 2, no. 3 (1940): 1–30.

– *Immigration to and Emigration from Nova Scotia 1815–1838.* Halifax: Public Archives of Nova Scotia, 1942.

Martin, J.L. *The Ross Farm Story: A Brief History of Agriculture in Nova Scotia with Particular Emphasis on Life on the Small Upland Farm.* Halifax: Nova Scotia Museum, 1974.

Martin, R.M. *History of Nova Scotia, Cape Breton, the Sable Islands, New Brunswick, Prince Edward Island, the Bermudas, Newfoundland, etc., etc.* London: Whittaker, 1837.

Meinig, D.W. *The Shaping of America: A Geographical Perspective on 500 Years of History*. Vol. 1, *Atlantic America, 1492–1800*. New Haven and London: Yale University Press, 1986.

Mewett, P.G. "Occupational Pluralism in Crofting: The Influence of Non-Croft Work on the Patterns of Crofting Agriculture in the Isle of Lewis Since about 1850." *Scottish Journal of Sociology* 2, no. 1 (1977): 31–49.

Meyer, D. "The National Integration of Regional Economies, 1860–1920." In *North America: The Historical Geography of a Changing Continent*, edited by R.D. Mitchell and P.A. Groves, 321–46. Totowa, NJ: Rowman and Littlefield, 1987.

Millward, H. "A Model of Coalfield Development: Six Stages Exemplified by the Sydney Field." *Canadian Geographer* 29, no. 3 (1985): 234–48.

– *Regional Patterns of Ethnicity in Nova Scotia: A Geographical Study*. Halifax: St Mary's University, 1981.

Mitchell, R.D., and P.A. Groves, eds. *North America: The Historical Geography of a Changing Continent*. Totowa, NJ: Rowman and Littlefield, 1987.

Molloy, M. "'No Inclination to Mix with Strangers': Marriage Patterns among Highland Scots Migrants to Cape Breton and New Zealand, 1800–1916." *Journal of Family History* 11, no. 3 (1986): 221–43.

Montgomery, D. *The Fall of the House of Labor: The Workplace, the State, and American Labor Activism, 1865–1925*. Cambridge: Cambridge University Press, 1987.

Moore, C. "The Other Louisbourg: Trade and Merchant Enterprise in Ile Royale 1713–58." *Histoire Sociale–Social History* 11 (1978): 79–96.

Moorsom, W. *Letters from Nova Scotia*. London: Colburn & Bentley, 1830.

Morgan, R.J. "The Loyalists of Cape Breton." *Dalhousie Review* 55, no. 1 (1975): 5–22.

– "Orphan Outpost: Cape Breton Colony, 1784–1820." PhD thesis, University of Ottawa, 1972.

– "'Poverty, wretchedness, and misery': The Great Famine on Cape Breton, 1845–1856." *Nova Scotia Historical Review* 6, no. 1 (1986): 88–104.

Muise, D.W. "The General Mining Association and Nova Scotia's Coal." *Bulletin of Canadian Studies* 6–7 (1983): 70–87.

– "The Making of an Industrial Community: Cape Breton Coal Towns, 1867–1900." In *Cape Breton Historical Essays*, edited by D. Macgillivray and B. Tennyson, 76–94. Sydney, NS: College of Cape Breton Press, 1980.

Muise, D.W., and C. Armour. *Shipping and Shipbuilding in the Maritime Provinces in the Nineteenth Century*. Canada's Visual History series 1, vol. 9. Ottawa: National Museum of Man/National Film Board of Canada, 1974.

Nash, M., ed. *Essays on Economic Development and Cultural Change in Honor of Bert F. Hoselitz*. Economic and Social Change series 25. Chicago: University of Chicago Press, 1977.

New Statistical Account of Scotland. Edinburgh: William Blackwood and Sons, 1845.

Nova Scotia Museum. *Cossit House.*

Ommer, R.E. "Highland Scots Migration to Southwestern Newfoundland: A Study of Kinship." In *The Peopling of Newfoundland: Essays in Historical Geography*, edited by J.J. Mannion, 212–33. St John's, Nfld: Institute of Social and Economic Research, Memorial University of Newfoundland, 1977.

– *From Outpost to Outport: A Structural Analysis of the Jersey-Gaspé Cod Fishery, 1767–1886.* Montreal and Kingston: McGill-Queen's University Press, 1991.

– "Primitive Accumulation and the Scottish Clann in the Old World and the New." *Journal of Historical Geography* 12, no. 2 (1986): 121–41.

Parker, J.P. *Cape Breton Ships and Men.* Toronto: McGraw-Hill Ryerson, 1967.

Potter, D.M. *People of Plenty: Economic Abundance and the American Character.* Chicago: University of Chicago Press, 1954.

Remiggi, F.W. "Ethnic Diversity and Settler Location on the Eastern Lower North Shore of Quebec." In *The Peopling of Newfoundland: Essays in Historical Geography*, edited by J.J. Mannion, 184–211. St John's, Nfld: Institute of Social and Economic Research, Memorial University of Newfoundland, 1977.

Richards, E. *A History of the Highland Clearances: Agrarian Transformation and the Evictions 1746–1886.* London: Croom Helm, 1982.

– *A History of the Highland Clearances.* Vol. 2, *Emigration, Protest, Reasons.* London: Croom Helm, 1985.

Riddell, R.G. "A Study in the Land Policy of the Colonial Office, 1763–1855." *Canadian Historical Review* 18, no. 4 (1937): 385–405.

Roach, T.R. "The Pulpwood Trade and the Settlers of the New Ontario, 1919–1938." *Journal of Canadian Studies* 22, no. 3 (1987): 78–88.

Rutman, D.B. "People in Process: The New Hampshire Towns in the Eighteenth Century." *Journal of Urban History* 1, no. 3 (1975): 268–92.

Ryan, S. *Fish out of Water: The Newfoundland Saltfish Trade 1814–1914.* St John's, Nfld: Breakwater Books, 1986.

Sabine, L. *Report of the Principal Fisheries of the American Seas.* Washington, DC: Armstrong, 1853.

Sager, E.W. "Dependency, Underdevelopment, and the Economic History of the Atlantic Provinces." *Acadiensis* 17, no. 1 (1987): 117–37.

Sager, E.W., and G.E. Panting. *Maritime Capital: The Shipping Industry in Atlantic Canada, 1820–1914.* Montreal and Kingston: McGill-Queen's University Press, 1990.

Salaman, R. *The History and Social Influence of the Potato.* 2nd ed. Cambridge: Cambridge University Press, 1985.

Samson, R. *Fishermen and Merchants in 19th Century Gaspé: The Fishermen-Dealers of William Hyman and Sons.* Ottawa: Parks Canada, 1984.

Shannon, F.A. *The Farmer's Last Frontier: Agriculture, 1860–1897.* New York: Farrar & Rinehart, 1945.

Sinclair, Sir J. *General View of the Agriculture of the Northern Counties and Islands of Scotland.* London: Board of Agriculture, 1795.

Skene, W.F. *Celtic Scotland: A History of Ancient Alban.* Vol. 3, *Land and People.* Edinburgh: 1880.

Smith, H.N. *Virgin Land: The American West As Symbol and Myth.* Cambridge, Mass.: Harvard University Press, 1950.

Stanley, L. *The Well-Watered Garden: The Presbyterian Church in Cape Breton, 1798–1860.* Sydney, NS: University College of Cape Breton Press, 1983.

Tennyson, B. *Impressions of Cape Breton.* Sydney, Nova Scotia: University College of Cape Breton Press, 1986.

Thompson, E.P. "The Moral Economy of the English Crowd in the Eighteenth Century." *Past and Present* 50 (1971): 76–136.

– "Time, Work Discipline and Industrial Capitalism." *Past and Present* 38 (1967): 56–97.

Thompson, J.H. "Bringing in the Sheaves: The Harvest Excursionists, 1890–1929." *Canadian Historical Review* 59, no. 4 (1978): 467–89.

Thornton, P.A. "The Problem of Out-Migration from Atlantic Canada, 1871–1921: A New Look." *Acadiensis* 15, no. 1 (1985): 3–34.

– "Some Preliminary Comments on the Extent and Consequences of Out-Migration from the Atlantic Region, 1870–1920." In *Merchant Shipping and Economic Development in Atlantic Canada*, edited by L.R. Fischer and E.W. Sager, 187–218. St John's, Nfld: Memorial University of Newfoundland, 1982.

Toward, L.M. "The Influence of Scottish Clergy on early Education in Cape Breton." *Collections of the Nova Scotia Historical Society* 29 (1951): 153–77.

Turner, F.J. "The Significance of the Frontier in American History." American Historical Association. *Annual Report 1893.* Washington, DC, 1894.

Vernon, C.W. *Cape Breton, Canada, at the Beginning of the Twentieth Century: A Treatise of Natural Resources and Development.* Toronto: Nation, 1903.

Vicero, R. *Immigration of French Canadians to New England, 1840–1900: A Geographical Analysis.* Ann Arbor, Mich.: University Microfilms, 1970.

Wagg, P.M. "Lawrence Kavanagh I: An Eighteenth-Century Cape Breton Entrepreneur." *Nova Scotia Historical Review* 10, no. 2 (1990): 124–32.

Warner, C.D. *Baddeck, and That Sort of Thing.* Boston: Houghton Mifflin, 1874.

Watkins, M.H. "A Staple Theory of Economic Growth." In *Approaches to Canadian Economic History*, edited by W.T. Easterbrook and M.H. Watkins, 49–73. Toronto: McClelland and Stewart, 1967.

Williams, R.H. *Historical Account of the Lobster Canning Industry.* Halifax, 1930.

Williams, T. "The Williams Lobster Factory at Neil's Harbour, 1901–1935." *Nova Scotia Historical Review* 8, no. 1 (1988): 77–83.

Withers, C.W.J. "Highland-Lowland Migration and the Making of the Crofting Community, 1755–1891." *Scottish Geographical Magazine* 103, no. 2 (1987): 76–83.

Wynn, G. "Administration in Adversity: The Deputy Surveyors and Control of the New Brunswick Crown Forest before 1844." *Acadiensis* 7, no. 1 (1977): 49–65.

– "'Deplorably Dark and Demoralized Lumberers'? Rhetoric and Reality in Early Nineteenth-Century New Brunswick." *Journal of Forest History* 24, no. 4 (1980): 168–87.

– "Ethnic Migrations and Atlantic Canada: Geographical Perspectives." *Canadian Ethnic Studies* 18, no. 1 (1986): 1–15.

– "Exciting a Spirit of Emulation among the 'Plodholes': Agricultural Reform in Pre-Confederation Nova Scotia." *Acadiensis* 20, no. 1 (1990): 5–51.

– "The Maritimes: The Geography of Fragmentation and Underdevelopment." In *Heartland and Hinterland: A Geography of Canada*, edited by L.D. McCann, 157–213. Scarborough, Ont.: Prentice-Hall Canada, 1982.

– "Notes on Society and Environment in Old Ontario." *Journal of Social History* 13, no. 1 (1979): 49–65.

– "A Province Too Much Dependent on New England." *Canadian Geographer* 31, no. 2 (1987): 98–113.

– "A Region of Scattered Settlements and Bounded Possibilities: Northeastern America 1775–1800." *Canadian Geographer* 31, no. 4 (1987): 319–38.

– "Settler Societies in Geographic Focus." *Historical Studies* 20, no. 80 (1983): 353–66.

– "A Share of the Necessaries of Life: Remarks on Migration, Development, and Dependency in Atlantic Canada." In *Beyond Anger and Longing: Community and Development in Atlantic Canada*, edited by B. Fleming, 17–52. Fredericton, NB: Acadiensis Press, 1988.

– *Timber Colony: A Historical Geography of Early Nineteenth Century New Brunswick*. Toronto: University of Toronto Press, 1981.

– , ed. *People, Places, Patterns, Processes: Geographical Perspectives on the Canadian Past*. Toronto: Copp Clark Pitman, 1990.

Youngson, A.J. *After the Forty-Five: The Economic Impact on the Scottish Highlands*. Edinburgh: Edinburgh University Press, 1973.

Index

Acadian Recorder, 187–8, 190

Acadians: emigration to Newfoundland, 186; employed in farming, 20; employed in fishery, 12, 93–4 *passim*, 204; occupations of, 14 (table); settlement of, 3, 5, 15, 48, 121, 168, 207

Agricultural exports, 23, 60–2, 128, 130

Agricultural implements, 69–70, 72, 134–7, 140

Agricultural improvement, 63, 66–7, 69, 131, 133–4

Agricultural markets, 23, 59–63, 128, 130–1

Agricultural settlement: in Canada, xxiii, 207–9; in Cape Breton, 19–25, 48–51, 123–5, 203; in the Thirteen Colonies, xxi–xxii

Agricultural societies, 78–9, 146; Broad Cove, 67; Cape Breton, 66; Mabou, 80; Port Hood, 69, 80; Richmond, 63; Sydney, 69

Agriculture: American competition in, 130–1; backland, 71–2, 139–40, 203; early, 23–4; extensive, 69; frontland, 63–71, 131–9, 203; outport, 92–3, 162–3

Aguire & Borando, 88

Anticosti, 90, 158

Antigonish, 60

Applecross, 31

Archbold, E.P., 170

Archibald & Co., 169–70, 184

Ardnamurchan, 31, 43

Argyll, 31, 32

Arichat, 83, 86, 115, 144; agricultural market in, 63, 80; agricultural society, 79; fishery at, 5; migrant labour at, 93; Roman Catholic Church at, 168; settlement of, 3, 13, 163–4 (figure); shipbuilding at, 19; shipping at, 19; trade at, 5

Arichat News Budget, 165

Arisaig, 31

Arnot & Co., 88

Aspy Bay, 51, 55

Baddeck, 63, 83, 144, 148–9 *passim*; emigration from, 187; fishery at, 86; granting land at, 51; oat mill at, 81; potato blight at, 118; potato famine at, 116–17 *passim*; tourism at, 150

Baddeck River, 3, 20, 48, 51

Ball's Bridge, 71–2 *passim*

Barbados, 11

Barra, 31, 32, 42, 44, 45

Benbecula, 31, 44

Blockhouse coal mine, 170, 172, 176, 178–9 (figure)

Boisdale Hills, 51, 71

Boston: agricultural implements from, 69; coal exports to, 108; emigration to, 194–5, 198; employment in, 141, 161, 204; industrial investment from, 201

Boularderie, 51, 116, 131, 187

Bourinot, Marshall, 170

Boyle, Dougald, 163, 165–6, 169, 197–8
Bracadale, 44
Bras d'Or Lake, 22, 50, 58, 80, 83, 86, 89, 90, 117, 149, 154
Brazil, 88, 154–5
Bridgeport, 51; coal mine at, 98–101 *passim*, 103, 176, 178; emigration from, 191
British Columbia, 190–1, 194, 195, 199, 201
Broad Cove: agricultural improvement at, 63; dairying at, 67; driving cattle from, 128; emigration from, 186, 197; oat mill at, 81; potato blight at, 112–13; potato famine at, 112–14 *passim*; Scots at, 76
Brown, R.H., 177–8
Brown, Richard, 96–7 *passim*, 103, 106, 173
Brymer, Arthur, 113

Caledonia coal mine, 172, 174 (figure), 176, 178
Campbell, Angus, 199–200
Campbell, Charles J., 148–9, 169
Campbell, Donald, 58, 71, 75, 76
Campbell, Hugh Oig and Hugh Ban, 197
Campbell, Lieutenant-Governor, 55
Campbell, Samuel, 55–6
Campbell Mountain, 114
Campbellton coal mine, 149, 169
Canadian Pacific Railway (CPR): "harvest specials," 193
Canna, 31, 45
Canning, King's County, NS, emigration from, 195, 197
Cape Ann Advertiser, 161–2

Cape Breton County: coal industry in, 202; emigration from, 190; famine relief in, 113, 115–16, 118; lobster fishery in, 160; squatters in, 126
Cape Mabou, 114
Cape North, 51, 59, 116, 155, 157
Caribou Cove, 157
Catalone Lake, 144
Central Board of Agriculture, 80
Chaleur Bay, 5
Channel Islands, 28; labour, 11–12, 93, 154, 201; merchants, xxv, 4–6, 11, 15, 86–8, 93, 154, 184, 201, 204–5
Charlottetown, 108
Chéticamp, 83; climate at, 23; farming at, 20; fishery at, 5, 11, 85, 89, 155, 167–8; migrant labour at, 93, 154; settlement of, 3, 13, 93
Chignecto Post, 189
Christmas Island, 128, 141, 149–50 (figure)
Clearances, 41–5, 204
Coal industry, 15–18, 95–107, 169–83, 202–3; indebtedness of miners in, 180–1; labour in, 16–17 (table), 95, 100–3, 176–7 (figure), 180; leases, 96, 169; settlement, 18, 95, 103–5, 178–9 (figure); strikes in, 106, 181–2; techniques and technology of, 16, 95, 98–100, 173, 176; trade, 15–16, 95, 96, 170–2; wages in, 18, 106, 180
Codroy Valley, Newfoundland, 186, 193, 197
Colchester County, 61
Coll, 31, 44
Colonization schemes, 125

Committee for Relief of Distressed Settlers, 115–16
Committee on Crown Property, 126
Corbet, David, 76
Corbet, William, 76
Cottars, 39–40
Courteau, Father, 94
Cow Bay, 81
Coxheath Hills, 51
Crawley, H.W., surveyor general of Cape Breton, 53–5 *passim*, 58, 125
Creighton & Grassie, 88
Creignish Hills, 51, 125
Crèvecour, Hector St John de, xxii
Crichton, William, 92
Crofting, 33–7, 40, 42, 44, 143
Crop failure, 74
Crown land: regulations, 51–3, 126–8; removing timber from, 58; sales of, 23, 126–8
Cumberland County, 61
Cunard, Samuel, 96–7 *passim*

DeCarteret & LeVesconte, 86, 88, 90, 93–4, 108–9, 154, 158, 166–7
D'Escousse, 5, 86
Diet, 39, 40, 71, 74, 142
Domestic service, 141
Dominion Coal Company, xvii, 183, 203
Doyle, James, 80
Drummond, Robert, 178, 181–2

East Bay, 149; granting land at, 48, 51; potato famine at, 116; squatter settlement at, 123, 125
Eastern Chronicle, 189
Eigg, 31, 44, 45
Emigration: from Cape Breton, 186–200; from coal industry, 106–7,

190–1; from Great Britain, 30; from the Highlands, 41–7; to United States, 194–7, 198; of women, 189, 195

Farm: establishing a, 57–8; labour, 59, 70, 72; mixed, 63; sales, 75
Farmers, number of, 123
Farquharson, Rev. Alexander, 117
Ferguson, John, 73
Finlayson, John, 197
Fishermen: destitution of, 94, 165; indebtedness of, 14–15, 165; kinship among, 155, 168; number of, 87 (figure), 152–3 (figure)
Fishery, xxiv, 4–15, 85–95, 152–69, 201–2; American, 92, 128, 161–2; bank, 90; exports, 5, 7, 11, 87–8, 154–5; herring, 11, 90, 91 (figure), 159–60; labour in, 11–13, 93, 154; lobster, 160–1 (figure), 168; mackerel, 11, 90, 91 (figure), 159–60; merchants in, xxv, 4–7, 11, 14–15, 86–9, 90, 92, 154–5, 166–8; planters in, 14–15; salmon, 11, 90, 159; seal, 11, 90, 92; settlements, 13, 93, 162–7 (figures); techniques and technology of, 7–11, 89–90, 155, 157–60; trade, 5–7, 87–9, 154–5
Forest cover, 22
Fort William, 32
Fourchu, 160
Framboise, 51
Frazer, Donald, 88
Frazer, Rev. James, 74, 117
Frye, Northrop, xxiii

Gabarus: fishery at, 85, 89–90 passim, 155; lobster fishery at, 160; potato famine at, 116; settlement of, 3, 5
Gaelic, 76, 144, 204–5
Gairloch, 31
Gaspé, 5
General Mining Association (GMA), 83, 95–106 passim, 169, 170, 172–3, 176–8 passim, 180, 184, 190, 203
Glace Bay, 86, 170, 172, 176, 178
Glace Bay Mining Company, 183
Glasgow Colonial Society, 77
Glencoe, 131
Glenelg, 31
Glengarry, 32
Glen Orchy, 32
Gloucester, Mass., 141, 161
Gowrie coal mine, 169–70, 172, 176, 178–9 (figure)
Graham & Taylor, 88
Grand Mira, 116
Grand Narrows, 51, 116, 131, 141
Grand River, 51, 76
Gut of Canso, 79, 86, 108

Haliburton, Thomas, 47, 83
Halifax, 15, 83, 206; currency, 16; emigration to, 191; employment in, 141–2 passim; merchants, 7, 88–9, 166–7, 205; shipping, 19; trade with, 7, 11, 15, 23, 61–3, 88–90 passim, 107–8, 128, 146, 206
Harrington, Charles, 116–17
Harris, 31, 44–6 passim
Harvey, Lieutenant-Governor, 114, 118, 187

Hebrides, 31, 33, 43, 76
Housing: in Cape Breton, 13, 24, 70, 74, 137–8, 142; in the Highlands, 39–40
Howley's Ferry, 86, 89

Indian Bay, 86
Indian Rear, 115
Ingonish: fishery at, 86, 152, 155; lobster fishery at, 160; granting land at, 51; potato famine at, 116
Intercolonial Railway, xvi, 144, 206
International coal mine, 170, 172, 176
Inverness County, 31, 63, 65, 125, 149, 198; emigration from, 189–90; famine relief in, 113, 115–16, 118–20; lobster fishery in, 160; meat-packing industry in, 146; squatters in, 126
Inverness-shire, 30
Ireland, 11
Irish: emigration from Cape Breton to Newfoundland, 186; employment in fishery, 94, 204; employment in mines, 16, 59, 180; settlement of, 5, 121–2, 168, 207
Île Madame: fishery, 5, 85, 89, 155; lobster fishery at, 160; merchants at, 155; settlement of, 3, 93, 162; shipbuilding on, 108
Île Petabe, 117

Janvrin, John, 114–15 passim, 117
Janvrin & Co., 5, 11, 86–7
Jefferson, Thomas, xxii
Jersey, 19, 83, 87, 109
Johnson, Dr, 76
Judique, 76, 157, 160

Kavanagh, Lawrence, 6–7
Kelp industry, 33, 37,
    41–3
Kempt Road, 55
Kingross, 51
Kin groups, 76, 143–4
Kintail, 31
Knoydart, 46

Labrador, 11, 90
Lake Ainslie, 51, 63, 67,
    113–14 passim, 117
Lake Uist, 125
Land: cost of clearing,
    57; occupied, 123; pur-
    chase of, 53–4
L'Archeveque, 73, 160
L'Ardoise, 5, 58, 85, 113–
    14 passim
LeVesconte, William, 161
Lewis, 31, 32, 42, 44, 46
Lewis Cove Road, 51
Lime kilns, 148
Lingan, 81, 86; coal mine
    at, 98–100 passim, 103,
    172, 182
Little Baddeck, 118
Little Bras d'Or, 86, 98
Little Glace Bay coal
    mine, 178, 190
Little Mabou, 157
Little Narrows, 72, 141,
    116, 193
Livestock: raising, 65–7,
    131–4; trade, 79, 146,
    208
Lochaber, 32
Loch Alsh, 31
Loch Carron, 31
Loch Linnhe, 31
Loch Lomond (Cape Bre-
    ton), 51, 113, 115, 125
Loch Torridon, 31
London, 83, 109
Louisbourg: colliery rail-
    way to, 176; emigration
    from, 190; farming at,
    92; fishery at, 86, 89,
    155; French regime at,
    xxiv–xxv; population
    of, 3, 5
Loyalists: employment in

farming, 20, 23, 204;
    employment in mines,
    16; settlement of, 3,
    19–20, 23, 48, 121
Lumbering, 58

Mabou: 56, 83, 149; agri-
    cultural improvement
    at, 63, 131; dairying at,
    67; emigration from,
    193, 197–8; granting
    land at, 48–9; oat mill
    at, 81; potato famine
    at, 114; tannery at, 79
Mabou Harbour, 20
McCoy, Robert, 76
McCulmot & Co., 88
MacDonald, Angus, 81
McDonald, John, 126
MacDonald, Lord, 42, 45
MacDonald, Roderick,
    160–1
MacDonald & Co., D.,
    146
McDougall, J.H., 199
McDougall, Malcolm, 141,
    149–50 (figure)
McKay, John, 73
McKeen, William, 119
MacKenzie, Charles, 81
McKinnon, Betsey, 141
McKinnon's Point, 76
MacLean of Coll, 45
McLellan Brothers, 146
McLeod, Rev. Norman,
    118, 187, 198–9
McNab's Cove, 49, 76
McNeil, Captain Donald,
    71, 186–7
McPherson, John, 56
Magdalen Islands, 5, 11,
    90, 157
Main-à-Dieu, 3, 5, 86, 90,
    92, 155
Maitland, Lieutenant-
    Governor, 73
Malagawatch, 50, 149,
    113–15 passim
Manitoba, 193, 195,
    205
Manufacturing, rural,
    79–82, 146–8, 203

Margaree: agricultural
    improvement at, 63;
    climate at, 23; dairying
    at, 67; emigration
    from, 186, 197; fishery
    at, 11; granting land at,
    48–9; potato blight at,
    112–13, 115, 118; po-
    tato famine at, 114, 118
Margaree, Northeast, 51,
    131, 81
Margaree, Southwest, 76–
    7 (figure), 131, 143–4
Margaree Harbour, 11,
    20, 83, 86, 90
Margaree Valley, 79
Mathewson, Farquhar, 76
Mathewson, John, 76
Meat-packing, 146
Merchants, 203, 205;
    coal, 15, 18; country,
    82–3, 148–9; fish, xxv,
    5–7, 11, 14–15, 86–9,
    154–5, 166–8, 201
Middle River, 75, 81–2
    passim, 137, 140, 193;
    agricultural improve-
    ment at, 131; emigra-
    tion from, 187;
    granting land at, 48–9
    passim; potato blight at,
    113, 115, 118; potato
    famine at, 116; settle-
    ment of, 52, 125
Mills: grist, 80–1; weav-
    ing and carding, 80
Mira Bay, 86
Miramichi: Irish settle-
    ment in, 207; lumber
    towns in, 205
Mira River, 48, 81, 123,
    141, 186
Moidart, 31, 76
Moncton, 193
Montreal, 88, 90, 172,
    193, 206–7 passim
Moore, John Belcher, 72,
    138–9
Moore, John and William,
    139
Morar, 76
Morvern, 43

Moullin & Co., Thoume, 86, 89, 93
Muck, 31
Mull, 31
Muller & Co., 88
Murray, Donald, 142

Nanaimo, BC, 190, 194, 196, 200
National Policy, 172, 189, 191
Neil's Harbour, 152, 155, 162–4 passim
New Brunswick, 83, 191
New Campbellton, 131
New Canada, 114
New England, 5, 94, 194–6, 204, 207–9 passim
Newfoundland, 11, 16, 122, 152, 208
New Glasgow, 191, 193, 206
New Haven, 154, 157, 162–4 passim
New York, 108
New Zealand, Waipu, 196–7, 205
North Mountain, 51
North River, 51
North Shore, 51, 79, 86, 158
North Sydney, 63, 83, 128, 138–9 passim, 149, 169
North Sydney Herald, 141, 161, 191, 193, 197, 199–200 passim
North Uist, 41, 45, 71
Nova Scotia, 31, 42, 56, 69, 130
Nova Scotia Coal Owners' Association, 172

Oban (Cape Breton), 142
Ontario, 84, 206–8 passim

Paint, Nicholas, 88
Pennsylvania, 96, 196
Petit-de-Grat, 5, 162, 165 (figure)
Philadelphia, 108

Physical geography of Cape Breton, 21, 51
Pictou, 69
Pictou County, 95, 191, 198–9 passim
Pleasant Bay, 51
Point Aconi, 98
Point Michaud, 160
Population of Cape Breton, 3, 48, 121, 188–9 (figure), 201, 202 (figure); urban, 83, 128, 149
Port Hawkesbury, 83, 144, 149; fishing station at, 93; merchant at, 88, 89; Scottish immigrants at, 45
Port Hood, 79, 83, 144, 149; emigrants from, 193; fishery at, 86, 157; lobster fishery at, 160, 168; meat-packing industry at, 146; potato blight at, 112
Port Hood Eastern Beacon, 188
Port Hood Referee, 189
Portland, 108
Port Morien, 51
Portugal, 11, 154
Potato famine, 111–20, 186
Prince Edward Island, 20, 31, 60, 63, 66, 130, 191, 201
Provincial Workmen's Association, 181–2 (figure), 204
Pryor & Sons, William, 89

Quebec, 207–8
Quebec City, 172

Raasay, 31
Railways, colliery, 175 (figure), 176
Reciprocity Treaty, 97, 159, 169–71 passim, 187
Red Islands, 51, 54, 71–2 passim, 112, 139, 144
Regional geography, xv

Religion, 40, 78, 94–5, 144–5 (figure), 146, 168–9, 204
Remon & Co., 5, 86
Reserve coal mine, 170, 172, 176, 178
Rhum, 31, 44–6 passim
Richmond County: emigration from, 189; famine relief in, 113, 115–16, 118; lobster fishery in, 160
River Bourgeois, 5, 85–6 passim, 93, 167
River Denys, 50–1 passim, 81, 113–15, 131, 197
River Inhabitants, 48, 65, 81, 131
Robertson, Forsyth & Co., 86–7
Robin & Co., 5–6, 86–7, 89–90 passim, 154–5, 157–8, 167–8
Ross, James, 142–3, 146
Rundell, Bridge & Rundell, 95

Sabine, Lorenzo, 94
St Andrew's Channel, 51, 118
St Anns, 51, 71–2 passim, 116, 118, 187, 199
St Helier, 83
St George's Bay, 90, 186
St George's Channel, 50
Saint John, 83, 108, 193, 205
St John's, 15, 19, 23, 58, 59–60, 89, 107–8, 128, 206
Saint John Valley, 83, 205–6 passim
St Patricks Channel, 72, 74, 112–13 passim
St Peters, 5, 81, 112, 117
St Peters Island, 160
St Pierre and Miquelon, 61, 108, 128
Salmon River, 51
Sanday, 45
Sawmills, 81, 147–8
Schooners, 7–9

Scots: emigration of, 31;
emigration from Cape
Breton to Newfound-
land, 186; settlement in
Cape Breton, 20, 48–
51, 121, 204; settle-
ment in Highlands, 33;
settlement in Mari-
times, 207
Seasonal employment,
72–3, 140–2
Settlement: European,
xx–xxiv, 207–8; in
Cape Breton, 3, 13, 18,
19–20, 24, 48–51, 121,
204; detailed pattern
of, 56–7 (figure), 128–
9 (figure); in High-
lands, 33
Shipbuilding, 18–19,
108–9, 183–4
(figure)
Shipping, 18–19, 107–8,
183–4
Skye, 31, 33, 40, 41, 44,
45
Skye Glen, 51, 114–15
passim
Skye Mountain, 142
Smith, Richard, 96
Smyth, Peter, 149
Society, rural, 75–9, 143–
6, 204
Sorel, Que., 208

South Mountain, 51, 125,
142
South Uist, 36, 38, 42,
44–6 passim
Spain, 87, 154
Squatters, 51–2 passim,
54–6, 123, 125–8
Staple trades, xix–xx,
xxiii, 85, 152, 203–8
passim
Stewart & Co., 89
Stillwater, Minn., 196
Strait of Canso, 11, 20,
90, 92, 145, 159, 162
Strath Glass, 32
Sunart, 43
Sutherlandshire, 32
Sydney, 15, 25–8, 41, 42,
63, 79, 83; climate at,
23; coal piers at, 176;
population of, 149; po-
tato blight at, 113, 115;
potato famine at, 116;
Scottish immigrants in,
46–7; settlement at, 3,
20, 24; shipping, 19
Sydney Harbour, 3, 15,
20, 24, 86
Sydney Mines, 16, 79,
95–107 passim, 172–3,
176–8 passim, 180–81,
182, 190, 200

Tanneries, 79

Timber trade, 58
Tiree, 31, 40
Toronto, 193, 206–7 pas-
sim
Trades Journal, 182, 189–
90 passim, 200
Treaty of Washington,
159
Tremain & Stout, 6–7,
15, 18
Turner, Frederick Jack-
son, xxii

Victoria, BC, 194, 199
Victoria coal mine, 178
Victoria County, 189–90
Vooght Brothers, 139

Washabuck Bridge, 51
West Arichat, 163, 168,
197
West Bay, 50–1 passim,
74, 150–1 (figure), 193
Wester Ross, 31
Whaleboat, 7–8
White Point, 154
Whycocomagh, 113–15
passim, 142–3, 193, 197
Whycocomagh Bay, 50
Wilson, Joseph, 88–9,
108

Young, John, 67, 80
Young, William, 114